The Essential
Guide to
Having a Baby

The Essential Guide to Having a Baby

KAREN EVENNETT

WARD LOCK

To my husband, Steve, and daughters, Coco and Bella, with love

A WARD LOCK BOOK

First published in the UK 1998 by
Ward Lock
Wellington House
125 Strand
London WC2R 0BB

A Cassell Imprint

British Library Cataloguing-in-Publication Data
A catalogue record for this book is available from the British Library

ISBN 0-7063-7741-9

Designed and typeset by Eric Drewery

Printed by Wing King Tong Co., Hong Kong

While every effort has been taken to ensure that the information in this book is accurate, this guide should not be used to replace a doctor or midwife's advice. Alternative remedies and exercises are suggestions only and should be checked against your personal needs with a relevant practitioner. The author and publishers take no responsibility for injury or damage incurred as a result of using this book.

Contents

Foreword   **7**

Author's acknowledgements   **8**

Introduction   **9**

PART 1 : PREGNANCY AND BEFORE

Chapter 1 : Getting Pregnant   13

Planning ahead ◆ Getting to know your fertile times ◆ Maximizing your chances of getting pregnant ◆ How conception takes place ◆ Difficulties in conceiving ◆ Your questions answered

Chapter 2 : The First Trimester   32

Booking in with your antenatal clinic or midwife ◆ Looking after yourself now you're pregnant ◆ Exercise in the first trimester ◆ Your baby's development in weeks 1–12 ◆ Changes to your body ◆ Changes to your emotions ◆ Common worries ◆ Your questions answered

Chapter 3 : The Second Trimester   65

Your baby's development in weeks 12–24 ◆ Changes to your body ◆ Common worries ◆ Sex in the second trimester ◆ Exercise in the second trimester ◆ Your questions answered

Chapter 4 : The Third Trimester   90

Your baby's development in weeks 25–38 ◆ Changes to your body ◆ Common worries ◆ Sex in the third trimester ◆ Prelabour and false labour ◆ Premature labour ◆ Overdue baby ◆ Your questions answered

Chapter 5: Antenatal Screening   113

What screening can do for you ◆ Which test and when? ◆ The ultrasound scan ◆ Terminating a pregnancy for abnormality ◆ Your questions answered

PART 2: BIRTH AND AFTERWARDS

Chapter 6: Preparing for Childbirth   137

Your options ◆ Coping with fear of childbirth ◆ Choosing a childbirth class ◆ Where's the best place to have your baby? ◆ Vaginal birth after caesarean ◆ Preparing your body the natural way ◆ Pain relief: what's available? ◆ What to take to hospital with you ◆ Do you want a birth plan? ◆ Your questions answered

Chapter 7: Labour and Delivery – What to Expect   164

Recognizing the real thing ◆ The stages of labour ◆ Emergency delivery ◆ Your newborn baby ◆ Your questions answered

Chapter 8: Coping with a Complicated Delivery   178

Prolonged labour ◆ Fetal distress ◆ Breech delivery ◆ Other awkward baby positions ◆ Forceps and ventouse ◆ Caesarean section ◆ Twins or more ◆ Your questions answered

Chapter 9: The First Three Months of Motherhood   189

The first few days ◆ Your body's recovery after the birth ◆ Recovering from a caesarean ◆ Breastfeeding your baby ◆ Choosing to bottle feed ◆ Monitoring your baby's health ◆ Sex talk ◆ Six weeks on ◆ Getting back into shape: exercises you can do ◆ Your questions answered

PART 3: A–Z OF PROBLEMS AND SOLUTIONS   219

Further Reading   251

Address Book   251

Index   253

Foreword

Lucilla Poston, Professor of Fetal Health, funded by Tommy's Campaign

Tommy's Campaign funds a major research programme nationwide aimed at understanding and preventing premature birth, miscarriage and stillbirth. It is the only UK charity focusing exclusively on the health of the unborn child. Tommy's Campaign also informs mothers-to-be about ways to reduce the risk of having a problem pregnancy.

I am delighted to have been asked to provide a foreword to this excellent and very informative new pregnancy guide. Until the relatively recent advent of modern technology such as scanning, women knew little of the miraculous changes which were taking place within their bodies and were dependent upon the expertise and involvement of their GP, obstetrician and midwife. Today's generation of mothers is far better informed and expect to operate in partnership with their ante-natal supporters. This is all to the good, and guides such as this are becoming an essential element in the preparation for motherhood.

Nowadays, most well-monitored pregnancies are, thankfully, trouble-free but the high expectation of 'sailing through' pregnancy can make it so much harder to accept the situation when things do go wrong. Given a prevailing sense that we can control so much in our lives it can seem shockingly cruel when a baby is lost during pregnancy or at birth. For the last six years Tommy's Campaign, the national medical research charity, has been doing a brilliant job raising funds for research projects at hospitals and universities throughout the UK. For three years I have been Professor of Fetal Health, based at St Thomas' Hospital in London. With help from Tommy's Campaign, I am fortunate to have been able to assemble a team of dedicated top-level researchers whose efforts, together with those of colleagues and collaborators world-wide, will, we hope, make significant advances in understanding why some pregnancies unfortunately develop problems.

Nonetheless, the majority of pregnancies are healthy and problem-free and this book will help you to achieve this. It is an informative and accessible introduction to pregnancy with plenty of common-sense advice but it will also help you to recognize difficulties when they arise.

Tommy's Campaign is also there to help those women who encounter problems along the way. So, have a healthy pregnancy, enjoy the delights of your new baby and the wonder of watching your child grow. Meanwhile, Tommy's Campaign will work harder than ever to ensure that every baby has the best possible start in life.

Tommy's Campaign receives no Government funding and depends entirely upon voluntary contributions. You can contact the charity at: 1 Kennington Road, London, SE1 7RR or phone 0171 620 0188.
Registered Charity No: 1060508

AUTHOR'S ACKNOWLEDGEMENTS

My very special thanks go to Helen Denholm, Zoë Hughes, Rosemary Anderson, Esther Jagger and Jo Murray who all put a lot of time into making this book work. I'm also indebted to the organizations listed in the Address Book, and the many women who have shared their personal experiences with me.

PICTURE CREDITS

Introduction

Pregnancy is a time of great joy, mixed, inevitably, with a degree of anxiety. I hope that, whether you're a first-time mother, or an experienced one wanting to see how ideas have progressed, this book will be a useful companion from the time you start planning your new baby to the weeks after delivery when he or she is firmly establishing a place in the family.

It won't take you too long to realize that once you become pregnant (or admit to people that you're even thinking about having a baby), you're no longer regarded as an individual who knows how to run her own life – but as someone who needs to be told! Mothers, friends and relatives love nothing more than to tell you what you should and shouldn't be doing, eating and even feeling. Of course most of this advice is well-intentioned, although often out-of-date and to be taken with a pinch of salt. Your doctor or your midwife are better able than the best-intentioned friend to answer any genuine concerns you may have about how to manage your pregnancy. But I hope that this book will also fill you in on all the basics you need to know, and give you the information you often need in order to ask the right questions and get the care you want.

This is a time of great change for you and your partner – and if you can encourage him to read sections of this book you will be in a good position to discuss matters which may be worrying either of you. For example, is he feeling aggrieved at your lack of libido? Is he cross that you're so tired? By understanding that what you're going through happens to most pregnant women, he may be able to overcome (or at least express) any negative feelings he's worried about.

You'll also want to discuss your plans for the birth with him. Does he want to be with you? Most men do stay with their partners in labour these days – but it's not obligatory, nor does being with you mean that he has to be actively involved in delivering the baby, or seeing things he'd rather were left to the imagination. Many men are happy to limit their involvement to holding their partner's hand, but it may help you both if you've discussed this first and have some idea of what to expect.

Finally, on the subject of anxiety in pregnancy – which is an entirely natural emotion – I'd like to point out that pregnancy isn't a medical condition. It's a stage in a woman's life, that, with care and attention, will almost always be a happy experience.

However, I've written this book as a mother and a journalist, both of which roles have brought home to me the fact that, while women need all the help they can get in staying healthy in pregnancy – how to eat well, exercise safely, and get all the vital relaxation they need, all of which are addressed in detail – most of us also want, and need, easy access to information when problems arise. And this is why I have included the A–Z of Problems and Solutions at the back of the book, for anyone who may need it.

As a first-time mother, I had no idea that a baby's growth in the womb could slow down – until my first baby did just that and suddenly I had to take on board the hitherto unmentioned and very complex-sounding subject of intra-uterine growth retardation (IUGR). With little information available to me, my mind was left to run riot wondering, 'Why don't people talk about these things?'

Likewise, as a journalist working on the health pages of a weekly women's magazine, I have received scores of letters from women telling me about difficult or worrying experiences in pregnancy. Time after time, their one regret is that they hadn't known about the condition before it struck . . . although, most, I'm pleased to report, have had a happy ending thanks to the excellent obstetric care now available.

In fact, of course, doctors don't mention many of the problems that can occur in pregnancy because they're so rare, which is a comfort to know. But equally comforting is the fact that in most cases there's a solution to the problem. My own IUGR baby was born very healthy at term, and I went on to have a second beautiful baby eight years later, despite different complications arising – this time to do with me.

If this book achieves nothing else, I hope it will raise issues that will enable you to ask questions and get the excellent care in pregnancy that we are all entitled to.

NOTE: To avoid sex discrimination, 'he' and 'she' are used throughout the book when talking about the baby.

Part 1

PREGNANCY
AND BEFORE

1 *Getting Pregnant*

Take time to plan ahead for your baby. Paying special attention to your diet, exercise and lifestyle will maximize your chances of conceiving when you want to, and of producing a healthy baby.

PLANNING AHEAD

Most doctors advise couples to start looking after themselves at least three months before they plan to conceive – but six months is even better. There are a number of good reasons for doing so.

General Health and Nutrition

First, it takes at least three months to improve the health of red blood cells, which boosts the immune system and strengthens the body against infection. In addition, both the egg and sperm are at their most vulnerable during the hundred days prior to conception – if you're not in general good health, both their quality and your fertility will be poor.

Secondly, poor nutrition and bad health at the time of conception can hinder your baby's growth. The national average weight for a newborn in the UK is now around 3.6 kg (8 lb), though anything between 3.5 kg (7 lb 8 oz) and 4.5 kg (9 lb 9 oz) is considered healthy. However, 7 per cent of British babies weigh in at less than 2.5 kg (5 lb 5 oz), the official low birth weight figure.

Low birth weight can be life-threatening to a baby – in 1993, 57 per cent of stillbirths and 61 per cent of neonatal deaths were amongst low birth weight babies. Researchers have also demonstrated that children tend to perform less well at school if they were small at birth. And in later life, people who were small at birth are at greater risk of heart disease, diabetes and strokes.

Both you and your partner should:

♦ Avoid taking any drugs without first consulting your doctor.
♦ Keep alcohol drinking to an absolute minimum.
♦ Give up smoking.

HOW TO GIVE UP SMOKING STEP-BY-STEP

1. Make a date to stop completely – and stick to it.
2. Throw away all your ashtrays, unopened packs of cigarettes, matches and lighters.
3. Keep yourself busy to help you get through the first few days.
4. Drink lots of water, and keep a glass by your side which you can sip steadily.
5. Get more active, which will help you relax. Join an exercise class, take walks or go swimming.
6. Think positive – any withdrawal symptoms, although unpleasant, should be welcomed because they are positive indications that your body is recovering from the effects of tobacco. Common effects include headaches, sore throats and irritability – but they'll all disappear within a week or two.
7. Change your routine – if you bought your cigarettes on your usual route to work, go another way for a few days. If you smoked with friends at the pub at lunchtime, go somewhere else and do something different.
8. Don't make excuses – a crisis or a celebration is no excuse for 'just one' cigarette. One leads to another, and another . . .
9. Treat yourself – use the money you've saved on cigarettes for something special.
10. Watch what you eat – you're likely to feel peckish, so go for fruit instead of sugary snacks or you'll put on weight.
11. Take one day at a time – and remember each day is good news for your health, your family and your pocket.

Additionally, you as the potential mother should:

♦ Cut down on caffeine.
♦ Take folic acid.
♦ Take vitamin B12.

Caffeine can reduce your chances of becoming pregnant, and some studies have linked high caffeine intake with low birth weight babies. Women should stick to a maximum of four caffeine-containing drinks a day (tea, coffee, chocolate, cola).

Folic acid is available in fresh green leafy vegetables, fortified cereals and bread (check the nutrition labels), meat, oranges, orange juice and

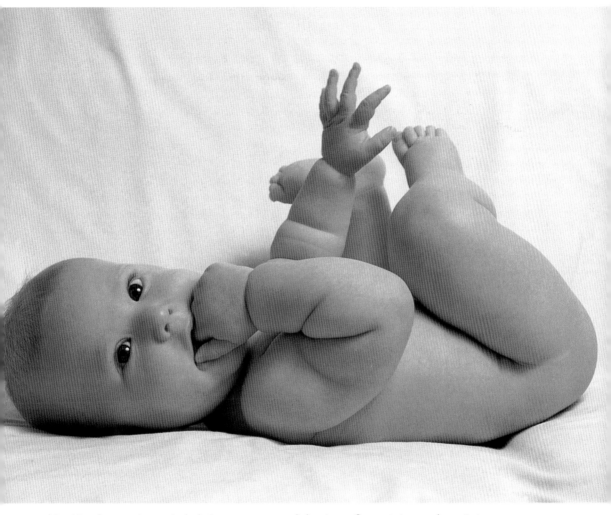

Nutritional status is particularly important around the time of conception, and maximizes your chances of having a healthy baby.

potatoes, and plays a crucial role in the prevention of neural tube defects such as spina bifida. It's difficult to get the full daily 600 mcg recommended for preconception through diet alone. But we tend to get about 200 mcg from our diet, and a 400 mcg tablet to make up the deficit is available over the counter to women planning a pregnancy, and on prescription once you're pregnant.

Vitamin B12 is found in meat, fish, eggs and dairy produce. It's vital for the production of the genetic material DNA, and works with folic acid to prevent neural tube defects.

MIRIAM'S STORY

My first daughter, Chloe, was very small at birth – weighing just under 5 lb. I didn't think too much of it, as my husband and I are both small too. Happily, Chloe had no health problems as a baby or child, and, now five years old, seems just as able as her peers at school.

However, when John and I were planning our second child, when Chloe was two, I read about some research that stressed the importance of eating well in pregnancy 'to make a big baby'. The report went on to point out that small birth weight babies are at greater risk of bad health in later life – and, alarmed to think that Chloe could have fallen into this category, I decided to take better care of myself this time round.

Looking back, I remembered that John and I were having building work done on the house when I was expecting Chloe, and this meant we resorted to a lot of cook-chill meals and take-aways when we couldn't get into the kitchen to prepare fresh food.

I read up some more, discovered that this was not the ideal diet for a pregnant woman, and made a determined effort to eat five portions of fresh fruit or vegetables every day, along with more fish, baked potatoes and pasta. I was already making sure Chloe was eating a lot of these things so it didn't cause too much disruption to our lives.

We started our new fresh food regime in the July. Ben was conceived in November and born the following July, weighing the perfect national average of 8 lb.

As a would-be mother you should include the following in your diet:

Calcium – from milk and milk products such as cheese and yogurt, tinned fish such as sardines whose bones are eaten too, green vegetables and beans. Calcium keeps your bones strong and healthy. As bone density seems to diminish during the first three months of pregnancy it's important to stock up before conception if possible. The equivalent of half a litre (one pint) of milk a day (680 mg calcium) should be enough.

Iron – from red meat, pilchards, beans, lentils, nuts, eggs, leafy green vegetables, fortified cereals, bread and dried fruit. Iron is important to prevent you becoming anaemic before and during pregnancy – anaemic women are more likely to have small, premature babies.

Vitamin C – from fresh fruit and vegetables – increases the amount of iron you absorb.

Vitamin D helps you absorb calcium. The body makes vitamin D in response to exposure to sunlight but dietary sources include oily fish such as salmon, herring and tuna, eggs and milk.

WHAT CAN AFFECT THE BIRTH WEIGHT OF YOUR BABY?

Genetics – if you are small and women in your family tend to have small babies, a below average weight baby may be normal for you.

Smoking – aim to give up six months before you plan to conceive as it reduces fertility levels.

Caffeine – stick to a maximum of four caffeine drinks (tea, coffee, chocolate, cola) a day.

Alcohol – limit yourself to a maximum of one small glass of wine, or equivalent, each day.

A below average weight mother – build yourself up by eating a healthy, regular diet before conceiving.

Poor diet – remember quality of food is more important than quantity. Mothers of babies weighing less than 2.5 kg (5 lb 5 oz) have often lacked vital nutrients including B vitamins, magnesium, iron, zinc and essential fatty acids.

Vitamins B6 and B12 – B6 from meat, fish, egg yolk, avocados, seeds and bananas; and B12 from eggs, dairy produce, meat including offal, fish, Marmite (or Vegemite) and some breakfast cereals – are important. Women whose diet is significantly low in these vitamins are more likely to produce low birth weight babies.

In addition to paying attention to diet potential mothers should check their immunity status for rubella and toxoplasmosis (see pp.29, 36 and 249). It's also advisable to attend for screening if in the past either partner has suffered from STDs (sexually transmitted diseases) or if the woman has had many sexual partners.

TAKE CARE WITH VITAMIN A

Liver is a rich source of iron, but because it's so high in vitamin A it's recommended that you avoid it before and during pregnancy because very high doses may cause birth defects.

Taking Exercise

Developing a good regular exercise programme will help you feel better, increase your stamina, and make labour and delivery easier. It's better to be fit and to have established an exercise routine before conception than to try and start something once you're expecting. But if you do have to start from scratch consult your doctor, especially if you've had medical problems or pregnancy complications in the past. And avoid contact sports or risky exercise such as water skiing or riding.

Regular exercise will build your strength for pregnancy and help you relax, too. Choosing a sport you enjoy is important. Keeping fit should not be a chore.

Wear comfortable clothing, and allow plenty of time for warming up and cooling down. Start gradually and increase as you build your strength. Check your pulse every 10–15 minutes while you are exercising, and don't let it exceed 120 beats a minute.

Exercise is important throughout pregnancy and after you give birth. Further guidelines will be given as appropriate in later chapters (see in particular p.41).

GETTING TO KNOW YOUR FERTILE TIMES

The Menstrual Cycle

A woman's menstrual cycle is divided into five phases:

Phase 1, days 1–5: the period – when the old lining of the womb or uterus is shed along with about 80 ml of blood.

Phase 2, days 6–12: the proliferative phase – during which the ovarian follicles develop and produce the hormone oestrogen, which makes the womb lining regrow.

Phase 3, days 13–14: the ovulatory phase – during which the follicle from one or other of the two ovaries bursts, releasing its egg.

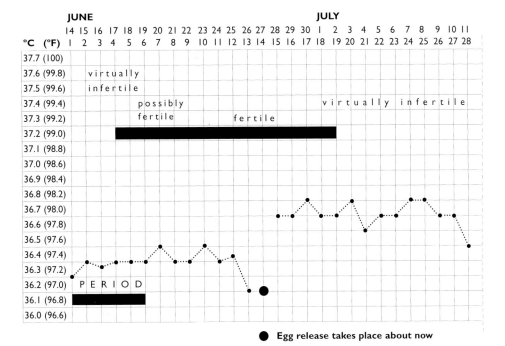

Plotting your temperature and your menstrual cycle will help you identify your most fertile time.

Phase 4, days 15–26: the secretory phase – during which less oestrogen and more progesterone is produced to prepare the body for pregnancy if the newly released egg has been fertilized.

Phase 5, days 27–28: the premenstrual phase – during which, if pregnancy has occurred, the womb lining continues to thicken. If there is no pregnancy, the lining breaks down to be shed again at the beginning of the new cycle.

The Fertile Days

Most women are fertile for two to seven days a month around the time of ovulation. You can identify these days by getting used to the changes in your cervical mucus or discharge. Similar to egg white in texture, fertile mucus is elastic and stretches to form a string. As well as being a sign of fertility, it forms a slippery lubrication to help sperm swim up through the vagina and cervix into the uterus and the fallopian tubes, where they wait for an egg to be released.

But this is not the only symptom of fertility. You may also know you are ovulating when you feel very interested in sex. Many women experience a surge in their libido around the time of ovulation.

Alternatively, you may recognize a subtle change in your body temperature. Some women plot these changes by taking their

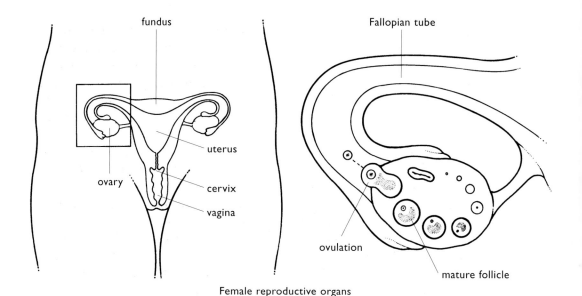

Female reproductive organs

At ovulation, an egg is released from one or other of the ovaries.

temperature first thing every morning. A couple of days after ovulation their temperature rises and stays at that very slightly higher level until their next period. So a woman can use her temperature chart to identify when ovulation took place, and once a pattern has been established over several months she will know when to expect ovulation in the menstrual cycle in which she plans to get pregnant.

Around the time of ovulation you may experience some kind of pain, in the lower part of your abdomen. Known as mittelschmerz, it varies greatly. Many women will go through a fertile lifetime and never have any inkling of pain at the time of ovulation. Others complain of a bursting type of pain which is mild in degree and duration, while others still suffer a more severe, cramp-like pain every month.

Ovulation Kits

These are available from pharmacists and work by detecting a substance called luteinizing hormone (LH) in the urine 24–36 hours before ovulation. But the presence of LH is no guarantee that a woman is ovulating, and the kits are also quite expensive.

MAXIMIZING YOUR CHANCES OF GETTING PREGNANT

Timing Intercourse

Experts differ in their opinions on timing and frequency of intercourse to maximize the chances of conception. But generally it is agreed that couples should make love at least every other day around the time of ovulation. Most sperm are capable of fertilizing an egg up to 48 hours after ejaculation (although some last much longer), and an egg can be fertilized for up to 24 hours after ovulation. This gives a period of three days in the cycle when intercourse should take place.

Regular sex during the rest of the cycle will strengthen male fertility, rather than weaken it. If couples abstain until the woman's next fertile phase, the semen is more likely to contain dead sperm.

Although some people believe that the contractions during female orgasm help carry the sperm up the vagina, it's actually not necessary for her to experience orgasm in order to conceive. Nor do different sexual positions enhance a couple's chances – although, in the hope that they will, some couples try ploys such as the woman lifting her bottom on to a pillow after intercourse to stop the sperm draining out. In fact, as long as the sperm is deposited in the vagina it will be able to penetrate the cervical mucus very quickly, regardless of position.

To make a body temperature chart take your temperature daily, preferably first thing in the morning, before you've had anything to eat or drink.

Choosing the Sex of Your Baby

The sex of a baby is determined by the sperm which fertilizes the egg. Most men produce equal amounts of male- and female-making sperm, though a few men have more of one kind than the other. Couples have tried various methods to obtain a baby of the sex of their choice, but none is particularly reliable.

To have a female baby, some couples have tried:

◆ having intercourse two or three days before ovulation, because female sperm live longer and are more likely to reach the egg, while male sperm die off in the race to get there.
◆ having frequent intercourse, which is said to lower the proportion of male sperm.
◆ douching the vagina with a weak vinegar solution (one part vinegar to 10 parts water) before intercourse, as female sperm thrive in an acid environment.

To have a male baby, some couples have tried:

◆ having intercourse as near as possible to ovulation, because the male sperm are believed to reach the egg before the females.
◆ having intercourse infrequently, to increase the proportion of males.
◆ douching the vagina before intercourse with an alkaline solution of one teaspoon bicarbonate of soda to half a litre (one pint) of water.

A modern scientific line is that the ovum will, on different days of the month, be receptive only to boy or girl sperm. With the help of a questionnaire about the woman's blood group, date of birth and menstrual pattern, Patrick Schoun the scientist behind the research (see Address Book), claims to be able to work out the days on which you can expect to conceive boys or girls. If used properly it is 98.7 per cent successful, although it will never work if your partner is one of the minute number of men who produce only one gender of sperm.

HOW CONCEPTION TAKES PLACE

The process of fertilization is apparently very straightforward. Semen, containing sperm, is deposited inside the vagina of a woman. If she has recently ovulated, an egg is now waiting to be penetrated by the first sperm to reach it. However, the process is notoriously inefficient in humans. We do not, by nature, have high levels of natural fertility – and our individual fertility levels only have to drop slightly for us to be unable to have children.

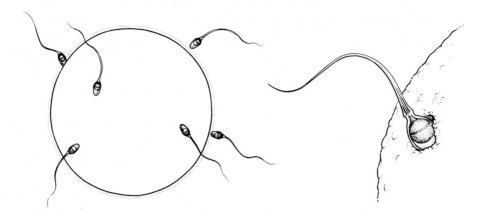

Many sperm reach the ovum, but only one will succeed in penetrating it.

The Journey of the Sperm

After being ejaculated into the vagina it can take the sperm several hours or even days to make the short 15–18 cm (6–7 in) journey to the fallopian tubes where they hope to meet the waiting ovum. Some high-speed swimmers can reach their destination in just half an hour, but the majority will struggle to get there and most will get lost or die along the way.

Their voyage is hindered by numerous hidden dangers. First, the sperm encounter acidic secretions in the vagina which slow them down before they meet the more welcoming alkaline environment of the uterus. Then, many will enter the wrong fallopian tube – the one which does not contain that month's released ovum – or lose their way completely, ending up by swimming around the abdominal cavity until they die.

Out of an average of 300 million sperm which start the journey, only about 500 will reach the correct fallopian tube and fewer still will reach the egg. Those still in the race at this stage are helped by substances in the cervix, uterus and fallopian tubes which make them capable of fertilizing the ovum. But even so, sperm can swim past the ovum, oblivious to its presence.

Sperm Meets Egg

After being released from its follicle at ovulation, the egg, or ovum, travels one third of the length of the fallopian tube where it waits to be fertilized by the first sperm to arrive. As we have seen, this is likely to be some hours after intercourse. The sperm breaks through the membrane of the ovum by releasing enzymes which create a hole in it. It then prepares to penetrate the oocyte, the innermost part of the ovum, and sheds its body and tail as it finally joins its chromosomes – the strands which contain its DNA or genetic material – to those of the ovum. As it enters, a chemical reaction occurs in the ovum, making it impossible for another sperm to penetrate. Once the sperm's head, or nucleus, is inside the ovum, the two nuclei are drawn together until they fuse. This is the point at which fertilization takes place.

Several hours later the fertilized egg divides for the first time, becoming what is known as a morula. The cells of the morula divide every 12–15 hours until it is composed of about a hundred cells, at which point it is known as a blastocyst.

During this process a growing number of unsuccessful sperm attempt to penetrate the outer membrane. It's thought that the frenzied activity of these 'loser' sperm helps to move the blastocyst from the fallopian tube to the uterus.

DOUBLE FERTILIZATION CAUSES TWINS

In most cases a woman releases just one ovum, which eventually becomes a single baby. If she produces two or more ova which are each fertilized by separate sperm, the conception will result in a multiple birth of non-identical or 'fraternal' siblings (twins), each nurtured during pregnancy by their own separate placenta. But when one egg divides to produce two or more embryos the twin siblings will be identical, sharing a single placenta.

Implantation

The journey of the fertilized egg or blastocyst from the fallopian tube to the uterus, where it will grow to become a fetus, begins about three days after conception. But movement is hindered by a sphincter (circular) muscle through which the tiny blastocyst cannot pass. However, the increasing levels of the pregnancy hormone progesterone flooding the body allow the muscle to relax and open, so the blastocyst can continue with its journey. Rarely, a damaged or blocked fallopian tube may bar the blastocyst's route and result in what is called an ectopic pregnancy (see p.226). Assuming its journey is successful, however, the blastocyst enters the womb or uterus, rupturing and shedding its protective shell as it does so, and then implants itself in the thickened lining (endometrium) of the womb. Hormones immediately alert the body to the fact that the blastocyst is not an alien intrusion (for which, because of the genetic material from the father's cells, it could be mistaken) and should be nurtured rather than expelled. The growth of the fetus begins.

Confirming Pregnancy

If you have been planning a pregnancy you will be on red alert for any changes which indicate that your attempts have been successful. Breast tenderness and swelling, vaginal secretions, constipation and nausea can all be very early signs. Some women experience them only a week after conception – i.e. around week 3 of a typical 28-day cycle.

A missed period at the beginning of the next cycle is a more definite sign of pregnancy, but some women do experience a scanty bleed even though they are pregnant. If you have got into the habit of taking your temperature every day and it is still raised 20–22 days after ovulation (one week into the next cycle), it is very likely that you are pregnant.

Pregnancy tests can be carried out on a sample of urine from the first day of a missed period – about two weeks after conception. The test works by picking up the hormone HCG (human chorionic gonadotrophin), which is produced by the placenta and appears in the blood and urine of pregnant women.

DIFFICULTIES IN CONCEIVING

It is the natural expectation of any couple planning a pregnancy that, sooner or later, they will have a baby – and that, with birth control, they will be able to pace their family, choosing when the woman gives birth and how many children she has. But it's not always so easy.

It has been calculated that if a fertile couple have intercourse with no contraception on the most fertile day possible, the woman has a one-in-three to one-in-four chance of a baby (the chances of starting a pregnancy are slightly higher, as not all pregnancies come to term). This means that three times out of four, intercourse, even without contraception, will not produce a baby. Doctors expect couples to have been 'trying for a baby' for an average of six months before conceiving, and it won't be considered a problem worth further investigation until they have been trying for about 18 months without success.

Even then, there is a strong chance that the couple will conceive naturally and without medical intervention. Approximately 70 per cent of couples have conceived after one year of trying; 80 per cent after eighteen months; and 90 per cent after two years. After two years of trying to conceive, the remaining 10 per cent of couples discover they are labelled as 'infertile', but with medical help the chance of achieving a pregnancy is still very realistic.

Orthodox medical treatment is not the only option for couples who have trouble conceiving. Homeopathy, aromatherapy and herbalism can also help. See p.233.

The Effects of Age on Fertility

Both men and women become fertile at puberty, which usually occurs between the ages of ten and fifteen in both sexes. A woman will remain fertile until she reaches menopause, usually between the age of forty-five and fifty-five, when the ovaries run out of eggs and she can no longer have children. But her fertility will have declined fairly drastically before this age. Doctors estimate that a normally fertile woman under the age of twenty-five will need, on average, two to three months to conceive. Over the age of thirty-five she will need six months or longer.

One reason it takes longer to become pregnant as a woman gets older is that the quality of her eggs is gradually deteriorating. Fewer eggs are released which are capable of being fertilized and achieving a pregnancy.

Age is far less of a factor in male fertility. Although the quality of sperm deteriorates with age, this only becomes significant beyond the age of sixty.

The Chances of Conception

Not every woman releases an egg in every menstrual cycle. Some release eggs irregularly, which may cause difficulty in conceiving and require investigation. However, most women are fertile for between two and seven days every month, around the time of ovulation (see pp.19–20).

When Might You Need Infertility Treatment?

The best way to get pregnant is to have sex as often as you can. Although there are only a few days each month when you can conceive, the quality of sperm deteriorates the longer they remain in the body. So there's no benefit in abstaining in the hope of increasing the number of sperm available when you're ovulating. Try to separate sex for pleasure from sex for baby-making (learn to predict your fertile period and make sure you have sex at that time) . . . and enjoy them both!

Ninety per cent of women who have regular unprotected sex become pregnant within one year. If you haven't conceived after 12–18 months of timed sexual intercourse, see your doctor. But go earlier if:

- you have absent or irregular periods, or a history of pelvic inflammatory disease or endometriosis.
- you're overweight or underweight.
- you're over thirty-five.
- your partner's had groin surgery or a testicle injury at any time in his life.
- either of you has a history of sexually transmitted infection, or drug or alcohol abuse.

Remember, it's just as likely to be the man's problem as the woman's. Your doctor can send a sample of your partner's semen for tests to check the number of sperm and how well they move.

One in six couples in the UK seek medical help to have a baby, but not all of them end up having so-called test tube babies. Treatments range from simple advice and easy-to-take medicines to more complicated hi-tech procedures. The pattern of treatment depends on which of you has the problem, and what it is. But be warned: infertility treatment can be stressful, time-consuming and expensive – privately, it can be as much as £20,000 – and there's no guarantee you'll have a baby at the end. For more details see pp.232–33.

YOUR QUESTIONS ANSWERED

Q: *Should I see my doctor before I get pregnant?*

A: If you're confident that you're looking after your health and have no questions to ask, then you may as well wait until you are pregnant. However, a visit now is very useful if you're worried about anything such as past medical history or medicines you're taking; or if you want to know more about looking after yourself during these vital months.

Q: *Will I need any tests before getting pregnant?*

A: If the following information is unknown, consider:

- ◆ Cervical smear test.
- ◆ Rhesus factor test (see pp.245–46).
- ◆ Blood typing.
- ◆ Rubella status, to see if you are Rubella immune or need immunizaton. If you do, you will have to wait three months before conceiving.

If you may have been exposed to hepatitis or Aids, have tests for these too.

Q: *I've had previous miscarriages – do these affect my plans to have another baby?*

A: Although it isn't always possible to prevent problems like these recurring, you should discuss any past pregnancy complications with your doctor before you try to conceive.

Q: *When should I stop using contraception before trying to conceive?*

A: If you're using barrier methods such as condoms or the cap, you can continue with these right up to the time you want to conceive. If you're using an IUD, wait for a couple of normal cycles after it's removed, and use barrier methods during this time. Likewise use a barrier method for two or three cycles after coming off the birth control pill, or having Norplant removed.

Q: *I've recently been vaccinated against rubella. Is it OK to try to get pregnant?*

A: No. Most doctors advise waiting for at least three months after any type of vaccination.

Q: *I regularly use certain medicines – will it be safe to use them while I'm trying to get pregnant?*

A: While you're still in the preconceptual phase (looking after your body but not yet trying to conceive), be cautious about medicines. Take them only as prescribed, and never use any left over from previous prescriptions. Take care with any over-the-counter medicines as they may contain caffeine, alcohol and other additives. Once you're trying to get pregnant and there's any possibility that you may have conceived, let your doctor know immediately if you are on a prescribed medicine; also, before buying any over-the-counter treatments check their safety with the pharmacist or with your doctor.

Q: *I take vitamin and herbal supplements – are these safe when I'm preparing for pregnancy?*

A: Excessive amounts of some vitamins – notably vitamin A – can increase the risk of birth defects. Aim to get most of your vitamins from a healthy diet. However, a folic acid supplement is necessary as you can't get all you need from food alone, and some women like to take a multivitamin preparation too. Before buying, check their safety during pregnancy with your doctor or pharmacist. Check any herbal preparations you are thinking of using with a herbalist.

Q: *I don't drink much alcohol – do I have to stop altogether before getting pregnant?*

A: Pregnant and pre-pregnant women may now drink a small amount of alcohol without harming their unborn baby, according to the Royal College of Obstetricians. In its first guidelines on drinking in pregnancy the college says there's no evidence that drinking up to 15 units a week will harm the baby. To be on the safe side, however, pregnant women should stick to one unit a day – that is, half a pint of ordinary beer, a small glass of wine or a single measure of spirits. Drinking more than 15 units a week may harm the brain of an unborn baby and has been linked to lower birth weight.

Q: *My work exposes me to chemicals and an X-ray machine – will this be a problem when I'm pregnant?*

A: Many forms of workplace exposure can be harmful, so discuss your situation with your doctor or occupational health nurse at work, preferably before getting pregnant.

Q: *I'm on my feet for ten hours a day at work, and don't find it a problem now. But will it cause complications in my pregnancy?*

A: Studies have shown that women who stand for long periods have smaller babies. If in the past you've had premature deliveries or an incompetent cervix (see pp.231–32) discuss this with your doctor. If you have a tendency towards varicose veins (see p.56) a standing job can make them worse. Wear support tights and try to take regular breaks and put your feet up.

Q: *I do a lot of yoga — will the head stands and shoulder stands be safe to do if I've just conceived?*

A: If you've been doing yoga regularly for at least six months, and you're used to doing head and shoulder stands, it will be quite safe to continue with these now. But tell your teacher you may be pregnant so she can show you some more comfortable postures.

2 *The First Trimester*

In the first three months you will show few, if any, visible changes to the outside world, though you may well feel tired and nauseous. This is a time for having routine tests and examinations, for reading about what is going to happen to you and your baby in the next nine months, for making plans and discussing lifestyle changes with your partner.

BOOKING IN WITH YOUR ANTENATAL CLINIC OR MIDWIFE

As soon as your pregnancy is confirmed you will need to make your first appointment with your antenatal clinic or midwife. This visit (the earlier the better) is likely to be long – mainly because of the huge amount of paperwork involved in putting together a picture of you and your pregnancy so that any special risks can be spotted and the appropriate support or advice given. You will be asked a number of standard questions, all relevant even if they don't seem to be, about:

- ◆ your past and present state of health.
- ◆ any illnesses and operations you've had.
- ◆ any previous pregnancies or miscarriages.
- ◆ whether there are twins or inherited disorders in either family.
- ◆ your ethnic origin, because certain inherited conditions are more common in some ethnic groups.
- ◆ your work, and that of your partner.
- ◆ your home, and who you live with.

The doctor or midwife will also want to know the first day of your last period, in order to work out when the baby is due. In fact you can also work this out yourself by starting with the date of your last period, then adding seven and counting back three months for the date when your

January	1 2 3 4 5 6 7 8 9 10 11 12 13 14 15 16 17 18 19 20 21 22 23 24 25 26 27 28 29 30 31	**January**
October	8 9 10 11 12 13 14 15 16 17 18 19 20 21 22 23 24 25 26 27 28 29 30 31 1 2 3 4 5 6 7	November
February	1 2 3 4 5 6 7 8 9 10 11 12 13 14 15 16 17 18 19 20 21 22 23 24 25 26 27 28	**February**
November	8 9 10 11 12 13 14 15 16 17 18 19 20 21 22 23 24 25 26 27 28 29 30 1 2 3 4 5	December
March	1 2 3 4 5 6 7 8 9 10 11 12 13 14 15 16 17 18 19 20 21 22 23 24 25 26 27 28 29 30 31	**March**
December	6 7 8 9 10 11 12 13 14 15 16 17 18 19 20 21 22 23 24 25 26 27 28 29 30 31 1 2 3 4 5	January
April	1 2 3 4 5 6 7 8 9 10 11 12 13 14 15 16 17 18 19 20 21 22 23 24 25 26 27 28 29 30	**April**
January	6 7 8 9 10 11 12 13 14 15 16 17 18 19 20 21 22 23 24 25 26 27 28 29 30 31 1 2 3 4	February
May	1 2 3 4 5 6 7 8 9 10 11 12 13 14 15 16 17 18 19 20 21 22 23 24 25 26 27 28 29 30 31	**May**
February	5 6 7 8 9 10 11 12 13 14 15 16 17 18 19 20 21 22 23 24 25 26 27 28 1 2 3 4 5 6 7	March
June	1 2 3 4 5 6 7 8 9 10 11 12 13 14 15 16 17 18 19 20 21 22 23 24 25 26 27 28 29 30	**June**
March	8 9 10 11 12 13 14 15 16 17 18 19 20 21 22 23 24 25 26 27 28 29 30 31 1 2 3 4 5 6	April
July	1 2 3 4 5 6 7 8 9 10 11 12 13 14 15 16 17 18 19 20 21 22 23 24 25 26 27 28 29 30 31	**July**
April	7 8 9 10 11 12 13 14 15 16 17 18 19 20 21 22 23 24 25 26 27 28 29 30 1 2 3 4 5 6 7	May
August	1 2 3 4 5 6 7 8 9 10 11 12 13 14 15 16 17 18 19 20 21 22 23 24 25 26 27 28 29 30 31	**August**
May	8 9 10 11 12 13 14 15 16 17 18 19 20 21 22 23 24 25 26 27 28 29 30 31 1 2 3 4 5 6 7	June
September	1 2 3 4 5 6 7 8 9 10 11 12 13 14 15 16 17 18 19 20 21 22 23 24 25 26 27 28 29 30	**September**
June	8 9 10 11 12 13 14 15 16 17 18 19 20 21 22 23 24 25 26 27 28 29 30 1 2 3 4 5 6 7	July
October	1 2 3 4 5 6 7 8 9 10 11 12 13 14 15 16 17 18 19 20 21 22 23 24 25 26 27 28 29 30 31	**October**
July	8 9 10 11 12 13 14 15 16 17 18 19 20 21 22 23 24 25 26 27 28 29 30 31 1 2 3 4 5 6 7	August
November	1 2 3 4 5 6 7 8 9 10 11 12 13 14 15 16 17 18 19 20 21 22 23 24 25 26 27 28 29 30	**November**
August	8 9 10 11 12 13 14 15 16 17 18 19 20 21 22 23 24 25 26 27 28 29 30 31 1 2 3 4 5 6	September
December	1 2 3 4 5 6 7 8 9 10 11 12 13 14 15 16 17 18 19 20 21 22 23 24 25 26 27 28 29 30 31	**December**
September	7 8 9 10 11 12 13 14 15 16 17 18 19 20 21 22 23 24 25 26 27 28 29 30 1 2 3 4 5 6 7	October

Using an Estimated Date of Delivery chart, you can work out when your baby should be born by finding the date of the first day of your last period in bold type – the figure immediately below will give you your expected delivery date.

baby will be born. For example, if your period started on 1 January your baby should be born on 8 October.

However, charts do vary between professionals. In fact some studies say only 4 per cent of women deliver on their due date anyway. A normal full-term pregnancy lasts anything from 37 to 42 weeks, and you can expect to deliver at any time in that four-week period around your EDD.

If you have a regular 28-day cycle you're more likely to deliver close to your EDD, and if your cycle is always longer than that you'll probably deliver late. But if your menstrual cycle is irregular the dating system may not work for you at all. In this case your first ultrasound scan at 10–12 weeks (if you decide to have one, see p.125) should give you a realistic idea of when you will give birth.

Your weight will be taken at this visit to establish whether you are under or over the normal weight for your height, and whether this may pose any problems for you and your growing baby. It used to be routine to check weight at every antenatal visit, but some health authorities have stopped doing this because many women worry that they're getting too big or not big enough. Most women put on between 10 and 12.5 kg (22–28 lb) in pregnancy, the majority of it after week 20. A gradual, steady weight gain may help prevent a variety of complications, including diabetes, hypertension, varicose veins, haemorrhoids, low birth weight and difficult delivery of a big baby. The most important thing, of course, is to eat sensibly and look after yourself throughout the pregnancy.

Your height will be measured as it is a rough guide to the size of your pelvis – if you're small you may need to discuss your baby's delivery with your midwife or doctor. But not every small woman will have a problem giving birth. At 4 ft 11 in (1.5 m)and taking a size 2 shoe (also thought to indicate difficulties), I had no problems delivering my two babies.

Your general health will also be assessed, with a check on your heart and lungs.

A sample of urine will be tested for the presence of:

◆ protein, which can be a sign of infection or hypertension.
◆ sugar, which may necessitate further tests to rule out diabetes.

Your blood pressure will be taken at this and every subsequent antenatal visit, as high blood pressure can endanger both you and your baby.

A blood sample will be taken to test for your blood group and whether your blood is rhesus positive or negative (see pp.245–46). It will also establish whether you're anaemic – if you are you'll be given iron tablets, as anaemia can make you tired and also affect your ability to cope with the standard loss of blood when you deliver the baby.

Other tests: If tests for rubella, syphilis, hepatitis B and HIV have not already been carried out and you are at all unsure about your status, your blood could be checked for these now.

An internal examination may be carried out with your permission, though this is no longer routine. If you do have one, it's straightforward. The doctor puts one or two fingers inside your vagina and presses the other hand on your abdomen to feel the size of your womb and judge the age of your baby. The ultrasound scan at around ten weeks is becoming a more common way of assessing the age.

A cervical smear may be taken now if it's more than three years since you've had a test.

Genital herpes: if you or your partner have ever had this condition mention it to your doctor at this visit in case the infection is passed on to the baby. But this risk is very small, and greatest if you develop genital lesions near to delivery – in which case you may be advised to have a caesarean if it is a primary infection and active.

Your blood pressure will be checked at every antenatal visit. Slight fluctuations are normal in pregnancy, but a significant rise may be an early indication of pre-eclampsia (see pp.243–244).

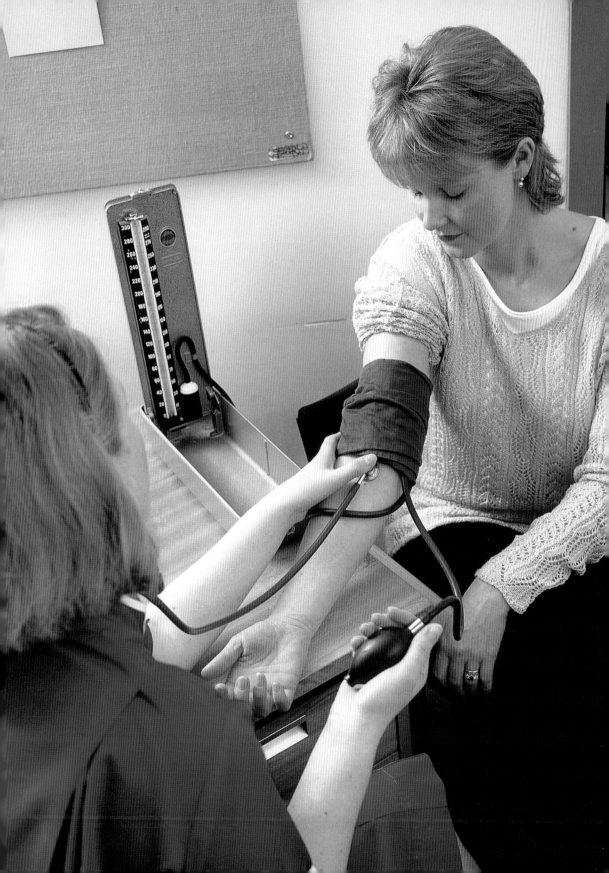

SOPHIE'S STORY

I began to feel pregnant the day after my twenty-sixth birthday, when I suddenly went off the coffee cake my husband Charlie had bought me to celebrate. Even though our baby was planned, I was shocked at how quickly we'd conceived – we'd only been trying in one cycle. And I also felt a sense of panic, as if I'd gone beyond the point of no return.

I don't think I felt excited at all – only dazed – until I went for a pregnancy test at a clinic and was told by the nurse, 'It's positive – you're going to have a baby!' After that, Charlie and I became extremely concerned and possessive about our unborn baby. He didn't want to have intercourse with me for a couple of weeks, because he was so scared of damaging our child. But happily we soon overcame that hurdle!

Having decided to wait until I was twelve weeks pregnant and had had the first scan before telling anyone, we felt as if we were guarding a naughty secret. When other people talked about their babies, or the word 'pregnant' came up in dinner party conversation, we exchanged glances and could barely stop ourselves from blurting it out.

LOOKING AFTER YOURSELF NOW YOU'RE PREGNANT

A good diet, sensible exercise and some hygiene do's and don'ts will ease your path through pregnancy.

To Avoid Toxoplasmosis

Toxoplasmosis is an infection caused by a microscopic parasite which lives in meat, cat faeces and the soil where cats defecate. It can cause severe damage to an unborn baby, resulting in miscarriage, stillbirth or brain damage (see p.249). However, following these straightforward guidelines will considerably reduce the risk:

- only eat meat which has been cooked right through, with no trace of blood remaining.
- wash your hands and all cooking equipment after preparing raw meat.
- wash fruit and vegetables thoroughly to remove all traces of soil.
- avoid unpasteurized goats' milk and cheese.
- wear rubber gloves to handle cat litter and always wash your hands and the gloves afterwards (but preferably get someone else to do the job for you).
- wear gloves for gardening.
- keep children's sandpits covered to prevent cats using them as litter boxes.

To Avoid Listeriosis

Listeriosis is an infection from the bacteria listeria, which can thrive in unpasteurized cheeses, meat pâtés, cold prepared meats, ready prepared cook-chill meals and chicken carcasses. Although it causes only mild flu-like symptoms in an adult it can lead to miscarriage in early pregnancy or premature labour mid-pregnancy, resulting in the stillbirth of your baby. However, listeriosis is very rare – it affects only one pregnancy in every 20,000, and if infection is suspected you can be treated with antibiotics. Avoid the possibility of infection by not eating or drinking:

◆ unpasteurized milk.
◆ unpasteurized cheese.
◆ food which has not been properly refrigerated.
◆ pâté.
◆ cook-chill foods.
◆ ready prepared salads.

To Avoid Salmonella

Salmonella, found in eggs and chickens, causes severe diarrhoea in adults and should be avoided in pregnancy, so:

◆ cook all eggs solid (no poached, scrambled, soft boiled etc.).
◆ wash your hands after handling raw chicken.
◆ make sure chicken is fully cooked.

To Avoid Chlamydiosis

The bacteria Chlamydia psittaci is found in sheep which have recently lambed, their placentas and newborn lambs. It can cause pregnant women to miscarry, so avoid all contact with sheep and lambs during pregnancy. Their meat and dairy products, however, are perfectly safe in pregnancy provided you follow the usual rules about such foods (see pp.38 and 40). (Despite the similarity in names this bacteria has nothing to do with the sexually transmitted condition known as chlamydia.)

Your Pregnancy Diet

Start as you mean to go on and follow these healthy eating guidelines right through pregnancy. From the following groups, try to aim for a variety of foods each day to ensure that you get all the nutrients you and your baby need.

Bread, Other Cereals and Potatoes

The various breads, cereals, rice, pasta, noodles and potatoes are good sources of carbohydrates, protein and B vitamins. They're also low in fat, filling and relatively cheap. Aim for four to six servings per day.

Fruit and Vegetables

Aim to eat four to six servings per day and try to include dark green vegetables such as spinach or broccoli, and orange-coloured vegetables and fruit. Examples of one serving are one orange or apple, two average tomatoes, and six to eight grapes.

◆ Always wash fruit and vegetables before you cook them.
◆ Don't store fruit and vegetables for too long because the vitamin content goes.
◆ Eat some raw vegetables each day.
◆ Steaming or microwaving vegetables is preferable to boiling them, which destroys a lot of the vitamins.

Meat, Fish and Other Sources of Protein

Poultry, meat, fish, eggs, nuts and pulses (baked beans, lentils, chick peas and red kidney beans) are a major source of protein, vitamins and minerals. Aim to eat two to three servings per day. Cook meat, fish and eggs right through, and refuse pâté. Avoid peanuts if food allergies run in your family – eating peanuts while pregnant may contribute to a nut allergy in your child.

Dairy Products

Milk, yogurt and cheese are high in calcium and also provide protein. Aim for two to three servings per day, but avoid unpasteurized products. One serving is equivalent to 0.2 litres (⅓ pint) of milk, a small pot of yogurt or 40 g (1½oz) Cheddar cheese. The low-fat varieties supply just as much calcium as their high-fat alternatives.

Cheeses which are best avoided in pregnancy are ripened soft ones such as Brie and Camembert, and all blue-veined cheeses (even pasteurized) such as Stilton, Roquefort, Danish Blue and Dolcelatte. You can safely eat hard cheeses like Cheddar, Babybel, Gruyère, Edam and Parmesan; and soft cheeses such as Philadelphia, Mozzarella and processed cheese spreads.

Avoid Too Many Fatty and Sugary Foods

◆ Remove visible fat from meat and take the skin off chicken.
◆ Grill rather than fry.
◆ Steam or bake fish for the healthiest results.

Before you pick up a snack, ask yourself if it's good for your baby. Choose fresh fruit and vegetables in season and try to eat some raw fruit and vegetables every day.

INVOLVING YOUR PARTNER

Make the most of every opportunity to involve your partner in these early weeks of pregnancy. If he cooks regularly, he should be aware of the importance of hygiene in the kitchen. Encourage him to eat the same foods as you, to give up smoking, and cut down on the amount he drinks. He may even be persuaded to take up exercising with you, too ...

Most men these days do enjoy being involved and included in the pregnancy – and most will be happy to attend the delivery too, although this is not essential and nobody should be made to feel obliged to be at the birth if it's likely to make them feel uncomfortable.

Even if he's not keen to attend the birth, he may want to:

- join you for antenatal appointments with your midwife, and any hospital outpatient visits (for example, your ultrasound scans).
- read all the pregnancy books and join in with antenatal classes.
- plan the baby's nursery and have a say in the furnishings and layette.
- talk about his anxieties as well as yours – give him the opportunity to speak to the midwife if there's anything he's concerned about and needs reassurance.

- Cut down on fatty spreads. Low-fat equivalents can taste just as good in a sandwich.
- Keep puddings, biscuits and cakes for occasional treats rather than having them every day.

Kitchen Hygiene

- Keep the kitchen clean and dry.
- Wash your hands before preparing food.
- Keep the fridge temperature below 5 degrees C and the freezer below -18 degrees C.
- Store raw meat, covered, in the bottom of the fridge so that it can't drip on to other foods. Always keep it completely separate from any cooked meat (which should be stored on upper shelves).
- Cook foods thoroughly.
- Always stick to the 'use-by' guidelines.
- Keep pets out of the kitchen.

EXERCISE IN THE FIRST TRIMESTER

Your grandmother may have been warned not to take exercise during pregnancy, but it's now generally agreed that exercise is good for most pregnant women. However, this is not the time to start anything new; and, if you've been used to doing fairly strenuous sports, you must be prepared to adapt to a gentler routine during the next nine months. It's worth making a point of discussing the types of exercise you enjoy with your midwife or doctor when you attend your first appointment at the antenatal clinic. The goal of exercising in pregnancy is to improve your overall health. It will make you feel better physically and emotionally.

Some women should not exercise during pregnancy, and you're advised not to do so if:

◆ You have a history of an incompetent cervix (see pp.231–32), repeated miscarriages or premature deliveries.
◆ You have high blood pressure in early pregnancy.
◆ You're expecting twins or more.
◆ You have a heart disease.
◆ You've had vaginal bleeding.

Specific Forms of Exercise

Aerobics – If you've been doing aerobics regularly before you became pregnant you can continue until you feel too big. But don't exert yourself too much or become overheated, and drink plenty of water before and after classes. Limit yourself to thirty minutes per session and ensure your teacher knows you're pregnant, so she can adapt exercises for you. Don't jump up and down – always try to keep one foot on the ground. Consider switching to a low-impact class for your pregnancy.

Badminton – The game is more strenuous than it looks, so take it easy. Your biggest risk is overstretching and pulling muscles and ligaments, which are more supple in pregnancy. As with aerobics, you must take care not to jump up and down.

Cycling – This is safe in pregnancy, as long as you don't fall off. Be careful how you go, and remember as you get bigger you'll have more weight at the front which could make you topple off.

Golf – The average nine-hole golf course is about 4 km (2½ miles) long, so this is the perfect form of exercise at a gentle pace. But be careful not to twist your knees and pelvis too much.

HOW MUCH EXERCISE?

Recommendations for pregnant women are to exercise three times a week for no more than thirty minutes per session. If you miss a day or two, don't be put off. A little exercise is better than none.

Jogging – If you're a fan and have been jogging regularly for a long time, you may carry on with it. But try to develop a low stride which avoids jarring.

Swimming – A perfect exercise for pregnancy as your weight is supported by the water. But be careful not to widen your legs too much during breast stroke, as this opens up the pelvis.

Tennis – Fine for the first trimester, but later you should stick to practising shots rather than playing a game.

Walking – A great low-impact aerobic exercise. If you hate all other types of keep-fit, try to take a twenty-minute walk every day.

Now is also the time to start your important pelvic floor exercises (see below).

Keep Your Pelvic Floor Strong

The pelvic floor is the sling of muscles that helps hold the pelvic organs in place, and pelvic floor exercises are important throughout your life. If the muscles in this area are allowed to become slack you may enjoy sexual intercourse less and may have more difficulty than before in reaching orgasm. Your partner may also find lovemaking less enjoyable. A particularly weak pelvic floor can lead to incontinence and sagging vaginal walls.

A strong pelvic floor is especially important during pregnancy because the increase in progesterone softens tissues and ligaments and allows the body to stretch more easily. The pelvic floor softens too, and the weight from your growing baby may weaken it. Strengthening the pelvic floor now will help you avoid 'leaking' when you laugh or sneeze after the baby is born, and will also help the vagina to return to normal soon after pregnancy – and enable you to heal faster if you have to have stitches.

Test the strength of your pelvic floor during intercourse by squeezing your partner's penis in your vagina; or, when you are urinating, stop the flow and restart it. If you can stop completely in mid-flow, your muscles are in good shape. (But avoid doing this if you suffer regular bladder infections.)

The Drawbridge Exercise

This, the essential pelvic floor exercise, is best learned when you're lying down on the floor.

- Lie down with your knees bent up, hip-width apart, and your feet flat on the floor. Let your arms relax.
- Tighten the vagina as if you're clamping it around a tampon.

◆ Tighten the urethra as if you're trying to hold a flow of urine.
◆ Tighten the anus as if you're trying to hold back a bowel movement.
◆ Now think of these three tightened areas as one bridge or lift, and imagine you are lifting the drawbridge up inside you. Tighten a little, then stop (without relaxing), then tighten a little more and stop again. Hold this squeeze and breathe slowly in and out, then let your drawbridge down in as many stages as you can manage.

Once you've mastered the exercise lying down, you can try it sitting, standing or walking. Aim to do it whenever you can – when you make a cup of tea, do the washing up, take the dog for a walk, brush your teeth or watch your favourite TV programme. Getting into a habit will make you do the exercise without even thinking about it. One postnatal exercise class got mothers to do their pelvic floor exercise to the tune of 'Bridge Over Troubled Water'. The idea was that, since this is still one of the world's most-played recordings, women would find themselves automatically doing their exercise while queuing at supermarket checkouts or sitting in cafés where the song was being played!

Further exercises to do during pregnancy will be found on pp.82–86. You can do these further exercises in the first trimester if you're already fairly fit, but most women find they're more geared up to them during the second trimester.

YOUR BABY'S DEVELOPMENT IN WEEKS 1–12

Week 2

Around fourteen days after the first day of your last period conception takes place.

Week 3

The embryo implants in the wall of the uterus. In just one week it has grown from a single cell to a mass of over a hundred cells and is still growing. The outer cells reach out like roots to link with your blood supply. The inner cells separate into two, then three, layers which develop into different parts of the baby's body. One layer becomes the brain and nervous system, skin, eyes and ears; the second becomes the lungs, gut and stomach; and the third becomes the heart, blood, muscles and bones.

Week 4

Eyes and ears start to form, and the baby's head and 'tail' are present.

Week 5

The arms start to form. The baby already has some of its own blood vessels and a string of these connect the baby to you, forming the umbilical cord.

Week 6

The spinal canal closes around the spinal cord. If you were to have an ultrasound scan now to confirm the pregnancy, it would be able to pick up the baby's heart movements and the embryo should be visible.

Week 7

The head and body are now well established and the baby is about 13 mm long from head to bottom, though it's too early to see different structures of the embryo on an ultrasound scan.

Week 8

The embryo begins to move and the head can be differentiated from the body on an ultrasound scan. A face is slowly forming. The eyes are more obvious and have some colour in them. There's a mouth with a tongue. The embryo has the beginnings of hands and feet, with ridges where the fingers and toes will be.

Week 9

Your baby is now about 30 mm long from head to bottom. The fingers have separated but the toes are still stuck together. The arms and legs can be seen on a scan.

Week 10

The heart is fully formed and the embryo is now called a fetus. It has a human appearance with eyes, eyelids and ears, and on an ultrasound – if you choose to have one – now looks like a little human.

Week 11

The spine, skull and some internal organs are now visible on a scan.

Week 12

The fetus can produce urine and it's possible to identify its sex.

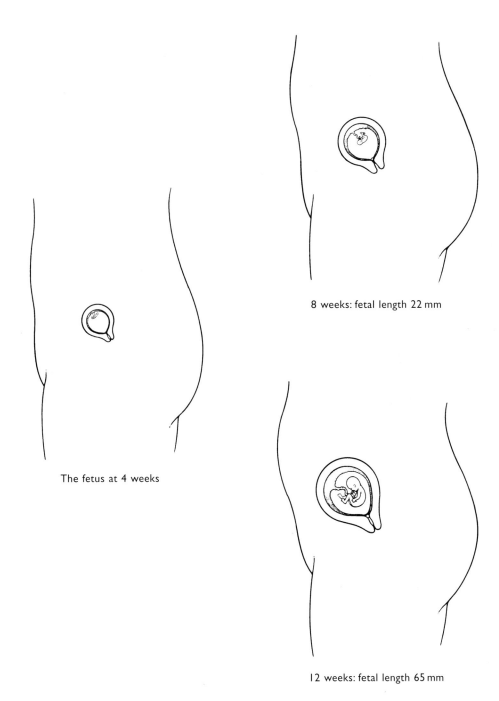

8 weeks: fetal length 22 mm

The fetus at 4 weeks

12 weeks: fetal length 65 mm

Although you may be barely aware of your pregnancy in the early weeks, dramatic changes are taking place – and, by the 12th week, your baby has sexual organs and even 32 permanent tooth buds!

CHANGES TO YOUR BODY

Absence of Periods

Missing your period is usually the first sign of pregnancy. But you may experience some slight spotting when your period should have been – and this can happen when the fertilized egg implants in your womb.

Appetite Increase

The desire to eat more is normal. Don't fight it – pregnancy is not the time to diet (see pp.37–40). But do eat sensibly.

Braxton Hicks Contractions

From very early in the pregnancy (as soon as eight weeks) the uterus begins making practice contractions. They will become more noticeable as the pregnancy progresses, but at this early stage are very slight, and are rarely noticed by women before the 28th week.

Breast Changes

Especially in your first pregnancy, the growth of your breasts is likely to be one of the first signs of impending motherhood. Some women experience swelling and hardening of their breasts premenstrually, and the hormones which govern pregnancy have the same effect.

These changes are aimed at preparing you to feed your baby when it arrives. If they are less pronounced in a second or subsequent pregnancy, it doesn't mean that you will be less capable of breastfeeding. Having gone through one pregnancy already, they may need less preparation time (although some women balloon from the first month with every pregnancy) and may gradually grow along with your baby, or may hold off until after delivery when milk production begins.

As well as getting bigger, your breasts will probably undergo other changes:

- The areola (the pigmented area around the nipple) will darken and spread. This darkening may fade but not disappear entirely after the baby's birth.
- The little bumps on the areola, which are sweat glands, may also enlarge. They will return to normal after you've had your baby, or after you've stopped breastfeeding.

At the end of your first trimester, your pregnancy is just beginning to show.

◆ Blue veins on your breasts may become more noticeable, but the skin will eventually return to normal.

◆ Especially during the first trimester, your breasts may be agonizingly tender to touch. Fortunately this tends to pass after week 12.

TO ALLEVIATE SORE BREASTS

Soothe sore breasts with warm water compresses, or compresses of damask rose flower water. Make sure your bra still fits. If not, change it.

Complexion Changes

Some women have a glowing skin in pregnancy. Others, unfortunately, suffer acne. Both states are brought about by the increased secretion of oils due to hormonal changes. If you get premenstrual acne, you're more likely to break out in spots now too. But sticking to a healthy diet and drinking plenty of water will help keep your skin as clear as possible.

Constipation

This is a very common problem in pregnancy. Elimination is sluggish now that the muscles around the bowel are beginning to relax, and the pressure from your growing womb also inhibits normal bowel activity. Do all you can to avoid being constipated, though, as it can lead to haemorrhoids (see pp.78–79).

Plenty of fruit and fibre in your diet, washed down with the recommended 2 litres (4 pints) of still drinking water every day, will help fight constipation. Regular exercise – for example a brisk half-hour walk or a swim – will also help.

Don't worry if you don't get constipated! It's not an obligatory symptom of pregnancy, and its absence is most likely to be a sign that you've acted on the advice for changing your diet and lifestyle before getting pregnant. However, if your stools are very frequent (more than twice a day) or loose, or watery, or contain blood or mucus, consult your doctor. Diarrhoea during pregnancy should not be ignored.

Cravings

Don't expect to start craving coal or disinfectant now you're pregnant. Although they exist in popular belief there are very few recorded cases of these bizarre cravings, which are known as pica. The records are mostly from research carried out in the 1950s, when women's nutrition was generally not as good as it is now. Pica, if it happens, can be a sign of nutritional deficiency, particularly of iron, so it should be reported to your doctor or midwife.

The more common cravings are for ice cream, chocolate, citrus fruits and juices, and sweets. Some research suggests that women who crave foods in pregnancy are more likely to develop nausea than those who don't. But most women stop experiencing cravings after the first trimester. (See also Food Aversions on p.50.)

Dizziness or Faintness

Common in the first trimester, dizziness may be related to the pressure on your blood supply to meet your rapidly expanding circulatory system. You may also feel dizzy if your blood sugar is low because you've gone too long without food. If you suffer in this way eat something rich in protein at every meal to keep your blood sugar stable, and try taking more frequent, smaller meals or snacks between meals. You should also try not to get up too quickly when you've been sitting or lying down, as a sudden shift of blood away from the brain causes dizziness.

If you think you're going to faint, increase the circulation to your brain by lying down. Actual fainting is rare, but if you do faint it won't affect the baby. Recover from fainting by lying down on your side, to take the weight of pregnancy off the major blood vessels in your abdomen. But report actual fainting promptly to your doctor, or let him know at your routine visit about any dizziness you've been experiencing.

Fatigue and Sleepiness

Even when you're resting, your body is working harder than it ever did before you were pregnant. During this first trimester it's working extra hard to produce the placenta which will be your baby's life support system (and will be complete around the fourth month), so during this time you may need to give in and take more rest than you'd planned. Don't overdo it – fatigue is a sign that your body needs time off. If you're at home without other children to look after, indulge in a regular afternoon nap during the first three months. Even if you can't afford this luxury you can go to bed an hour earlier at night, and if possible enlist the help of your partner in the morning so you can sleep in. But don't miss out on exercise because you're tired. A walk will do you good – too much rest and not enough activity will make you even more tired. But remember not to push yourself too far.

Flatulence (Wind)

If you have wind it will not affect your baby, unless it prevents you from eating regularly and properly. But you can prevent the situation, and save yourself a lot of embarrassment, by taking the following measures:

◆ Fight constipation (see p.48).
◆ Eat six small meals a day instead of three larger ones.
◆ Don't rush your eating.
◆ Keep calm at mealtimes to avoid swallowing air.
◆ Avoid the obvious culprits – onions, beans and fried foods.

Food Aversions

Mercifully a lot of women tend to go off the things which are bad for them in pregnancy, such as coffee and alcohol, and this makes keeping off them a whole lot easier. It's more of a problem if you go off healthy foods which you know you should be eating. Don't force feed yourself, but do try to compensate with suitable alternatives from the same food group. If you notice that certain foods smell or taste peculiar now you're pregnant it could be a sign of zinc deficiency, according to one study – check that you're eating enough zinc-rich foods, e.g. red meat and nuts.

Frequent Urination

Most pregnant women notice that they need to urinate more than usual, particularly in the first and last trimesters. First, you're producing a greater volume of body fluids and the kidneys are responding by speeding up the process by which they get rid of waste products. Secondly, the growing uterus is putting pressure on the bladder while the two organs are still next to each other in the pelvis during the first trimester. You may not have to go to the loo quite so often once the uterus has risen into the abdominal cavity around the fourth month. In the meantime, try leaning forward when you urinate to make sure you empty your bladder completely.

Headaches

Pregnancy headaches are commonly caused by hormonal changes but can also be the result of fatigue, tension, stress and hunger. Make sure you get plenty of rest and eat regularly.

Aromatherapy is a relaxing treatment in pregnancy, but some essential oils are not suitable for use in the first trimester. Seek expert advice before using oils in your bath or for massage. (See also p.110.)

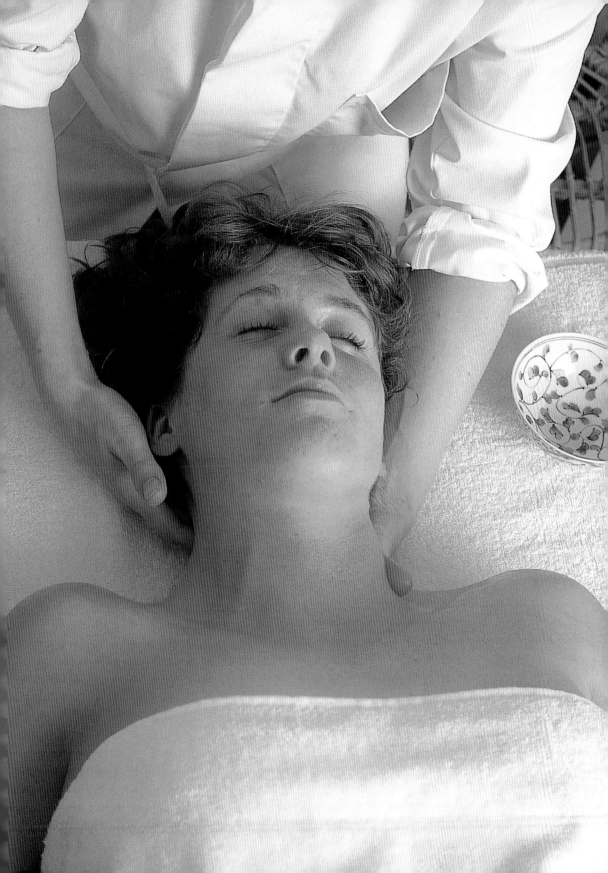

To Relieve Headaches

Give yourself a facial massage. With your eyes shut and your hands in front of your face, palms towards you, apply the middle finger pad all along the outer edges of your eye socket zone. (If you wear contact lenses, remove them first.) With your hands in the same position, bring your middle finger forward to press up against the bottom edge of the cheekbone, and out to the temple. Afterwards lie down with your eyes covered by pads soaked in lavender flower water, and use a hot water compress on your forehead.

Heartburn

The oesophagus is the tube that carries food from your mouth to your stomach. When the ring of muscle that separates the oesophagus from the stomach relaxes (see Indigestion below), it allows partially digested food and harsh digestive juices to travel back up from the stomach to the oesophagus. These stomach acids irritate its sensitive lining, causing a burning sensation about where the heart is – hence the name, which has nothing to do with your heart.

Ten Ways to Avoid Heartburn and Indigestion

- Avoid gaining too much weight – it will put more pressure on your stomach.
- Wear loose clothing, so your stomach isn't squeezed.
- Eat six small meals a day rather than three larger ones.
- Eat slowly, taking small mouthfuls, and chew thoroughly.
- Avoid fried and fatty foods, processed meat such as sausages and bacon, chocolate, coffee, alcohol and fizzy drinks.
- Don't smoke.
- Relax.
- Sleep with your head supported – use an extra pillow or put a firm block under your pillow (I used the wedge seat which, by day, I used on my office chair to support my back).
- Bend at the knees instead of the waist.
- Ask your doctor or pharmacist to recommend a low-sodium antacid which is safe in pregnancy.

Indigestion

Early in pregnancy your body produces large amounts of progesterone and oestrogen which relax the muscles everywhere, including the gastro-intestinal tract. This can cause food to move more slowly through your system, leading to bloating and indigestion. Although uncomfortable for you, the slowing down of the digestive process results in better absorption of nutrients into your bloodstream and subsequently the placenta, which feeds your baby. So you can console yourself with the knowledge that while you may hate the effects, they're in a good cause.

Libido Changes

If you've never had an enormous appetite for sex you may be surprised to discover how it has increased since becoming pregnant. Feeling sexier is one of the nicest symptoms many women experience, but it may not happen until the second trimester (see Chapter 3), especially if you experience nausea, excess fatigue and painful breasts.

SEX IN PREGNANCY

Most couples find their sexual relationship changes, for better or worse, during a pregnancy. For some it's better than ever before. For others, it's right off the agenda. The 'typical' pattern, however, is for sexual interest to drop off in the first trimester when you feel nauseous and tired, to pick up in the second trimester, then to tail off again in the third trimester.

Milk Intolerance

Many women go off milk in pregnancy, but don't worry if it happens to you. Although you need calcium for your baby, it doesn't have to come from milk. See the lists of food on pp.16 and 38 for ideas. If you can't tolerate any of these, talk to your doctor about taking a supplement.

Nausea

Over 80 per cent of pregnant women suffer from morning sickness in some way. Nobody knows why it happens or why some women are affected while others are not. But you're more likely to suffer if you also get nauseous on the contraceptive pill, suffer travel sickness or get sick with migraines.

Symptoms linked to morning sickness include hunger, cravings, pica (the desire to eat something inedible, like coal), an aversion to certain foods (usually coffee and alcohol), burping, heartburn, and feeling queasy at the touch, sight or smell of something unpleasant.

The most severe form of morning sickness, known as Hyperemesis Gravidarum, is discussed on pp.230–31. Fortunately it is quite rare.

PREVENTING MORNING SICKNESS

- Get as much rest as possible.
- Take your time getting out of bed.
- Indulge your cravings.
- Get plenty of exercise and fresh air.
- Separate drinks from meals.
- Avoid cooking as far as possible.
- Steer clear of fried foods and caffeine.
- Ginger can help food pass more rapidly through the digestive system, as well as reducing stimulation to the part of the brain which prompts nausea. Try sucking a lentil-sized pellet of ginger root, or sip fizzy ginger ale.
- Don't brush your teeth straight after a meal as this can make you gag.

Saliva

You may find you produce excessive saliva during the first trimester. This is known as ptyalism, and can be so excessive that it's impossible to swallow the saliva produced without being sick. It's more common in women experiencing morning sickness than in those who aren't, but usually disappears after the first few months.

Sleeping Difficulties

It's one of the ironies of early pregnancy that, despite increased fatigue during the day, you find you cannot sleep well at night. The following tips may help:

- Develop a bedtime routine with a slow pace after dinner, and have a relaxing bath before bed. Try to go to bed at the same time every night.
- Don't take work to bed with you – it will make your mind race and prevent you sleeping. Instead read something light, listen to soothing music or watch light TV.
- Naturopaths associate iron deficiency with poor sleep. An iron-rich diet with plenty of pulses, dark green leafy vegetables and nuts can help.
- Too much caffeine is a classic culprit for a restless night. Although people who drink a lot of coffee develop a tolerance to caffeine and sleep well, you should try to avoid too much coffee, tea, chocolate or cola in the evening.
- Going to bed feeling hungry, or over-full, will keep you awake. Try to eat early in the evening, and, if you're hungry just before bedtime, eat something sleep-inducing like a banana.

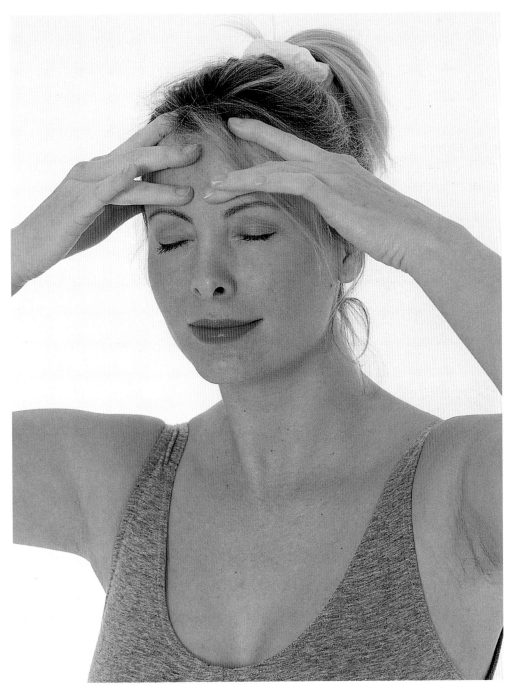

Headaches in pregnancy may be caused by hormonal changes, or a higher level of sensitivity in your sinuses. A gentle facial massage can make a difference (see p.52) and avoids the need to use unnecessary painkillers (see p.87).

◆ A sweetened milk drink at bedtime will help you sleep because the sugars enable the brain cells to absorb more tryptophan (provided by the milk protein) from the bloodstream. This is converted into a substance called serotonin, which is calming.

◆ Starchy foods – pasta, rice and potatoes – balance blood sugar levels and also encourage the release of serotonin.

Vein Changes

Blue lines on your breasts and abdomen are normal – they are signs that your body is doing what it should and expanding its network of veins to carry the increased blood supply of pregnancy. They may be especially noticeable if you're very slim or pale-skinned.

Spider naevi – purplish red lines, usually on the thighs – can result from the hormone changes in pregnancy and often fade after delivery. If they don't, they can be removed.

Varicose veins affect about 15 per cent of adults, mostly women. They are caused by pooling of blood in the surface veins when the valves which normally prevent blood from draining back down the leg are defective. The hormonal changes which occur in pregnancy can contribute to this happening.

The disorder tends to run in families, and usually the veins appear blue and visibly enlarged on the backs of your calves or the insides of your legs. Where the vein is prominent you may get a severe ache (especially if you've been standing a long time), your feet and ankles may swell, and your skin is likely to be itchy. These symptoms are often particularly bad in pregnancy, and sitting with your legs up is the best way to ease any discomfort.

DEALING WITH VARICOSE VEINS

◆ Wear support stockings or tights.
◆ Walk regularly.
◆ Stand still as little as possible.
◆ Sit with your feet up when you're resting.
◆ Get plenty of vitamin C, which is said to keep veins healthy and elastic.

Swollen 'varicose' veins can occur around the vulva in pregnancy. To avoid them, try not to sit with your legs crossed, to stand for long periods or to put on too much weight. Sleeping with your legs on a pillow can help.

Waistline Expansion

If you started out very slim, your waistline may begin to expand very early in pregnancy as you have little excess flesh for your growing uterus to hide behind. But it could be a sign that you're gaining too much weight too soon. If you've put on 1.7 kg (3 lb) by the second month, look at your diet and cut out items such as cakes and sweets.

Weight Gain

Some weight gain is normal, but not obligatory, in the first three months. Even if morning sickness has prevented you gaining any weight your baby will be OK, as his or her need for calories and certain nutrients is not as great now as it will be later. But not gaining weight from the end of the third month onwards can have an effect. So try to eat well from now on, aiming to gain 0.6 kg (1 lb) a week through to your eighth month.

If you've already gained too much weight by your third month, there's little you can do about it now. Dieting is not an option in pregnancy. But from now on eat sensibly, cutting out sweet, high-fat and junk foods.

CHANGES TO YOUR EMOTIONS

Anxiety

Feeling anxious about your baby's health is par for the course. Every expectant mother is concerned that her baby will be normal, but it is only a problem if it becomes an obsession and you can't look after yourself properly. In this case discuss the matter with your doctor or midwife, who will do all they can to allay your fears.

Premenstrual-type Emotions

Irritability, irrationality, weepiness and moodiness are normal in pregnant women, especially at the very early stages and if you normally suffer from PMS (premenstrual syndrome). Ambivalence about the pregnancy is also quite usual, even if the baby is planned and longed for. The usual rules – eating sensibly, exercising regularly and getting enough rest – apply to mood swings too. Doing these things should help keep your feelings in perspective. If your depression seems consistent in spite of your efforts to fight it, discuss it with your doctor or midwife who may refer you to a counsellor. It's important to take all the help available: if you're depressed you may not be able to take full care of yourself and your growing baby.

COMMON WORRIES

Age at First Pregnancy

Any doctor will tell you there's no 'right age' to have a baby. You've got to feel you're at the right time in your life – and that might be when you're twenty, thirty or forty, according to personal circumstances.

In the past, women usually got married young and started having babies straightaway. But nowadays we often want to travel, develop careers and build our own lives, so we take our time about deciding when to start a family. More and more women are postponing that moment until they're approaching thirty, when their friends and workmates are also having babies.

The female body has long been thought to cope best with pregnancy and childbirth when it's young – eighteen to twenty-two. This is the age at which there are fewest complications in pregnancy – the risk of having a baby with Down's syndrome, for example, is 1 in 2000 for a twenty-year-old; 3 in 1000 for a thirty-five-year-old; and 1 in 100 for a forty-year-old. The risk of miscarriage is lower in young women too.

But the average age for first-time mums in England and Wales is creeping up. It currently stands at twenty-nine, with over a quarter of first babies being born to women in the thirty to thirty-four age group. And once the pregnancy is established, even women who have their first baby when they are over thirty-five are no more likely to have problems than young mothers.

You're just as likely to have a short and problem-free labour and delivery. Despite being labelled 'high-risk' at the first antenatal visit a first-time mother of thirty-five is no more likely to have a ventouse or forceps delivery (see pp.184–85), or an emergency caesarean, than a first-time mum of twenty.

The main difference in older women is in their recovery after the birth. Older mums suffer extreme tiredness, stress incontinence (see pp.247–48) and pain in the legs. But younger mothers are not completely free of problems, and are far more likely to suffer headaches in the first year after the baby's birth.

However late you leave it before having a baby, medical advances are on your side. Potential birth defects can be identified early on (see Chapter 5) if you are concerned and choose to have the ultrasound scans and other tests now routinely offered to expectant mothers. But screening is not obligatory, and you are entitled to refuse any test. Perhaps even more important are the steps older mothers can take to improve the odds for themselves and their babies, through exercise, diet and quality antenatal care.

To reduce the risk in your pregnancy:

♦ Seeing your doctor or midwife regularly is vital – and make sure you ask lots of questions and report any symptoms.
♦ Follow a healthy diet. Avoid too many fatty and sugary foods, and try to eat a range of foods from each of the following groups: bread, other cereals and potatoes; fruit and vegetables; meat, fish and other sources of protein; dairy products.
♦ Take regular exercise to improve circulation and muscle tone.
♦ Stop smoking, and cut down on the amount you drink – no more than one small glass of wine a day.
♦ Take plenty of rest before your body begs you to.

Bleeding

Staining around the time you would have had your period can be a sign of implantation. It may alternatively be that the pregnancy hormones are not yet high enough to prevent spotting. Cut out unnecessary exertion and rest if you can. Bleeding that's as heavy as a period, or staining that continues for more than three days, may be a sign of miscarriage (see pp.234–36), although this is not always the case – talk to your midwife or doctor anyway.

Blighted Ovum

See p.222.

Breasts

If your breasts enlarge, then suddenly shrink again, especially if other pregnancy symptoms disappear, contact your doctor or midwife.

Caesarean History

It's no longer the case that if you have had one caesarean every subsequent baby will be delivered the same way (see Chapter 6).

Cats

See Toxoplasmosis (p.249).

Contraceptive Pill

Ideally you should try to come off the pill two or three months before conceiving. However, there is no statistical evidence of increased risk of damage to babies conceived while their mothers were on the pill.

Cramp after Orgasm

Suffering cramp during and after orgasm is very common and harmless during a low-risk pregnancy. It's caused by congestion of the sexual organs during arousal and orgasm, and congestion of the veins in the pelvic area. If you experience cramp and your pregnancy has been designated high-risk, talk to your doctor about it – particularly if you have had previous premature labours.

Ectopic Pregnancy

See p.226.

Fibroids

About 1–2 per cent of women have fibroids in pregnancy, and most go to full term without complications. But occasionally these benign growths in the uterus can slightly increase your risk of ectopic pregnancy, miscarriage, placenta praevia, abruptio placenta and problems with labour and delivery. For more information see Part 3.

If your doctor thinks your fibroids might interfere with a safe vaginal delivery, he may suggest a caesarean. If you've had extensive surgery for fibroids in the past, this could have weakened the uterus and make labour difficult. Again your obstetrician may suggest a caesarean. But you should also get to know what to expect of an early labour (see pp.107–109) – just in case it starts before your planned caesarean.

Hydatiform Mole

Very rarely (about 1 in 1800 pregnancies) a defective egg cell with no nucleus becomes fertilized and begins to develop as if it were a normal pregnancy. This is called a hydatiform mole. There is no embryo, but the placenta develops as if there was – producing pregnancy hormones and making you feel pregnant – until, at between eight and sixteen weeks, when the body realizes there is something wrong, the mole is miscarried. Other signs may include very severe morning sickness due to the high level of hormones, or vaginal bleeding.

If the mole is diagnosed before you miscarry, it will be removed either with a D and C (see p.131), or with pessaries or a drip to speed up the miscarriage. In about 3 per cent of cases the mole can become cancerous – but this is easy to detect and there is an almost 100 per cent cure rate. However, you will have to send regular samples of urine to be monitored for up to fifteen months.

See also Choriocarcinoma (p.222).

Incompetent Cervix

See pp.231–32.

IUD Still in Place

If your IUD was still in place when you conceived, you have two options. You can have the coil taken out if the removal cord is protruding from the cervix. Or if it's not visible you can leave it in place – in which case your pregnancy still has a good chance of proceeding uneventfully. The IUD will simply be pushed against the wall of the uterus by the expanding amniotic sac surrounding the baby, and during childbirth it will be delivered with the placenta.

If the coil is visible at the cervix in the early stages, your chances of a safe and successful pregnancy are greater if the coil is removed as soon as possible. The risk of miscarrying with its removal is 20 per cent (no higher than the rate of miscarriage for all known pregnancies). Your risk increases if it's left in place – so you should be extra vigilant about any bleeding, cramps or fever and notify your doctor or midwife immediately if you experience any of these symptoms.

Jacuzzis and Hot Baths

Anything that raises the body temperature over 38.9 degrees C and keeps it high is potentially hazardous to your baby, especially in the early months. You should be all right if you have the water at a reasonable temperature and keep your head and shoulders outside it. In practice too hot a bath is likely to make you feel uncomfortable, so you would get out anyway. Public jacuzzis are not recommended because of the risk of infection from germs. See also Saunas (p.62).

Miscarriage

The most common causes of miscarriage in the first trimester are ectopic pregnancy, blighted ovum and hormonal problems. High levels of luteinizing hormone (LH), particularly likely if you suffer from any condition caused by hormone imbalance, such as polycystic ovaries, can increase the likelihood of miscarriage. Daily urine tests will detect if you have a high level of LH, and treatment can be prescribed to prevent too much being secreted.

A miscarriage in the first sixteen weeks of pregnancy may be due to low levels of either progesterone or HCG (human chorionic gonadotrophin), the hormones which help maintain a pregnancy. Hormone injections, once thought to prevent miscarriage in subsequent pregnancies, are no longer considered safe. See also pp.234–36.

Obesity

Health risks do multiply with excess weight – in and out of pregnancy. The risk of hypertension and diabetes is higher, and it can also be difficult for the doctor to determine the baby's size by feeling your abdomen if it's over-padded. Even if you don't over-eat in pregnancy, your obesity can produce a much larger than average baby. And if a caesarean section is necessary, your size can complicate both surgery and your recovery.

Right from the start of pregnancy obese mothers have to undergo more tests than those of normal weight, and both mother and baby will be closely monitored throughout the pregnancy. Dieting now is inadvisable, but you may be told to restrict yourself to 1800–2000 calories a day, and these should all be packed with nutrition for your optimum health. If you're planning to have another baby after this one, you'll be advised to get as close as possible to your ideal weight before you conceive.

Picking Up Other Children

In second and subsequent pregnancies picking up other children early in pregnancy is often inevitable. But it shouldn't pose a risk unless, because of your medical history, your doctor has advised you to avoid lifting.

Rhesus Incompatibility

See pp.245–46.

Saunas

The weekly sauna is customary in Finland, even for pregnant women. Yet defects to babies' central nervous systems caused by hyperthermia (a dangerous rise in body temperature) aren't common in that country. So although many experts advise mothers to avoid saunas, the evidence of risk is unclear. However, until more is known on this subject it's best to play safe.

Spermicides

Many women become pregnant while using spermicides around the time of conception, but there has been little evidence of this having a detrimental effect on babies.

STDs (Sexually Transmitted Diseases)

Gonorrhoea, syphilis, chlamydia, nonspecific vaginitis, genital warts and HIV can all harm your unborn baby. But all can be treated even in pregnancy. Report unusual symptoms, such as an abnormal vaginal discharge, as soon as possible. If you feel there is a risk of HIV, discuss it with your midwife who will refer you to a specialist. Treatment can reduce the risk of transmission to your baby.

Vomiting Excessively

See Hyperemesis Gravidarum (pp.230–31).

X-rays

Although X-rays can be harmful to your unborn baby, the level of risk depends on a number of factors. No damage appears to occur if the dose is lower than 10 rads. The stage in the pregnancy when the exposure occurs is also relevant (and then only if the dose is high). Finally, it depends on whether the uterus itself is exposed to the X-ray (but even if it is, the level of radiation is usually below 10 rads, so the risk is minimized). Even so, you should always inform the doctor ordering the X-ray, and the technician performing it, that you are pregnant. And only have an X-ray if the benefit outweighs the risk and there is no safer alternative procedure.

YOUR QUESTIONS ANSWERED

Q: *How often must I see my doctor or midwife in pregnancy?*

A: Unless there are particular problems, you will be advised to see your doctor or midwife every four weeks during the first seven months, then every two weeks until the last month, then once a week.

Q: *Am I likely to be referred to a perinatologist?*

A: Probably not – although most pregnant women see their consultant obstetrician at some time in the pregnancy, only about 10 per cent are referred to a perinatologist, who's a specialist in high-risk pregnancies. But if you've had problems with past pregnancies, for example, you may be referred this time round.

Q: *Will my morning sickness last all through the pregnancy?*

A: It's usually far worse in the first trimester, starting around week 6 and finishing or lessening around week 12 or 13.

Q: *If I catch an infection, what harm will it do to my baby?*

A: Some infections are more damaging than others – the main high-risk ones are listed here, but always remind your doctor you're pregnant even if you're contacting him about something which appears to you to be unrelated to pregnancy.

- **Chicken pox** can cause heart problems in the baby.
- **Cytomegalovirus** can cause brain damage, microcephaly, and hearing loss (see pp.222–23).
- **Fifth disease** slightly increases your risk of miscarriage (see p.228).
- **Group B streptococcus** can cause pneumonia, meningitis, cerebral palsy, and damage to the lungs or kidneys.
- **Hepatitis** can cause liver damage or the death of your baby.
- **Lyme disease** can cause premature birth or stillbirth, or a rash in the newborn baby.
- **Rubella (German measles)** can cause cataracts, deafness and heart lesions.
- **Syphilis** can cause skin defects and stillbirth.
- **Toxoplasmosis** can damage all the baby's organs (see p.249).

Q: *What's my risk of miscarriage, having previously suffered one?*

A: Having had one miscarriage, you are bound to feel anxious this time round. The good news is that you have no greater risk than any other woman – one in four. This risk increases very slightly, but not enough to affect the statistics greatly, with every subsequent miscarriage. But even after having lost several babies in pregnancy you are still more likely to go to full term and have a healthy child than to have another miscarriage. After three miscarriages some doctors refer their patients for investigation by a gynaecologist.

Q: *If I have a fever, will it affect my baby?*

A: Your baby relies on you for his or her temperature control, so a fever can be a problem if it's prolonged, especially in the first trimester. To bring a fever down, drink lots of fluids, take paracetamol (see p.87) and wear cooler clothing.

Q: *Is a stuffed-up nose a normal symptom of pregnancy?*

A: A lot of women complain of stuffiness or nosebleeds in pregnancy – it's thought to be because the hormonal changes alter your circulation and make the mucous membranes of the nose and nasal passages swell and bleed more easily. Don't use decongestants or nasal sprays, because many of these contain drugs which shouldn't be used in pregnancy. Instead, try using a humidifier to relieve stuffiness, increase your fluid intake, and use a gentle lubricant such as Vaseline. If these tips don't work, talk to your doctor or midwife about alternative solutions.

3 *The Second Trimester*

Now you're into your second trimester, your pregnancy may finally seem more real. You can see changes in your figure, and may have seen your baby's outline on an ultrasound scan. Many women report feeling more energetic in this stage of their pregnancy. So if you haven't already started on a course of exercises, now is a good time to do so.

YOUR BABY'S DEVELOPMENT IN WEEKS 12–24

Weeks 12–14

Just 12 weeks after conception the fetus is fully formed, with all its organs, muscles, limbs and bones. At 14 weeks it's about 7.5 cm long from head to bottom. It's still impossible to make out the baby's sex on an ultrasound scan, even though the sex organs are well developed. The baby is already moving about, but you won't be able to feel this for another month or so. By 14 weeks the heartbeat should be strong and can be heard on ultrasound – it's twice as fast as your own heartbeat!

Weeks 15–22

The baby's body is now growing quite rapidly, so that the head and body are in better proportion and the baby doesn't look so top-heavy. The face begins to look more human and the baby's hair, eyebrows and eyelashes are all beginning to grow. The eyelids are still closed over the eyes and won't open until the 26th week, nearly always revealing the dark blue eyes that characterize all newborns.

The lines on the skin of the fingers are now formed, so the baby already has his or her own unique fingerprint. Toenails and fingernails are growing and the baby has a firm hand grip.

At about 22 weeks the baby is around 25 cm long and becomes covered in very fine hair, known as lanugo, which is thought to keep the child at the right temperature. Usually this hair disappears before birth, but sometimes a little is left – especially on the ears and back – and only disappears when the baby's a few weeks old.

CLAIRE'S STORY

Like many first-time mums I know, I found it difficult to get really excited about my pregnancy until after I'd had my first scan. Then, having seen the baby moving around in the womb, I felt an instant surge of love for it.

My morning sickness was subsiding by the 12th week. I felt less tired, and ready to throw myself into a pregnant lifestyle. I enrolled in an aquanatal exercise class, bought pregnancy magazines as if they were going out of fashion, and became obsessed with maternity catalogues.

I felt great – especially when I began to feel the baby moving, around the 18th week. The first feeling was like bubbles low down in my abdomen. I told my friend, who's a doctor, about it, and she laughed and said, 'I'm sure all pregnant women like to think their baby's advanced . . . but you can't feel the baby move until 20 weeks.' A doctor she may be, but Julie hasn't had any babies of her own – and, talking to my friends, I've discovered this early feeling is unusual, but not abnormal.

The bubbles developed into a butterfly feeling around the 19th week, and then, by the 20th week, I felt my first firm kick. Soon I was getting used to feeling the baby move at different times of day. Occasionally I'd worry if I'd been too busy with my work to notice for a few hours. But putting my feet up for a rest always seemed to elicit a response. And, come evening, when I watched TV with my husband, I felt there were definitely three of us, rather than just a couple, sitting on the sofa!

Weeks 23–28

The baby is moving more vigorously and will jump at an unexpected loud noise. He's swallowing small amounts of amniotic fluid, and passing tiny amounts of urine. Sometimes the baby gets hiccups, which you may feel. He may also begin to develop a waking and sleeping pattern – often, ironically, choosing to be awake and kicking when you want to sleep. The baby's heartbeat can be heard on a stethoscope.

Take pride in your pregnant profile and adopt the best posture for the activity you're doing (see pp.73–74). It will keep your back strong and free of pain.

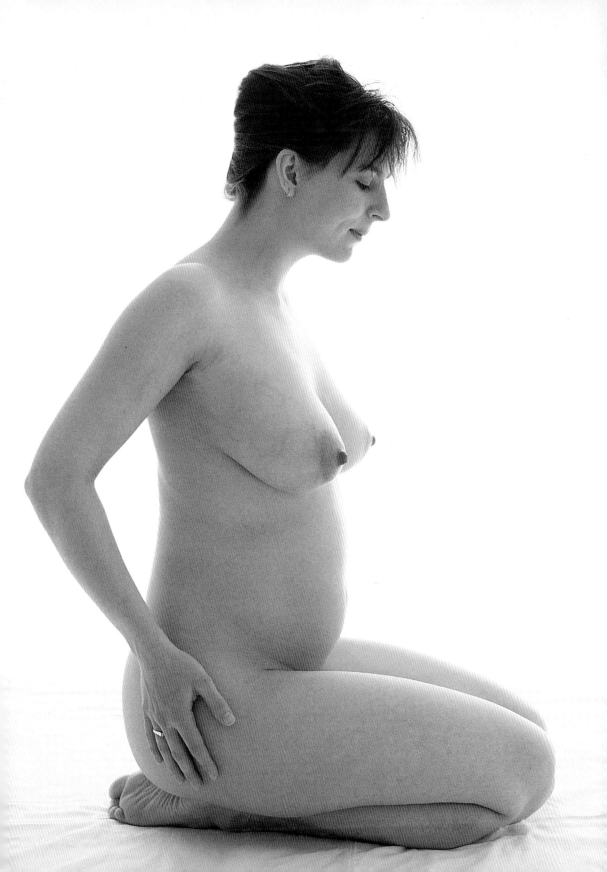

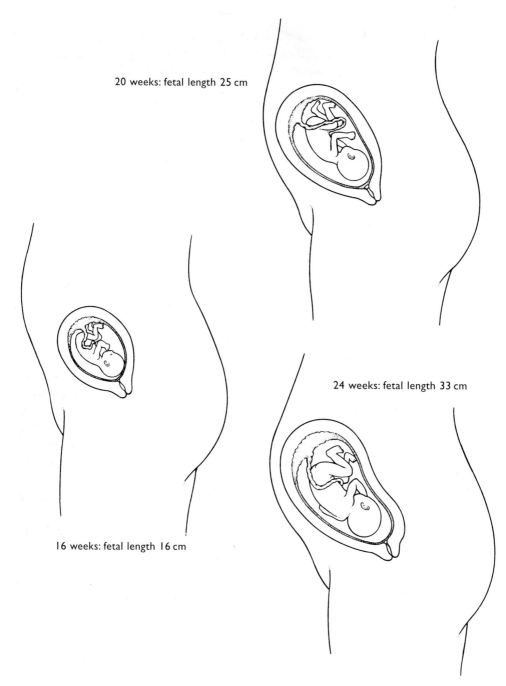

20 weeks: fetal length 25 cm

24 weeks: fetal length 33 cm

16 weeks: fetal length 16 cm

The baby's growth continues to be rapid until around the 20th week, when it slows down a little. He can now kick, twist and do somersaults – and every movement is a pleasure for you. By 24 weeks, many babies are able to survive outside the womb – although they will need intensive care for the first few months.

At 24 weeks the baby is about the length of your telephone receiver and may respond to loud noises and music by leaping around. He is now 'viable' – in other words, he now has a chance of survival if born prematurely. Before 24 weeks, the lungs and other vital organs are rarely strong enough to cope with life outside the womb. The baby's covered in a greasy white substance called vernix, which protects the skin while floating in the amniotic fluid and prevents it from becoming waterlogged. The vernix sticks to the hairy parts and some of this may still be present at birth.

CHANGES TO YOUR BODY

Baby Kicking

Expectant mothers love to feel their babies moving! More than your expanding abdomen, or even the sight of the baby on the ultrasound scan, feeling the fetus move is your main reassurance that all is well . . . even though, rationally, you know these other things count just as much.

The embryo is in fact moving as early as the seventh week, but you will not feel these movements (often as a fluttering or bubbling) until some time between the 14th and 26th weeks. A woman who's had a baby before may recognize the first movements earlier, and, because her uterine muscles are more lax, it's easier for her to feel them. You may also feel early, weaker, movements if you are very slim. Conversely, if you are quite well padded you may have to wait for the baby to move more vigorously before you are aware of it.

Having felt the baby move, it can be worrying if some time passes before you feel it again. This may be because the baby has been active when you've been asleep, or because you've been busy with other things and haven't noticed the baby. If you haven't noticed any movements all day, lie down quietly after an evening snack and see if that has any effect. If not, don't worry. Before the 20th week, many mothers go two or three days without feeling their baby move. If you've previously found the baby quite active and are concerned because you have now gone twenty-four hours without noticing anything, a visit to your doctor or midwife will reassure you that all's well.

Clumsiness

It's normal to become more clumsy in pregnancy. This is due to a combination of factors: loosening joints, water retention and lack of concentration, all of which are an inevitable part of pregnancy.

Forgetfulness

Not remembering appointments, feeling as if you're losing brain cells, and experiencing difficulty in concentrating on tasks are normal in pregnancy – all are caused by hormonal changes. Recognizing that it's normal should help you through what is, after all, a temporary phase. But to minimize the disruption to your life and reduce stress get into the habit of writing yourself To Do lists, and ticking off the tasks as you go.

Looking and Feeling Pregnant

Many women wait until the second trimester to tell friends and relatives that they're pregnant. And although you may have been feeling 'below par' during the first trimester it may only be now, when your abdomen is beginning to bulge, you've seen the baby on the ultrasound and it's finally making its presence felt in fluttery movements, that the reality sinks in. Ironically it is often now that mums-to-be start to have their first misgivings about the pregnancy and the imminent disruption of their lives. But studies show that not only is a little ambivalence, or even fear, normal, it's also quite healthy – as long as these feelings are confronted. This is a good time to talk any worries through with your partner, and work out how you will deal with your new life as a family instead of a couple.

More Energy

The second trimester is well known for being the 'energetic phase' of pregnancy – but don't expect to feel more energetic than you did before the pregnancy! Although your body is less tired now that it has got through the strenuous first weeks of manufacturing the baby, and morning sickness may also be subsiding, a lot of your energy is still going towards nurturing your baby.

This is, however, a safe time to enjoy exercise such as walking or swimming (but don't overdo it if you are new to it) and you may finally be feeling as if you are beginning to 'bloom'. See pp.82–86 for some specific exercises for this stage of your pregnancy.

Skin Changes

Pregnancy hormones can cause various changes to your skin. Some women experience the following:

- a darkening complexion (known as chloasma or the mask of pregnancy).
- a dark line down your abdomen (linea nigra).

While you are pregnant, moving in water can be a pleasure, both as an aid to relaxation and wellbeing and as a way of exercising safely. Even if you can't swim, exercising in water can be pleasurable and satisfying. See p.85 for specific exercises you can do.

- hyperpigmentation – darkening of the skin – in high-friction areas such as between the thighs.
- red, itchy palms.
- blue and blotchy legs and feet, due to increases in oestrogen.
- skin tags – floppy benign growths – usually where something like a bra strap has been rubbing.
- heat rash – caused by the increase in eccrine perspiration (the type that covers the whole body and regulates body temperature).
- diminished body odour – apocrine perspiration (the kind produced by glands under the arms and breasts, and in the genital area) lessens in pregnancy.

WEIGHT GAIN IN PREGNANCY

Normal weight gain in pregnancy is 11–13 kg (24–28 lb) and includes the weight of the baby, placenta, amniotic fluid and your own body changes.

If you start the pregnancy under-weight expect to gain 12–16 kg (26–35 lb).

If you're normal weight, your gain will be 11–13 kg (24–28 lb).

If you're overweight, expect to gain 7–10 kg (15–22 lb).

Total Weight Gain at Full Term	
Baby	3.5 kg (7½ lb)
Placenta	.7 kg (1½ lb)
Amniotic fluid	.8 kg (1¾ lb)
Growing womb	.9 kg (2 lb)
Bigger breasts	.45 kg (1 lb)
Increased blood	1.4 kg (3 lb)
Increased body fluids	1.4 kg (3 lb)
Fat gain	3.25 kg (7 lb)
Total:	**12.4 kg (26¾ lb)**

COMMON WORRIES

Abdominal Pain

Most pregnant women experience some degree of lower abdominal pain caused by the stretching of the muscles and ligaments supporting the uterus. It may be a sharp or cramp-like pain, and often most noticeable when you are standing up after sitting or lying, or when you cough. Mention the pain to your doctor or midwife at your next appointment, but there's no need to seek urgent medical help unless the pain is persistent or accompanied by other symptoms such as fever, bleeding, vaginal discharge or faintness. Persistent upper abdominal pain, just under your ribs, could indicate pre-eclampsia (see pp.243–44) and should be reported to your midwife or antenatal clinic immediately.

Anaemia

It is normal – and healthy – for your haemoglobin level to fall during pregnancy. So, although iron supplements used to be prescribed routinely to pregnant women, this practice is no longer considered safe. There are some suggestions that it may do more harm than good for pregnant women to take unnecessary iron supplements – when a woman's iron level does not fall in pregnancy she is more likely to give birth prematurely. You should never take them on the off-chance that you may need them, or because your friend says you look 'peaky'.

If you are genuinely anaemic, you may become extremely tired, pale, weak, breathless and faint (see p.221), although this is usually very rare in the UK.

Check that your diet contains enough iron-rich foods and vitamin C (see p.16), and if you have any reason to suspect you are deficient ask your doctor or midwife to order a blood test and/or prescribe one of the supplements specially formulated for pregnant women.

Backache

During pregnancy, backache is one of the side-effects of your joints loosening up to enable you to deliver your baby. If the weight of your uterus makes you stand back on your heels, with your bottom stuck out and your shoulders back, your spine hollows and you get low backache. To keep your back healthy, you need to use it sensibly. Correcting your posture will help prevent and minimize unnecessary pain. Lift shopping and small children from a squatting position; and get on all fours now and again to take the weight off your spine – especially if your job means you spend a lot of time sitting in one position.

The Best Way to Get Out of Bed

Stretch the length of your body, bend your knees and roll on to the side you get up from. Stay put for a few moments, then slowly come up to a sitting position with your legs over the side of the bed. Place your feet on the floor and gently push with your hands to lift yourself up.

The Best Way to Stand at a Kitchen Work Surface

Stand on both feet, hip-width apart, with your legs straight and your weight evenly distributed. Avoid stooping by bringing the work surface up to the right height for you (use a thick chopping block) or use the table instead – tables are always lower – if you're very short. This will help you keep your spine erect and your upper chest free to breathe.

The Best Way to Sit at a Desk

Keep your desk or table at the correct height for you to work without slumping forward. Your feet should be on the floor, a little apart, and your knees should be lower than your hips. A wedge cushion on your chair will help (but isn't essential) to push your spine into the correct position, so that you don't sink into your pelvis.

If you don't want to buy a wedge, imagine your pelvis as a bowl of water and keep it in a position which would keep the water level. Doing this will push your spine up straight, keeping your chest open so you can breathe and work in comfort.

The Best Way to Stand Comfortably

Keep your feet slightly apart and your legs straight with your hands by your side or behind you. This helps you to roll your shoulders back and open your upper chest so you can breathe easily.

The Best Way to Walk

Walk with your spine and head erect, looking straight ahead. Wear flat, comfortable shoes, carry your bag across your body, or else distribute the weight between two bags so both hands are balanced. Roll your shoulders back and down towards your waist, without bending your spine backwards.

The Best Way to Relax in Front of the TV

Using the back of the sofa or a block of cushions, support your spine, neck and head so they are in a straight line and aren't twisted or slumping. Keep your feet up in front of you. This will make you more comfortable and ensure your shoulders aren't rounded, so you can breathe deeply which will help you relax.

Blood Pressure

A 'normal' blood pressure is anything between 100/60 to 135/85. The first figure is called the systolic, measuring the pressure inside the arteries the instant the heart beats. The second figure is called the diastolic, measuring the pressure in the arteries when the heart is resting. If your systolic measurement is 140 or higher and the diastolic is 90 or higher you have high blood pressure (hypertension).

It's normal for your blood pressure to change slightly in pregnancy. It often goes down in the second trimester and rises in the third.

Low blood pressure (hypotension) may be supine hypotension, meaning that the enlarging uterus is putting pressure on the large blood vessels such as the aorta and the vena cava. It may be most noticeable when you're lying on your back. Alternatively it may be postural hypotension, meaning that your blood pressure drops as you get up after sitting. The main symptom is dizziness but hypotension can be avoided by not sleeping or lying on your back, and rising slowly when you get up.

High blood pressure (hypertension) can be a sign of pre-eclampsia (see pp.243–44). But many women develop high blood pressure in pregnancy without pre-eclampsia. Drinking lots of water and taking plenty of bed rest can help bring high blood pressure down, and it's important to follow your doctor's or midwife's advice about this. If they're concerned, you may be admitted to hospital for enforced bed rest and

Good posture is essential if you sit at a desk for long periods – but you should also make the most of every opportunity to get up and move around which will take the pressure off your back.

to enable your blood pressure to be monitored every few hours. You may be prescribed drugs if it is very high.

Breasts 'Leaking'

Your breasts start to produce colostrum, early breast milk, from the second trimester. Some women find it begins to leak – and this is entirely normal – while others have no obvious sign of milk production until after the baby's born. Leave your breasts alone instead of trying to squeeze the colostrum out, and wear breast pads if it's becoming an embarrassing problem.

Breathlessness

Mild breathlessness is a common experience in the second trimester. It's caused by hormonal influences swelling the capillaries in the respiratory tract and relaxing the muscles of the lungs and bronchial tubes.

Later in pregnancy, when your uterus is bigger and pushing up against the diaphragm, the lungs become more restricted and can't expand fully. But this type of breathlessness is also quite normal.

ALLEVIATING BREATHLESSNESS

Use a few drops of frankincense essential oil in your bath to help your breathing.

What *is* of concern is severe breathlessness which includes rapid breathing and chest pain and/or a rapid pulse and bluish lips or fingertips. If you experience this, call your doctor or midwife or go to a hospital Accident and Emergency Dept.

Dental Problems

Pregnancy hormones tend to make your gums swell, and it's not unusual to have more tooth worries while you're pregnant. In the UK you're entitled to free NHS dental treatment during pregnancy, so take advantage of it. Attend to any problems promptly, as any infection in your mouth risks spreading through your system and could be a potential hazard to your baby.

TIP FOR ORAL HYGIENE

A flower water mouthwash or herbal tea will clean and freshen your mouth and keep your gums stable.

Diabetes

See pp.223–25.

Growing Feet

Normal fluid retention and weight gain can make your feet fuller than they were before pregnancy. This is exacerbated by the hormone relaxin loosening all joints, including those in the feet, as it starts to loosen the pelvis in preparation for delivery. Wear comfortable, low-heeled, shoes in leather or canvas – synthetic materials will not allow your feet to breathe.

Itchy Abdomen

An itchy abdomen is normal in pregnancy, and you may have to apply calamine lotion to stop yourself scratching too much. Itchy limbs are not normal, however (see Obstetric Cholestasis on p.237).

Itchy Genitals

If you are extra-sweaty and suffer with itchiness keep the relevant areas very clean, and use a pad soaked in flower water (e.g. rose water) to cool the area. If the itching persists, it could be due to thrush, so seek advice from your midwife or doctor.

Leg Cramps

The second and third trimesters are often disrupted by leg cramps which can propel you out of bed in the middle of the night. They are sometimes thought to be caused by excess phosphorus and too little calcium in the blood, so reducing your phosphorus intake (less meat and milk) and increasing your calcium from other sources (see p.38) may help. But discuss dietary changes with your doctor or midwife first.

The pressure of the growing uterus on your nerves is another cause. Alternating periods of exercise with periods of rest during the day may help relieve the pain at night.

If you do suffer an attack of cramp, try to straighten your leg and then slowly flex your toes and ankle towards your nose. Alternatively, circle your ankles clockwise and anticlockwise. If you can't get rid of the pain, see your doctor. A continuous pain in the calf may be a sign of a blood clot, which needs urgent medical treatment.

Low-lying Placenta

The risk posed by a low-lying placenta is that you will have placenta praevia (see p.239), which puts you in danger of a haemorrhage and makes vaginal delivery almost always impossible, because the placenta is so low that it's covering the os or opening of the uterus. Having said that, 20–30 per cent of placentas are moderately low in the second trimester, and the majority move into the upper segment of the womb, where they should be, as the mother-to-be approaches her EDD. You will be offered regular scans (see Chapter 5) while the placenta is low, especially if you've had any slight bleeding, and may be advised to take plenty of rest and avoid doing anything remotely strenuous until you have the all-clear.

Miscarriage

See pp.234–36.

Painful Hands

Another side-effect of swelling in pregnancy is what is known as carpal tunnel syndrome. The carpal tunnel in the wrist becomes swollen, and this puts pressure on the nerve running through it to your fingers. The pain can radiate right up your arm and down through your fingers and is often more severe at night. If you wake with pain in your hands at night, dangle them over the side of the bed and shake them vigorously. If they're still painful, investigate wearing a wrist splint which can bring a lot of relief and can be obtained through your antenatal clinic.

Perineal Pressure

This can increase as your baby grows and presses on the perineum. Lying on your side can help relieve the pressure; massaging the area with sweet almond oil and then applying a lavender flower water pad is soothing.

Pre-eclampsia

See pp.243–44.

Rectal Bleeding

In pregnancy rectal bleeding is most likely to be a sign of haemorrhoids (piles), which are varicose veins of the rectum and also cause itchiness and sometimes pain. Another cause may be fissures – cracks in the anus caused by constipation – but these are usually extremely painful. Either way, see your doctor to confirm the diagnosis and get his advice on treatment. In addition to anything he offers, you can:

◆ avoid getting constipated (see p.48).
◆ avoid long hours of standing or sitting.
◆ sleep on your side to relieve pressure on your bottom.
◆ apply witch-hazel compresses or ice packs to ease the pain.
◆ keep your perineal area very clean.

Only use topical medications or suppositories prescribed by your doctor for use in pregnancy, or one of the alternative remedies below.

ALTERNATIVE REMEDIES FOR HAEMORRHOIDS

The medical herbalist Carol Rogers, recommends pilewort (*ranunculus ficaria*), which you can buy as an ointment cream from health food shops, or tincture of witch-hazel, available through herbal suppliers.

Or you might prefer to use a homeopathic remedy. Suggestions may include horse chestnut, poison nut, peony and sulphur, all of which should be prescribed by a homeopathic doctor.

Vaginal Discharge

The normal increase in vaginal discharge or secretion in pregnancy is called leucorrhoea and is white or creamy-coloured and fairly thick. It's caused by increased blood flow to the skin and muscles around the vagina, which also produces the blue coloration to your vagina (known as Chadwick's sign) in early pregnancy. If the discharge is very heavy, wear sanitary towels for protection and avoid nylon underwear. But don't douche your vagina. Your discharge is unlikely to be a sign of infection unless it causes itchiness or is foul-smelling and greeny yellow in colour. If you have these symptoms, see your doctor. Many treatments are safe to use in pregnancy, but you'll need his advice.

Warning Signs

Always ask your midwife for advice on any of the following:

◆ vaginal bleeding – needs prompt attention (see p.86).
◆ pain on urinating, which could be a sign of infection needing treatment.
◆ severe abdominal pain – urgently, particularly if it is in the upper abdomen.
◆ fluid from the vagina, which could be leakage of your waters.
◆ change of baby movement – especially lack of it.

- high fever (over 38 degrees C) or chills.
- severe vomiting.
- blurred vision.
- severely swollen face or fingers.
- severe headache.
- any injury or accident such as a fall or car crash which you fear could have harmed the baby (see p.86).
- breast lumps.
- a pain in the leg, especially when squeezing the calf or walking, which could be a sign of deep vein thrombosis and is urgent (see p.223).
- dizziness, which could be linked to high blood pressure.
- excessive itchiness.

SEX IN THE SECOND TRIMESTER

As long as your pregnancy is uncomplicated, and your doctor hasn't advised abstaining from intercourse, it is safe to enjoy sex to your heart's desire!

The engorgement of your genitals, caused by increased blood flow to the pelvic area, heightens sexual response in many women and can also increase the pleasure your partner gets from a tighter fit around his penis. But if you are not among the couples who benefit from this aspect of the pregnant body, you are neither alone nor abnormal. For some women, having engorged genitalia causes a feeling of residual fullness after orgasm – making them feel they haven't quite reached their climax. And, for some men, the fit can be so tight they lose their erection.

Breast tenderness enhances sexual pleasure for many couples. This is particularly so in the second trimester, when the pain often felt early in pregnancy has diminished and the breasts are no longer a no-go zone.

Vaginal secretions change in pregnancy (see p.79). This can have the effect of making your vagina more moist and receptive to lovemaking, or it might make it so slippery your partner has trouble keeping his erection. The odour and taste of your discharge changes, too, and, while oral sex is safe in pregnancy, it may not be pleasant-tasting to some men. Try massaging scented oils into your inner thighs or pubic area to improve your smell!

Deep penetration occasionally causes bleeding from the cervix. Any bleeding must be checked out by your doctor. But, as long as complications are ruled out and there is no need to abstain from intercourse, you can continue having sex, but avoid deep penetration.

Your growing baby is not going to be hurt by intercourse – although many couples fear that it will. The fetus is well protected inside the amniotic sac and uterus, and the uterus is sealed off from the outside world by a plug of mucus at the mouth of the cervix – so he can't harm your partner either!

Orgasm cannot trigger a miscarriage. Despite the very intense uterine contractions felt by some women after climax, the baby is completely safe in a normal, risk-free pregnancy. If you've had a history of miscarriages or premature labour, however, talk to your doctor about any potential risks.

Intercourse is unlikely to introduce an infection at this stage, unless your partner has a sexually transmittable disease.

You may be advised to cut down, or cut out, lovemaking if:

◆   you've had any unexplained bleeding.
◆   you have a history of miscarriages.
◆   you've shown any signs of threatened early labour in this pregnancy.

Each case is individual, so always ask your doctor for advice.

Use your pregnancy to your advantage, whatever the effects on your libido, or restrictions imposed by doctors. This can be a time to revive kissing and cuddling if full sex is out. Make sure you talk openly with each other about any problems, fears or misgivings arising from this temporary change in your sex life. Remember that making love is a good physical preparation for labour and delivery. Finally, experiment with new positions. Woman on top, front to front and front to back are all popular in pregnancy.

POSITIONS FOR LOVEMAKING IN PREGNANCY

Man on top: this can still be achieved if your partner supports his weight on his arms so he doesn't press down on your abdomen.

Spoons: you lie on your side with your partner lying behind you and entering you from behind. This is a great position for him to stroke your breasts and clitoris.

Woman on top: lying on top of your partner means you can support your weight on your arms and you have the advantage of being able to control the angle and speed of movement of the penis, allowing you to reach your orgasm when you want. Your partner also has easy access to your breasts, which many pregnant women enjoy.

All fours: this position takes pressure off your abdomen. You kneel on all fours with your head on your arms, and your partner kneels behind you, entering from behind. His hands are also free to caress you and give your clitoris extra stimulation.

EXERCISE IN THE SECOND TRIMESTER

If you were fit and active before getting pregnant you may already have established an exercise routine you enjoy, following the detailed advice in Chapter 2. If not, or if tiredness and nausea took their toll in the first three months, now's the time to start preparing your body for childbirth. If you're not already doing the Drawbridge Exercise (see pp.42–43), start now – it's the most important exercise on your list.

Other Exercises for the Pelvis

Learning to move your pelvis with greater ease and confidence will help you find the best position for yourself in labour.

Pelvic Lift

Stand with your feet a little way from a wall, hip-width apart, and back to the wall. Bend your knees slightly and rest your back, shoulders and head against the wall. Breathe in and, as you breathe out, press your lower back firmly against the wall, pulling in your abdomen and lifting your pubic bone so your buttocks tighten and leave the wall. Keep your shoulders on the wall, so you learn to move the pelvis only. Once you've mastered the lift you can do it in any position – kneeling, sitting, bending forward, or on all fours.

Lazy Dog

Kneel on all fours, with a cushion under your knees if necessary. Move your pelvis slowly from side to side like a lazy dog wagging a very heavy tail. Look round at each hip as you bring it forward, and keep your back horizontal, not curved or caving.

Back Strengthening

Sit upright and lift your ribs away from your hips, so your back lengthens. Lift your chest, pull your shoulders down, and feel the back of your neck lengthen upwards. Hold your chin at about a right angle to the front of your neck. Check that your shoulders are directly above your hips, then centre your pelvis so you are sitting evenly on both buttocks and can feel the bones pressing into the floor. Try to hold the position for a few moments, but don't let your back become stiff or rigid. Relax and then try again. Breathe slowly and evenly.

To help, sit against a wall at first. If your back is straight you will feel the length of your spine against the wall. If you can't you know you're rounding your back.

Yoga exercises are popular in pregnancy, but you should consult a yoga teacher for advice before adopting new postures. Regular practice should improve your energy and stamina, tone muscles, enhance your concentration and help you deal with stress. It's also the ideal preparation for labour.

Squatting

You may want to squat in labour, and if you've become used to doing this in pregnancy it won't be too difficult (but, if you find it awkward, don't do it). It also strengthens your thighs and feet and stretches your Achilles tendons, calves and inner thigh muscles. Always get up slowly, preferably holding on to a chair or table, or you may feel dizzy.

Squat down, keeping your back lengthened. If you can, keep your heels on the floor and balance your weight evenly between the balls of your feet and the heels, not allowing your feet to roll inward or outward. Press your arms against your thighs to increase the stretch on the groin and inner thighs. Start by squatting against a wall, or holding hands with your partner (facing each other).

Incorporate squatting into your routine when you're playing or working at floor level, lifting from the oven or a low drawer or shelf, or there's no chair at hand.

Dromedary Droop

Use this exercise throughout pregnancy and into labour to relieve the pressure of your enlarged uterus on your spine. Get down on your hands and knees, with your back relaxed but not sagging. Keep your head straight with your neck aligned to your spine. Then tighten your abdomen and buttocks and allow your head to droop. Gradually release your back and raise your head back to where it started. Repeat several times.

Neck Relaxer

This is a great exercise to aid general relaxation, as tension gathers in the neck. Sit in a comfortable position with your eyes closed. Gently roll your head around full circle, and breathe in. As you breathe out, relax and let your head drop forward to a comfortable position. Repeat four or five times, alternating the direction of the roll and relaxing between rolls. Aim to do the exercise several times a day.

Leg Lifts

Lie on your right side with your shoulders, hips and knees in a straight line. Place your left hand on the floor in front of your chest and support your head with your right. Relax and inhale; then exhale while slowly raising your leg as high as you can, with your foot pointing upward towards your body and your inner ankle facing down. Inhale while slowly lowering your leg. Repeat ten times on each side.

Ten-minute Pick-me-up

Use this quick routine to ward off tiredness until you can get to bed for a proper rest.

- Lie on your back facing a wall, with legs bent. Raise and straighten your feet, one by one, on the wall about 60 cm (2 ft) above your heart (no higher). Shut your eyes and take a few deep breaths. Relax in this position for about three minutes.
- Bring your feet down the wall a little, bending your knees. Then, feet still firmly against the wall, push away a little and do a pelvic lift, tightening your buttocks and abdomen. Repeat a few times with the Drawbridge Exercise (see pp.42–43).
- Straighten your legs and push up with your hips, so your body forms a straight line from shoulders to feet. Hold for a few moments, clenching your buttock muscles. Repeat a few times.
- Feet still on the wall, legs slightly bent, roll your pelvis from side to side. Push with your right foot to roll to the left, straightening the right leg and tightening your right buttock as you roll. Repeat several times on both sides, then bring your legs down one at a time, bending as you do so.
- Bend your knees, bring the soles of your feet together and let your thighs drop outwards. Rub your inner thighs and relax for a couple of minutes.
- Take three slow breaths, tightening your abdomen as you breathe out. Turn on your side and slowly get up, rolling on to your side first (for the correct way to get out of bed see p.73). Do a final Pelvic Lift and have a big stretch.

Exercises for the Swimming Pool

Using the pool for swimming and water exercises is a good way of maintaining tone and fitness in pregnancy.

- Swimming on your back with a life-saving leg kick is good for your back and will strengthen your legs.
- Avoid breast stroke unless you keep your face in the water. If it sticks out it will make your lower back arch.
- Cycle your legs with your back to the side of the pool and your arms on the rail.
- Float in the water, facing the side of the pool and holding the rail, then slowly kick your legs, lifting one at a time and keeping them straight.

Head-to-toe Relaxation

Lie on your back on the floor, and, starting with your pelvis, take one body part at a time, tense it, pressing into the floor, and then relax it. Once you've done your external body and face, close your eyes and shift your concentration to the inside of your body, working down through your trunk and back to the pelvis, adjusting any area that feels tense. When your whole body is relaxed, your mind should also be slowing down. If it continues to race it will tense your body again. To empty your mind of the everyday thoughts, try one of the following:

- concentrating on a tranquil scene such as a favourite beach or garden.
- repeating a mantra (a sound like 'Om') to exclude intrusive thoughts.
- focusing on your breathing.

YOUR QUESTIONS ANSWERED

Q: *I've had some very slight bleeding – does this mean my baby's life is at risk?*

A: Bleeding during pregnancy is not unusual and isn't always a problem – but you should always check with your doctor or midwife anyway. A scan may be ordered to see if there's any problem such as a low-lying placenta (see p.78). Bed rest and no sex until things settle down may also be recommended. With luck, after a couple of weeks you will be given the OK to do all the things you normally enjoy!

Q: *Should I call my doctor after falling over?*

A: It's always a good idea to let your doctor know what's happened, so he can check everything's OK. But a fall rarely causes serious injury to the baby, and feeling the baby move as normal, afterwards, will reassure you. If you've had a fall, these are warning signs to look out for:

- bleeding.
- a gush of water from the vagina.
- severe abdominal pain.

Q: *I've had bad sciatic nerve pain in the last month – what can I do about it?*

A: Sciatic nerve pain – an excruciating but occasional pain in the buttocks and back of the leg – can get worse as the pregnancy progresses and is due to the pressure of the growing uterus on the sciatic nerve. If it's very bad, take some rest, lying on the opposite side to the pain to relieve the pressure. You can also ask to be referred to an obstetric physiotherapist.

PAINKILLERS DURING PREGNANCY

Check with your doctor before taking painkillers. Paracetamol is generally thought to be safe, but large doses can cause liver and kidney damage, and Aspirin can produce difficulties in blood clotting for you and your baby. Neither drug should be taken regularly – although a few are unlikely to be harmful.

Q: *I still can't believe I'm having a baby – when will my bump begin to feel real?*

A: Some women are attached to their baby from the very beginning of the pregnancy. Others only start to feel that the baby is real when they've heard its heartbeat on an ultrasound (around 12 or 13 weeks) or felt it move (16–20 weeks).

Q: *I thought my mood swings would stop at the end of the first trimester. Why haven't they?*

A: There's a continuous flow of changing hormones throughout pregnancy, and mood swings may accompany them through the entire nine months.

Q: *I haven't a clue about maternity clothes. What should I be looking for?*

A: Expanding waistbands on skirts and trousers – elasticated, wrap-around, or drawstring – will grow with you through your pregnancy and are very comfortable. Over these you can wear loose shirts or T-shirts. Most maternity shops and catalogues also have ranges that are suitable for smart office wear and won't make you look like the old woman who lived in a shoe, if you are working while pregnant.

If your breasts are uncomfortable you'll need to buy a larger, more supportive bra – or you could try a sports bra, which won't chafe your nipples. But a maternity/nursing bra will be fitted later in pregnancy, when your postnatal size can be more accurately predicted.

Q: ***Is it safe to fly while I'm pregnant?***

A: Check first with your doctor, but there should be no problem in your second trimester unless you have a pregnancy with complications. Later on, you may need a letter from your doctor before an airline will carry you.

In case of sudden complications arising, it's best not to travel long distances at all, by any means of transport:

♦ during your last month of pregnancy.
♦ if you've had any bleeding or cramping.
♦ if you've had a lot of swelling.

Q: ***How safe is it to wear a seat belt in the car?***

A: Car restraints are as important as ever when you're pregnant, and there's no evidence that they can cause fetal or uterine injury. For maximum comfort and safety place the lap belt below your abdomen and across your upper thighs, and position the shoulder strap between your breasts.

Q: ***Is it safe to get a sun tan in pregnancy?***

A: Pregnant or not, you should always be cautious in the sun. Wearing a sunscreen will protect against the 'mask of pregnancy' which causes darker skin pigmentation. Using a sunbed is not advisable while you're pregnant, as the risks to your baby are unknown.

Q: ***Is it safe to get my hair coloured or permed in pregnancy?***

A: There's no evidence that hair treatments can cause problems in pregnancy – but if you're still suffering from nausea the fumes could make you feel ill.

Q: ***Can I use the microwave?***

A: The dangers of using microwave ovens in pregnancy aren't fully understood at present. There's an increased risk of food poisoning with microwaved food, so make sure food (especially cook-chill meals and rice) is piping hot all the way through before you eat it, and always follow the manufacturer's instructions very carefully. It's also a good idea not to stand too close to the microwave while it's in use – there have been suggestions that the fetus is vulnerable to microwave damage as it cannot dissipate the heat that the waves generate.

Q: *Is it safe to continue with electrolysis for my facial hair?*

A: It's not clear whether this procedure is safe, so it's best to use other methods until after your baby's born.

Q: *Why are electric blankets thought to be unsafe in pregnancy?*

A: Electrically heated waterbeds have been linked with an increased risk of miscarriage because of the electromagnetic fields they emit, and there's a theory that the electromagnetic field created by electric blankets could also be risky. In addition to this, you should be taking steps to avoid your body overheating – and electric blankets can raise body temperature excessively. It's best to avoid using an electric blanket during pregnancy.

4 *The Third Trimester*

The last trimester often feels like the longest. Make good use of your time to plan for the birth and afterwards. And, if this is your first baby, enjoy your final few weeks with your partner as a couple.

This chapter covers the basics of what to expect at this stage of your pregnancy. For additional information read the chapters on Preparing for Childbirth (pp.137–63), Labour and Delivery (pp.164–77) and Coping with a Complicated Delivery (pp.178–88).

YOUR BABY'S DEVELOPMENT IN WEEKS 25–38

By the start of the third trimester your baby is fully formed but is growing bigger and stronger, ready for birth. At 30 weeks she's about 40 cm from head to bottom, and by 32 weeks she's likely to be lying head downwards. The skin, which was quite wrinkled before, is now smoother and both the vernix (see p.170) and lanugo (see p.66) are beginning to disappear.

Around the end of the seventh month, fat begins to deposit on the fetus. She may suck her thumb, hiccup and cry, and, according to researchers, taste sweet and sour. She responds to pain, light and sound.

Around the 36th week in first pregnancies the baby's head may move down into the pelvis and is then said to be 'engaged'. In subsequent pregnancies the baby's head may not engage until labour begins.

By the 30th week of your pregnancy, you will have gained about 75 per cent of your total weight gain (see p.72).

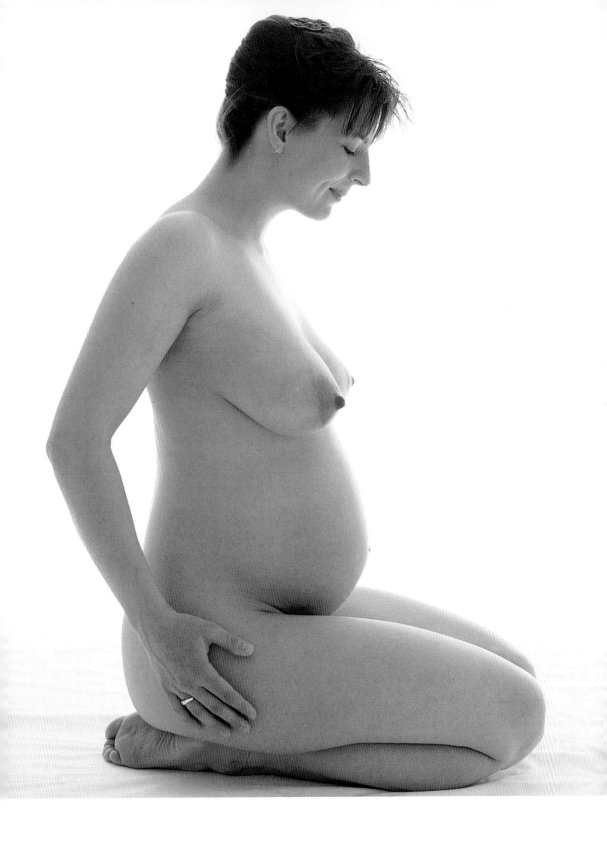

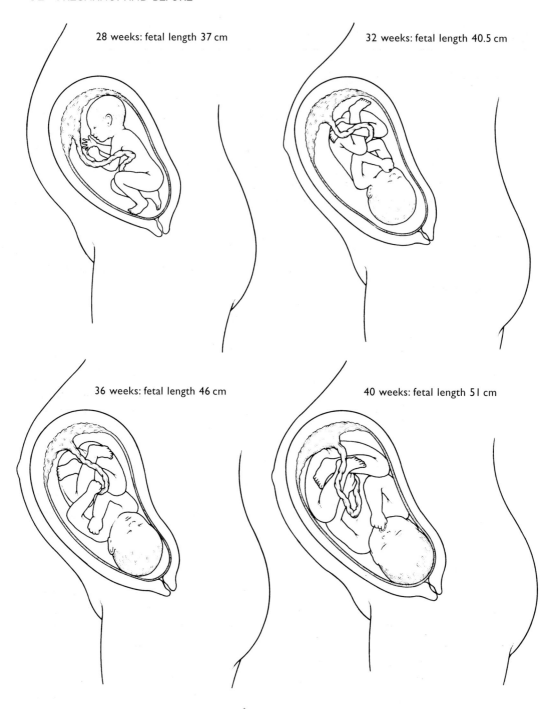

28 weeks: fetal length 37 cm

32 weeks: fetal length 40.5 cm

36 weeks: fetal length 46 cm

40 weeks: fetal length 51 cm

Your baby is now fully formed and has filled most of the available space in the uterus. By 32 weeks, the baby lacks only some lung surfactant and a layer of insulating fat before being ready to be born; and, after the 36th week, he or she will descend into the pelvis, ready for delivery.

CHANGES TO YOUR BODY

Abdominal Pain

As ever, you should take serious note of any unusual abdominal pain. But lower abdominal pain may be a symptom of your ligaments stretching to support your growing uterus. Mention it to your midwife or doctor, just to be sure. If it's a continuous problem, or very bad, you could wear a maternity belt which is designed to give your bump extra support. You can also avoid pain by supporting your abdomen with your hands when you get up from sitting down or lying.

ALTERNATIVE REMEDY FOR LIGAMENT PAIN

The homeopathic remedy Bellis perennis may be useful for ligament pain – consult a practitioner for advice.

Braxton Hicks Contractions

These practice contractions become more apparent as the pregnancy progresses, and can be quite strong by the third trimester. Early in the trimester, they should not be too painful or regular. True labour contractions are regular, intensifying, and similar in sensation to period cramps. This kind of pain is always reason to contact your doctor or midwife.

Women who've already been through one pregnancy are likely to feel Braxton Hicks earlier, and more intensely, than first-time mums.

As the EDD draws near, your Braxton Hicks may be more frequent, intense and even painful. To relieve any discomfort, change position – get up and walk around, or lie down.

Changes in Fetal Movements

Babies are at their most active between weeks 24 and 28, but these movements are often erratic and brief and, although always visible on ultrasound, you may not have been aware of them. In the third trimester fetal activity becomes more organized and consistent, with clearly defined periods of rest and activity – especially between weeks 28 and 32.

Comparing baby movements with other pregnant women is always a bad idea. Just like newborns, fetuses have their own individual patterns of development. Some are always active, others tend to be quite quiet. What matters is that there's no drastic change – for instance a previously lively baby becomes much slower or even stops moving.

Some doctors recommend testing for fetal movements twice a day – once in the morning, when activity tends to be sparser, and once in the evening, when many babies are active.

To check your baby's movements:

◆ Note the time when you start.
◆ Count any movements – kicks, flutters or rolls.
◆ Stop counting when you reach ten.
◆ Often you'll feel ten movements in ten minutes, but sometimes it will take longer.
◆ If you haven't felt ten movements by the end of an hour take a break, have a snack, then try again.

Changes in the ninth month may be more marked than before. For instance, your baby may seem to squirm instead of kicking. This is most likely to be because there's much less space for gymnastics than there was a few months ago. And, especially when the baby's head is engaged, she will be less mobile. At this stage the fact that you experience regular fetal movement is more important than the type of movement the baby makes.

Continue with tests for fetal movement, as above, because inactivity can be a sign of fetal distress. As long as you're getting your ten movements per test session, things should be going OK. If you don't, contact your doctor or midwife at once – picking up fetal distress early through movement testing can prevent serious consequences.

Constipation

If you're just beginning to suffer now, and haven't taken steps to improve your diet (see p.48), now's a good time to start. It will also get you in the habit of eating a healthy diet after your baby's born – when constipation can be extremely painful, especially if you've had stitches.

Fatigue

This is also likely to increase in the last trimester, for the following reasons:

◆ you're carrying around more weight than before.
◆ your bulk may be preventing you from sleeping properly.
◆ you may be worrying and losing sleep through that too.
◆ getting ready to have the baby (making work arrangements, childcare plans etc.) can be exhausting.

As always, though, fatigue is a sign that you should look after yourself. Rest and relax as much as you can, and save your strength for your delivery.

In the last three months of pregnancy you will probably feel more tired than usual. Try to rest before becoming so exhausted that you feel you cannot go on any longer.

If you feel no better after resting, report this to your doctor at your next check-up. Anaemia (see pp.72 and 221) sometimes strikes in the third trimester, and some antenatal clinics check for it in the seventh month.

Oedema

Some degree of swelling in the feet, ankles and lower legs is considered completely normal – 75 per cent of women experience oedema, especially towards the end of the day, in hot weather, or if they've been standing for a long time. Usually it disappears overnight.

You can help relieve the discomfort of oedema by putting your legs up, wearing comfortable shoes, and avoiding elastic-top socks or stockings. Support tights can also help – but put them on first thing in the morning, before the swelling has started.

Keep drinking plenty of water (2 litres/3½ pints a day), which helps prevent water retention, but don't drink it all at once. Two glasses at a time is sufficient.

If your hands or face become puffy notify your doctor or midwife, as this could be the first indication of pre-eclampsia (see pp.243–44) which will need speedy treatment.

Overheating

Your body is naturally warmer during pregnancy, so dress sensibly in layers of cotton clothing (avoid synthetics) to allow your skin to breathe. Take frequent baths and continue to drink plenty of water.

Skin Changes

The PUPPP (pruritic urticarial papules and plaques of pregnancy) lesions which sometimes gather in stretch marks, and on the thighs, buttocks and arms, aren't dangerous to you or your baby, and will disappear after delivery.

STRETCH MARKS

Whether you get stretch marks in pregnancy depends on whether you have an inherited tendency towards them. The stretch occurs in the collagen level of the skin and is thought to be linked to production of corticosteriods in pregnancy. The marks may appear on the abdomen, thighs, breasts and buttocks and, although quite alarmingly reddish purple to begin with, they usually fade within six months of delivery. Regular exercise (especially walking and swimming) will improve your circulation and help keep them under control. After the first three months, a daily massage with jojoba or wheatgerm oil will keep your skin supple and may reduce the marks.

COMMON WORRIES

Baby's Presentation

Towards the end of the third trimester your midwife will have told you of your baby's 'presentation' – in other words which part of her is facing the womb's exit. There are several possibilities, the first of which is the most frequently encountered.

Cephalic

The baby is head-down with the top of the head (the vertex) pointing towards your cervix, and her chin tucked into her chest. This is the best position for delivery, as the narrowest part of the head is coming out first and the baby's face is protected. This presentation can be described in

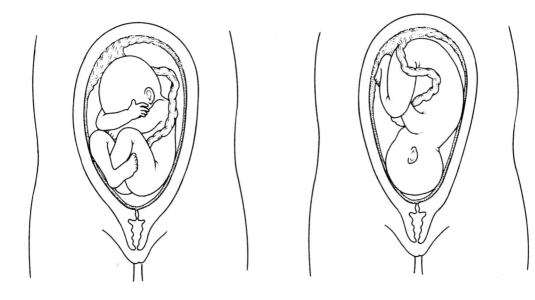

Breech presentation

Left occipito-anterior presentation

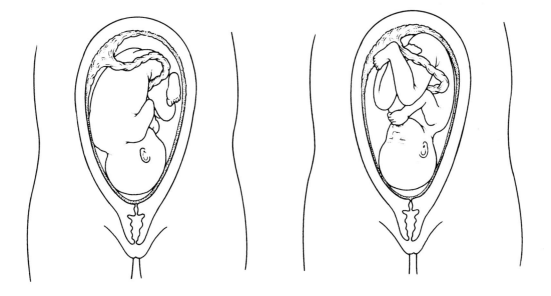

Right occipito-anterior presentation

Left occipito-posterior presentation

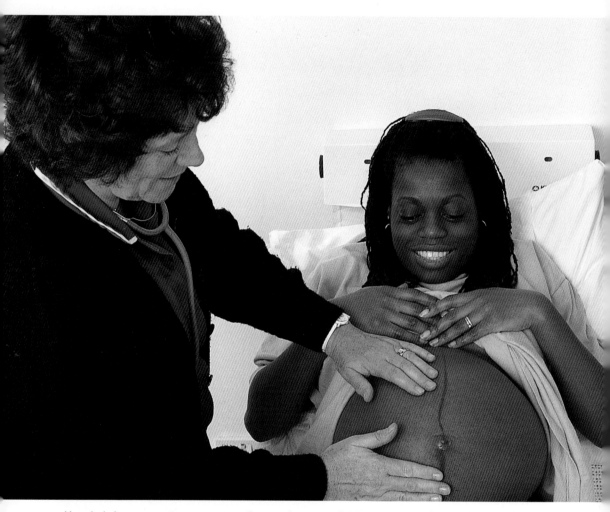

Your baby's presentation now may influence the type of delivery you have. If your baby is in a breech position, your doctor may advise a controlled labour with an epidural. But this is not the only option. See Hilary's story, opposite.

one of six ways, indicating where the back of the baby's head is during her descent down the birth canal:

LOA (left occipito-anterior): 15 per cent of babies are in this position at the start of labour.

ROA (right occipito-anterior): 10 per cent.

LOL (left occipito-lateral): 40 per cent.

ROL (right occipito-lateral): 24 per cent.

LOP (left occipito-posterior): 3 per cent.

ROP (right occipito-posterior): 8 per cent.

HILARY'S STORY

I didn't know much about breech presentation – until, late in my second pregnancy, my midwife announced that my baby was bottom-down. She realized for the first time at my 38-week check-up, but I've since wondered if Samuel had been breech for a few weeks before that, as I'd been suffering quite bad sciatic pain, and I hadn't experienced this with my first baby, Joshua.

I was worried, because this was something new to me – and I was scared the baby's breech presentation could cause complications. But my midwife was very reassuring, and said it shouldn't be a problem, although I'd have to see the doctor, and he may also want to X-ray my pelvis to check that a vaginal delivery would still be feasible.

That happened three days later. The X-ray was taken with great care, so that my baby wouldn't be harmed by the rays, and the results showed there was plenty of room for him to get out. My doctor warned me I'd have to have a controlled labour with an epidural, so that if a caesarean became necessary, I'd already be prepared for it.

In the event, however, things didn't work out quite according to plan! I went into labour in the middle of the night, and, by the time I reached the hospital, I was already starting to push. There wasn't time for an epidural and I was terrified because I thought that without the controlled labour I'd been promised, everything would go wrong. But there wasn't much time to think about that . . . Samuel was born within 20 minutes of our arrival on the labour ward. And, despite all the anticipated problems, and the fact that he was a whopping 9lbs 6oz, it was a lovely, quick and easy delivery.

Anterior

In this position the baby's back is facing out, lying inside the curve of the mother's abdomen.

Breech

About 3 per cent of babies are breech presentation – lying bottom-down rather than head-down at term. This used to mean an automatic caesarean section, but many mothers do now successfully deliver vaginally. But consider the options very carefully before making a decision, in particular the fact that you may still need an emergency caesarean if the labour doesn't proceed well.

Before 34 weeks there's no need to worry about your baby's breech presentation as she has ample room to turn round – and many babies do. But if, towards the end of your pregnancy, your baby seems to be

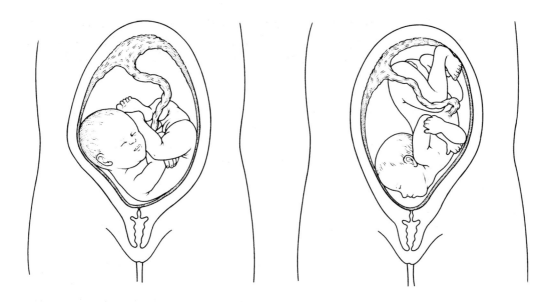

Shoulder presentation   Face presentation

sticking to a bottom first position, there are some steps you can take to help the baby turn head-down. These include:

Postural tilting: lie on the floor with a couple of cushions under your bottom, your knees bent and your feet flat. Remain like this for at least ten minutes. The position creates a little more room in the uterus and your baby may be tempted to turn around.

Acupuncture: the Freedom Fields Hospital in Plymouth had a 60–65 per cent success rate using acupuncture to turn a baby around, but you need the services of a qualified acupuncturist.

Homeopathy: one dose of Pulsatilla 30, every two hours for up to six doses (in one day only, then stopped), is recommended. Discuss this with a homeopathic doctor first.

External cephalic version (turning the baby from outside the mother's body): this requires the intervention of a midwife or doctor but is often unsuccessful as the baby is likely to turn back to his or her favoured position.

See also Breech Delivery on pp.181–82.

Brow

This presentation means that, although the baby is head-down, the neck is extended so that the brow or face is pointing to the cervix. If your baby is in this position in labour, you'll be closely monitored as the face is less robust than the top of the head. There may also be some facial bruising and/or elongation of the baby's head – but this will quickly subside.

Face

If the baby's face presents first, the delivery can be quite awkward and may lead to a delay in the second stage of labour. It's quite a stressful experience for the baby and, as the neck can be flexed backwards in the process, you may want to take your baby to a cranial osteopath in his early weeks.

Occipito-Anterior or Posterior

Occipito-Anterior means the back of your baby's head is facing the front of your pelvis as it comes down the birth canal. Occipito-Posterior means the back of your baby's head is lying against the back of your pelvis.

During delivery the baby's head will probably rotate into an occipito-anterior position, but if it remains occipito-posterior your progress through labour may be slower and more painful – this is known as a 'back labour' (see p. 167). It's demanding for both of you, and again may be a good reason to seek out the help of a cranial osteopath while your baby's still little.

CRANIAL OSTEOPATHY

This technique involves manipulating the bones of the skull with a touch so light that many people can barely feel it.

It is often used on pregnant and postnatal women. It can help them prepare for the birth and prevent problems like backache and stress incontinence after the baby's born. But because the head is so delicate and work in the cranial area is very gentle, it's particularly good for babies and young children.

A traumatic birth can have repercussions on a child such as colic in infancy, and hyperactivity later on. Cranial osteopathy is claimed to improve the body's ability to overcome these problems.

If there's compression in the spine and skull from a previous injury, or from the birth process, cranial osteopathy can release the blockages and pressure.

Parents of a child with a problem such as hyperactivity can see a dramatic change within weeks. But because each child is different it can take anything from two to two hundred sessions to treat the problem.

Transverse Lie

This describes the baby who's lying across the womb rather than head-down. If this is the case at the beginning of labour, a caesarean section is unavoidable. But transverse lie occurs in only 1 in 250 births (see p.182).

Unstable Lie

A baby is said to have an unstable lie if she keeps changing position between antenatal visits after 36 weeks. Ideally she should be adopting a head-down position around this time, even if the head isn't engaged. If you'd planned a home birth you may have to reconsider going to hospital as a caesarean may be necessary if the lie does not stabilize in early labour.

Bleeding or Spotting

Any bleeding or spotting in the last trimester is bound to concern you to some degree. How much of a concern it should be depends on the type of bleeding and the circumstances that surround it.

♦ pinkish-stained or red-streaked mucus soon after intercourse or vaginal examination, or brownish spotting within 48 hours, is most likely to be caused by bruising to your sensitive cervix. Report it to your doctor, but it's unlikely to be a danger sign – although you may be advised to abstain from sex until after the birth.

♦ bright red bleeding or persistent spotting could be coming from the placenta and must be checked immediately by your doctor. If he can't be reached, go to hospital.

♦ pinkish- or brownish-tinged or bloody mucus with contractions could be the first sign of labour. Call your midwife or hospital.

Cord Prolapse

The umbilical cord is the baby's lifeline, but occasionally it can slip down into the vagina when your waters break. If this happens the baby's life may be put in danger, so it's important to get to hospital as soon as you can. While this is very uncommon, it is life threatening for your baby. Call your hospital labour ward, or get someone else to do it if possible. Call an ambulance and, while waiting, get down on the floor or your bed on your hands and knees, then bend your elbows and lower your chest to the floor or bed, and *stay put*.

If you plan to work right up to your EDD, use the last few weeks of pregnancy to start delegating jobs to other people.

Stress Incontinence

As the baby's weight and the pressure of the growing womb push down on your bladder, stress incontinence may become more of a problem. Keep up your pelvic floor exercises (see p.42) to prevent postnatal incontinence, and see pp.247–48 for advice on coping if it does become a serious problem after the birth.

SEX IN THE THIRD TRIMESTER

A lot of women are confused about the advisability of having sex towards the end of pregnancy. But many doctors and midwives say there's no reason why women with healthy, uncomplicated pregnancies should not continue making love right up to their EDD. And most couples manage this without any problems. However if you're in a high-risk category for premature labour, intercourse may start you off early – talk to your doctor about the best course of action.

Sex is also sometimes linked to infection antenatally and postnatally. Most doctors believe it's safe to continue with unprotected intercourse right through to the ninth month (as long as your waters haven't broken, after which intercourse is a definite no-no). But because your waters could break at any time close to your EDD, and because of the possible risk of infection be extra vigilant about hygiene now – and ask your partner to wash or shower before sex.

You may be advised to cease sexual activity at this stage of your pregnancy if you've been diagnosed with placenta praevia (see p.239), or for any of the reasons listed on p.81. Whatever your worries, don't be afraid to discuss them with your doctor or midwife.

PRELABOUR AND FALSE LABOUR

Towards the end of pregnancy, it's only natural for any mum-to-be to search for signs that labour is imminent. The 'window' of term – when the baby can be expected to arrive – lasts from weeks 37 to 42. But from week 35 you may be anxious about any odd twinge that could be a sign that things are getting started.

Nobody knows exactly what triggers labour. Prostaglandins, natural substances made by the body, are thought to play an important part in the process. These are produced by the uterus during pregnancy and increase during spontaneous labour. They stimulate uterine muscle

JANE'S STORY

Life, for me, carried on pretty much as normal right through to the 38th week, when I went into labour. There were more hospital visits as the baby's EDD got nearer – but, as I'd decided to stay on at work right up to the baby's birth, the inevitably long waits in the antenatal clinic were a welcome chance to relax and read a few magazines.

Continuing with work was no problem. I was slightly slower than usual, but I saw that as a good thing – a chance to pace myself and start delegating jobs that would need to be passed on to other people when I was on maternity leave. At lunchtime I took the opportunity to go for a walk, have a swim, or (if nobody else was around) do a few relaxation exercises.

I must admit, though, I was much tireder than before in the evening, and took this as another warning sign that my body wanted me to slow down. I was always in bed by ten. Sex was still a pleasure, and I guess I was lucky in that respect. But my partner and I found new positions especially the 'spoons', more comfortable than others.

My only problem was not knowing exactly when my baby would come! I'd have loved to be able to tell everyone at work, 'I'm clearing my desk on Friday because the baby's due next Tuesday.' But my consultant said that, if he could predict the day any baby would come, he'd be a very rich man. In the event I was told to leave work in my 37th week, because my blood pressure was up slightly. This happens to a lot of first-time mums, I've discovered. And, though I had to spend the last week taking it easy at home, it presented no other problems. Once John had been born, my blood pressure soon returned to normal.

activity and trigger the release of a substance called oxytocin, both of which help to move the labour along. But prostaglandins alone do not bring labour about – a combination of fetal, placental and maternal factors are responsible for setting it in motion.

Prelabour symptoms, which can start a full month before the real thing (or sometimes only an hour before), include:

- engagement of the baby, two to four weeks before labour in first-time mothers, but often only just before labour with later births.
- crampiness in the pelvis and rectum.
- persistent low backache.
- slower weight gain.
- change in energy levels – for better or for worse (we don't all get the nesting instinct that makes pregnant women spring clean their homes just before giving birth).

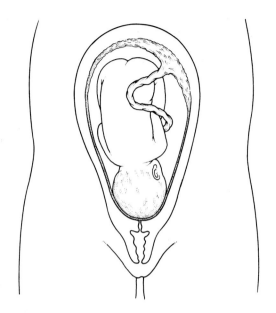

The engaged baby fits into the pelvis like an egg in an egg cup.

◆ thicker vaginal discharge.

◆ loss of mucous plug – the gelatinous chunk of mucus which has sealed the cervix comes loose because the cervix is beginning to thin and open for labour, and is sometimes passed through the vagina a week or two before the first real contractions. However, this may not happen until just before labour begins.

◆ 'show' – a pink or bloody discharge as the cervix effaces and dilates, rupturing capillaries. If this happens, labour is very close.

◆ more intense Braxton Hicks contractions.

◆ diarrhoea.

FALSE LABOUR

The symptoms of false labour include:

◆ irregular contractions which are not increasing in frequency or severity.

◆ pain in the lower abdomen, rather than the lower back.

◆ contractions are relieved by walking around, sitting or lying down.

◆ fetal movements intensify briefly with contractions – though be aware of excessive fetal activity, which could be a sign that the baby's distressed.

Your partner may enjoy massaging your shoulders, arms and lower back. It's something you may want him to do when you're in labour. Practising in advance means you will both know what is most comfortable for you.

PREMATURE LABOUR

Labour which begins before week 37 is premature. But only 7–10 per cent of babies are premature, and most of these are born to women who are already known to be at high risk.

What Might Put You at Risk of Premature Labour?

Predisposing factors include:

◆ smoking.
◆ alcohol.

- drug abuse.
- poor weight gain – if you were significantly underweight before getting pregnant you should aim to gain around 16 kg (35 lb) in pregnancy.
- poor nutrition – see the guidelines on pp.37–40.
- sexual intercourse (if you're already high-risk).
- hormonal imbalance.
- infections – early labour may be the body's way of getting the baby out of a dangerous environment. For this reason stay away from people who are ill, look after your own nutrition, and send your partner off for a wash before intercourse later in pregnancy.
- a weak or incompetent cervix (see pp.231–32).
- irritable uterus – this can set off untimely contractions. If the problem is diagnosed, bed rest should help delay labour.
- placenta praevia – a low-lying placenta.
- chronic illness such as high blood pressure, heart, liver or kidney disease, or diabetes.
- stress.
- age under seventeen.
- age over thirty-five.
- structural abnormalities of the uterus.
- multiple pregnancy.
- fetal abnormality.
- history of premature babies.

Occasionally, however, none of these risk factors is present. It's important, therefore, to take notice of the following symptoms of premature labour – however well things have been going thus far in your pregnancy.

Symptoms

- menstrual-like cramps.
- lower back pain or a change in the nature of lower backache.
- achiness in the pelvic floor, thighs or groin.
- a change in your vaginal discharge (especially if it is watery or bloody).
- broken waters – a trickle or rush of fluid from your vagina.

Treatment

Prompt medical attention is vital to postpone premature labour and give the baby a stronger chance of survival (unless there are very good reasons why the baby would be better off being nurtured outside the womb). If you have strong contractions but no bleeding, you may simply be admitted to hospital for supervised bed rest. If the membranes are intact and the cervix has not dilated, there's a good chance of carrying your baby to term.

OVERDUE BABY

It's distressing to think your baby is 'late'. And the phone never stops ringing because anxious friends and relatives want to know how you are – which merely adds to your stress. But studies show that, in spite of health professionals' efforts to pin down the right EDD, 70 per cent of apparently late babies are not late at all. They are only believed to be late because of a miscalculation of the time of conception.

If you reach 42 weeks, your doctor will check the size of the uterus and the height of fundus (the top of the uterus). He will then match these against the timing of the first fetal movements you felt and the first heartbeats detected by your midwife or ultrasound technician.

He will then want to be sure that the baby is continuing to grow and thriving well into the tenth month. But, even if he or she is, conditions in the uterus will begin to deteriorate as time goes by. The placenta can no longer provide adequate nutrition and oxygen, and the production of amniotic fluid also drops. You may recognize this because your clothes are looser over the 'bump', though this can also happen if the head engages.

Babies who are born after spending a long time in these less than perfect surroundings are called 'post-mature'. They are thin, with dry, flaky skin, and none of the vernix coating that most newborns have. They may also have long nails, thick hair and alert, open eyes.

Those who have been in the post-term uterus the longest – born at 42 or 43 weeks – may be yellow-stained and can be at greater risk during labour, or even before labour. Because of their size, they're likely to have a difficult delivery and may even have to spend some time in the special care baby unit.

If your doctor wants to induce the labour, ask him to explain his reasons. You may wish to ask for a second opinion.

YOUR QUESTIONS ANSWERED

Q: **Everyone says Braxton Hicks contractions are nothing to worry about — but mine are quite painful. What can I do?**

A: Talk to your midwife if you're worried, but you can also try a very gentle abdominal massage – stroking your bump slowly with mandarin oil.

Q: *My mind's racing at night and I can't sleep. What can I do?*

A: Try to have a warm aromatic bath at night. Ask your partner to massage your feet before bed, as this has a calming effect. Also give your bump a gentle goodnight massage. Avoid exercising within three hours of going to bed. Finally, try not to eat sweet food late at night.

Q: *I'm getting pubic pain in my last month. Is there a cure?*

A: Pubic pain is not unusual in the last two months as the cartilage between the two sides of the pelvis softens to allow the pelvis to move more freely in childbirth. Massaging the area with rosewood oil mixed with a carrier oil (such as sweet almond) may help. If the pain continues, report it to your midwife and stop doing yoga if you have been doing it.

Q: *Is there an alternative remedy I can use to help the soreness around my vulva?*

A: Soreness can indicate infection, so it's important to check this out with your doctor or midwife before taking any steps to remedy it yourself. But washing the area with lavender water, then swabbing with a dot of tea tree, rosewood or geranium oil blended in a base of jojoba, can help. Discuss these options with an aromatherapist. Some oils are suitable now that were contra-indicated earlier in pregnancy, so it's important to get expert advice.

AROMATHERAPY IN PREGNANCY

Many aromatherapy oils are unsuitable for use in pregnancy, so view them as medicines, not perfumes, and always consult a qualified aromatherapist before trying anything you're unsure about. However, the following oils are useful if you follow the guidelines given:

♦ Camomile (only in the last three months) is recommended as a relaxing oil. Camomile tea can help urinary tract infections such as cystitis.

♦ Mandarin (safe throughout pregnancy) is antiseptic and calming.

♦ Neroli or orange blossom oil (safe throughout pregnancy) helps calm nerves and reduce anxiety.

♦ Rose oil (only to be used in the last two to three weeks of pregnancy) is used in labour because it's thought to help women cope with contractions.

♦ Sandalwood (safe throughout pregnancy) is antiseptic, diuretic, tonic, sedative and aphrodisiac, though you may find it too strong if you're sensitive to smells during the first three months.

Q: *Will having sex in the last trimester make me go into labour early?*

A: Orgasm causes mild uterine contractions and chemicals in semen can also stimulate these. But in a normal pregnancy, even close to your EDD, sex does not cause problems – but send your partner for a wash.

Q: *My baby's due in about two weeks and I've noticed a change in the shape of my bump. Is this normal?*

A: It sounds as if your baby has engaged in the pelvis, ready for birth. This happens during the last month of the first pregnancy – though sometimes before, or even much later.

Q: *Why is it risky for the baby to be born prematurely?*

A: Statistics show that babies born early are more likely to suffer problems with their physical or mental development, and there's also an increased risk of neonatal death – although some babies born early thrive and have no problems.

5 Antenatal Screening

Antenatal screening exists to identify problems with the fetus. Where possible it will correct these in pregnancy, and if not it will give you, the parent or parents, the opportunity to come to terms with the prospect of having a child with a disability, or terminating the pregnancy if you wish. For further information on the conditions listed in the table below, see this chapter. The three tests used – amniocentesis (amnio), chorionic villus sampling (CVS) and ultrasound – are also all described in the following pages.

WHAT SCREENING CAN DO FOR YOU

Abnormalities Picked Up in Screening

Condition	Incidence per 100 Normal Babies	Test	Number Picked Up When Tested
Down's syndrome	1.5	Amnio/CVS Ultrasound	All Some
Turner's syndrome	0.2	Amnio/CVS Ultrasound	All Some
Cystic fibrosis	0.5	CVS	All in some families
Sex-linked conditions (e.g. haemophilia, Duchenne muscular dystrophy)	0.5	Amnio/CVS	Most in some families
Anencephaly	Varies	Amnio Ultrasound	All All

(table continues)

Condition	Incidence per 100 Normal Babies	Test	Number Picked Up When Tested
Spina bifida	Varies	Amnio Ultrasound	98% 95%
Hydrocephaly	0.5–3	Ultrasound	Most (after 20 weeks)
Cleft lip/palate	1.4	Ultrasound	Many
Heart abnormality	8	Ultrasound	33%
Abdominal wall deficiency	0.2	Ultrasound	Most
Kidney abnormalities	8	Ultrasound	Most
Dwarfism	0.2	Ultrasound	Most (after 20 weeks)
Club foot	1.2	Ultrasound	Many

There are, unfortunately, many other disabilities and severe health problems which cannot be identified during antenatal screening, so these tests are no guarantee that you will have a perfect child. And it is your right to refuse all tests offered, if you wish.

GENETIC COUNSELLING

This kind of counselling is offered in early pregnancy, or before conception, to couples who have previously had a malformed baby, or who have a history of inherited diseases, and also to women who have had more than three miscarriages. Detailed questions are asked about your medical history, previous pregnancies and the medical history of your family and your partner's family. Blood tests may also be taken for chromosome testing.

WHICH TEST AND WHEN?

Alpha-fetoprotein (AFP) Test: *weeks 16–20*

This is one of a number of blood tests offered routinely to pregnant women, though many health authorities have replaced it with the triple test or Bart's test (see p.117) which also screens for two other substances in the blood.

Alpha-fetoprotein is a substance produced by the unborn baby as it grows in the womb. Large amounts of it are found in amniotic fluid, and

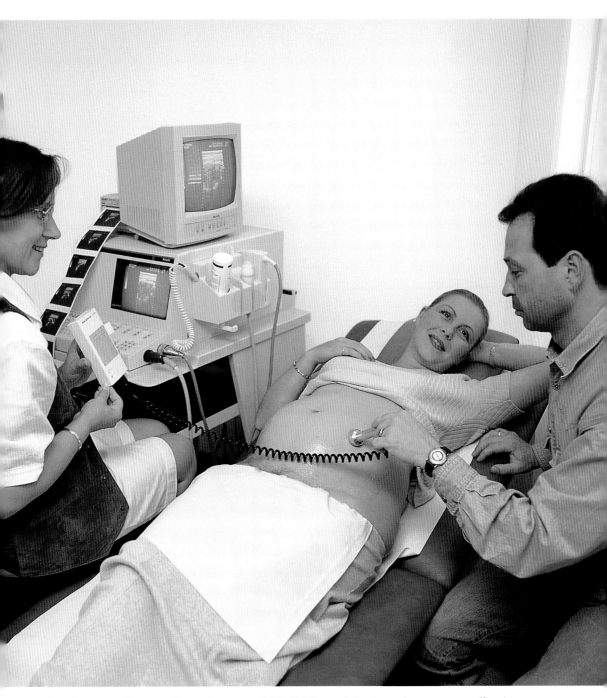

A wide range of antenatal tests is now available. Think carefully about those you are offered – your doctor or midwife will be happy to discuss any concerns you may have, and each test should be fully explained to you, so you can make up your own mind.

larger than normal amounts are found in the mother's bloodstream if the baby has neural tube defects.

Measuring the amount of alpha-fetoprotein can help your doctor predict the likelihood, but not the certainty, of problems. The test results must be combined with the mother's age and weight, and the age of the fetus, before the doctor comes up with a risk rating.

AFP can detect increased risk of:

- neural tube defects (e.g. spina bifida or anencephaly).
- severe kidney disease.
- severe liver disease.
- blockage in the oesophagus or intestines.
- Down's syndrome.
- urinary obstruction.
- osteogenesis imperfecta (fragile bones in the baby).

However, there's a chance that the AFP test will throw up an 'abnormal' result even if there are no problems. Out of 1000 women tested, about 40 will come back 'abnormal'. Of these 40, only one or two will actually have a problem. So if you have an AFP test and the result is abnormal, don't panic. Another AFP test will be done to verify the results, and an ultrasound scan will also be performed. Equally, because the AFP test is not infallible your result may show that you have a normal risk rating for your age, but this is no guarantee that your baby will not be born with one of the conditions mentioned above.

See also Serum Testing on p.122.

Routine Tests

- **AFP/Bart's test**, depending on the health authority's preference.
- **Amniocentesis**, depending on age.
- **Ultrasound**, at 10–12 weeks and 18–20 weeks.

Amniocentesis: weeks 16–18

This test is usually offered to women who:

- will be 35+ when they deliver.
- have had a previous high-risk rating in a blood test.
- have had a previous baby with a birth defect.
- have a family history of birth defects.
- have a birth defect themselves.
- have a partner with a birth defect.

Using an ultrasound scan (see p.125), the doctor will locate a pocket of fluid where the fetus and placenta are not in the way. Then he numbs your skin with a local anaesthetic, passes a hypodermic needle through the abdomen into the uterus, and with a syringe draws out fluid from the amniotic cavity.

Only a tiny amount of fluid (30 ml/1 fl oz) is needed. The fetal cells floating in it can be grown in cultures to confirm the health of your baby or to identify one of about forty abnormalities. But remember there are over four hundred abnormalities that babies can be born with so amniocentesis only detects 10 per cent of them. These include:

◆ chromosomal abnormalities, particularly Down's syndrome.
◆ skeletal diseases, such as osteogenesis imperfecta.
◆ fetal infections, such as herpes or rubella.
◆ central nervous system diseases, e.g. anencephaly.
◆ blood diseases.
◆ chemical problems or deficiencies.

The test can determine the baby's sex, but is not used for this purpose unless there's a risk that the sex of the baby could predict a problem such as muscular dystrophy.

The risk of the amniocentesis test is that it can cause trauma to the fetus, placenta or umbilical cord, infection, miscarriage or premature labour. But the risk of losing your baby as a result of the test is very small – only about 0.5–3 per cent.

Bart's Test: *week 16*

This test takes its name from Bart's, or St Bartholomew's Hospital in London, where it was developed. It's also known as the triple test.

A sample of the mother's blood is tested not only for its levels of AFP (see pp.114–16), but also for the two hormones oestriol and human chorionic gonadotrophin. It increases the possibility of assessing the risk of the baby having Down's syndrome.

See also Serum Testing on p.122.

Biophysical Profile: *third trimester, if there are suspected problems*

This is a comprehensive test to examine your baby while he or she's still in the womb. It's useful in checking the wellbeing of a baby in certain situations, for instance:

◆ The baby has intra-uterine growth retardation (IUGR; see p.234).
◆ The mother is diabetic.

- The baby hasn't been moving much.
- The pregnancy is high-risk for other reasons.
- The baby is overdue.

The test measures the baby's breathing and body movements, his muscle tone, and how his heart rate increases when he moves. It also looks at the amount of amniotic fluid surrounding him.

Each area is scored 0, 1 or 2, and the scores are added to give a total. The higher the total, the better the indications for the baby's health. A low score may mean there are problems, and if so the baby may have to be delivered immediately. If the score was reassuring, the test may be repeated at intervals.

Cardiotocogram: second or third trimesters if problems are suspected

This is a non-invasive procedure which can be done in the doctor's surgery or in the delivery room. While you are lying down, a fetal heart monitor is attached to your abdomen. Every time you feel the baby move, you push the button to make a mark on the monitor paper. At the same time the monitor records the baby's heartbeat on the same paper. The results show how well your baby is doing. If there's a problem with the cardiotocogram, you may be referred for a biophysical profile (p.117) or a contraction stress test (p.120).

Chorionic Villus Sampling (CVS Test): weeks 9–13

Chorionic villus sampling is an early test to detect genetic abnormalities such as Down's syndrome, Tay-Sachs disease (an inherited metabolic disorder which results in early death) and cystic fibrosis. It involves examining the placental fragments called chorionic villi, which, because the placenta and baby develop from the same cell, can be used to check the chromosomes of the baby.

You'll be given a local anaesthetic and then a fine needle is passed into the uterus, through the abdomen, and a sample of chorionic villi is taken. The needle is carefully watched with an ultrasound scan to ensure it doesn't injure the fetus. The whole procedure takes only two to three minutes and afterwards your baby's heart is checked to make sure it's beating properly.

After a CVS test you may experience a little crampiness, like period pain, or light bleeding. These are relatively common reactions, and in most cases the pregnancy continues without any problems. But you must call your doctor if you're in a lot of pain, or bleeding more than 'spotting'.

You're also likely to be emotionally and physically drained after the test, so it's best to have someone on hand to look after you and take you home so you can flop into bed.

The advantage over amniocentesis is that CVS can be done much earlier in pregnancy and the results are quickly available. So, if a considerable degree of abnormality is detected and you do opt for a termination, it can be done early – which is nearly always preferable.

However, although most studies conclude that CVS is safe and reliable, at least one testing centre in the USA has linked it to limb deformities in the fetus. The procedure also increases the risk of miscarriage slightly (more than amniocentesis). And there's a slim risk that the pregnancy could be terminated on the basis of incorrect information, as an abnormality known as mosaicism (which can give rise to conditions such as Down's syndrome) can be detected in the villi when it doesn't exist in the fetus. If mosaicism shows up on your test result, you may have to have an amniocentesis test later to confirm it or rule it out.

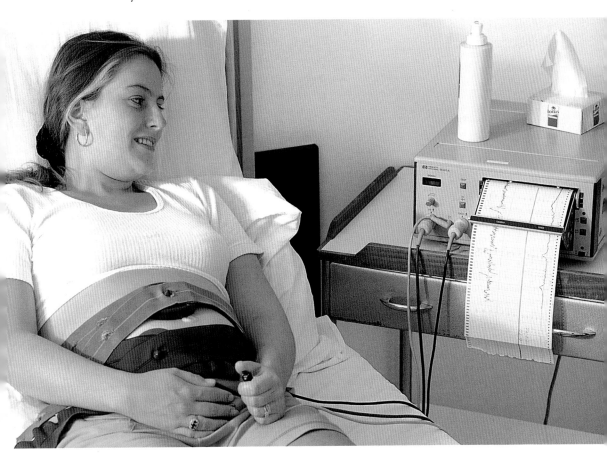

Fetal heart monitoring may be recommended if you've had a problem in pregnancy. In labour your contractions can also be recorded. Babies' hearts usually beat between 110 and 160 times a minute. During a contraction, or if the baby's under stress, the heartbeat slows down a bit.

Contraction Stress Test: *towards the end of pregnancy, where there have been problems – but rarely done in the UK*

This is a test to see how well the baby reacts to contractions. It may be necessary to trigger contractions through nipple stimulation or with an intravenous fluid infusion of small amounts of the hormone oxytocin. During these contractions the baby is tested with a fetal heart monitor, and the results show how well he or she will tolerate labour.

If the baby doesn't respond well it can be a sign of fetal distress. This will enable the doctors looking after you to make a decision about the baby's safety, which in some cases may mean having an emergency caesarean.

Cordocentesis: *weeks 18–20*

This test is rarely offered, but, if it is, it involves taking a sample of the baby's blood from the umbilical cord or vein, through your abdomen. It gives a quick chromosome result, within a week (chromosome abnormalities are linked with problems such as Down's syndrome), but can also be used to test for specific infections and blood disorders in your baby.

CVS

See Chorionic Villus Sampling (CVS Test) on pp.118–19.

STATE-OF-THE-ART SCREENING TESTS

Some very useful tests are currently being developed:

◆ **Early biochemical screening:** early pregnancy. Research is being carried out to develop earlier screening tests for chromosome abnormalities using samples of the mother's blood.

◆ **Fetal cells in maternal blood:** throughout pregnancy. It's known that some cells from the baby are present in the mother's blood, and these, when isolated, will hold accurate information about the baby's genetic make-up. Studies are also being carried out to develop ways of collecting fetal cells gathered from the mother's cervix.

◆ **Maternal blood test for gender:** early pregnancy. This test, although still experimental, could provide early screening for hereditary diseases that affect boy babies only.

◆ **MRI:** in place of ultrasound. Magnetic resonance imaging (MRI) may in the future be used in place of ultrasound to give a clearer picture of what the baby will be like, inside and out.

Fetal Tissue Sampling: *weeks 18–20*

It's possible to take samples of tissue from the baby for analysis at this time. But the test is only available at specialist centres and where there is a known high risk of certain genetic conditions.

Fetoscopy: *week 16+*

This is a test to diagnose, and sometimes treat or correct, certain blood and skin diseases that amniocentesis can't detect. But it's a high-risk procedure with a 3–5 per cent chance of miscarriage, and not widely used.

Your abdomen is swabbed with antiseptic and numbed with a local anaesthetic before tiny incisions are made in the abdomen and uterus. Then, with ultrasound monitoring to guide the instrument, a miniature telescope, called a fibre-optic endoscope, is passed through the incisions and into the uterus. The telescope allows the baby, placenta and amniotic fluid to be observed. Blood samples can be taken from the junction of the umbilical cord and the placenta, and a tiny piece of fetal tissue can also be removed for examination.

HCG Test: *first trimester*

The quantitative HCG (human chorionic gonadotrophin) test is a blood test taken when there's a concern about miscarriage or ectopic pregnancy. It measures the hormone HCG, which is made early in pregnancy and increases rapidly. Usually two or more tests are carried out a few days apart, as this shows any significant change in the hormone level. An ultrasound scan is often ordered as a matter of routine when the HCG test is carried out.

L/S Ratio: *when premature birth is imminent*

This is a test to check the maturity of the fetus's lungs, and involves measuring the ratio of two substances, lecithin and sphingomyelin, in the amniotic fluid. It is performed by amniocentesis.

Nuchal Fold Screening/Nuchal Translucency Scan: *week 11*

Research has shown that a slightly enlarged nuchal fold (a fold of skin on the back of the baby's neck) may be a marker for Down's syndrome in early pregnancy. The nuchal fold is measured using ultrasound, although it takes a trained scan operator. The test has an 85 per cent accuracy rate, but further tests may be needed for a diagnosis to be made.

Serum Testing: *weeks 15–22*

Up to four substances in your blood are measured and compared with average levels for your stage of pregnancy. These substances are AFP (see pp.114–16), unconjugated oestriol, inhibin A and human chorionic gonadotrophin (see p.121). The results, together with your age, indicate the level of risk of Down's syndrome in your baby. (The level of AFP is used to determine increased risk of spina bifida or anencephaly.)

The results, either 'screen negative' or 'screen positive', are usually ready in a week and are sent to your doctor or antenatal clinic. If your risk of Down's syndrome is lower than 1 in 300 and the AFP level is not high the result is screen negative, and a diagnostic test such as amniocentesis or CVS will not be offered. It means you are not at high risk of having a baby with Down's syndrome or a neural tube defect, but does not rule out this possibility altogether.

The result is called screen positive if your risk of Down's syndrome is 1 in 300 or greater (about 1 in 20 women screened will be in this risk group), or if the AFP level is more than two and a half times higher than normal (about 1 in 40 women screened will be in this risk group). A screen positive result means that you are in a higher risk group for having a baby with Down's syndrome or a neural tube defect, and will be offered a diagnostic test. But for every 50 women with screen positive results, only one will actually be carrying a baby with Down's syndrome.

Any woman could have a baby with Down's syndrome, whatever her age. But as you can see from the table the likelihood increases as you get older, which is why your age is used in working out your risk rating. It also means that an older woman is more likely to have a result in the higher risk group (screen positive) and to be offered a diagnostic test.

Screening for Down's Syndrome

Age of mother	Probability of a screen positive result for Down's syndrome	Actual Down's syndrome pregnancies among screen-positive women
Under 25	1 in 40	60%
25 – 29	1 in 30	65%
30 – 34	1 in 15	70%
35 – 39	1 in 5	85%
40 – 44	1 in 3	95%
45 +	more than 1 in 2	more than 99%

PENNY'S STORY

My second baby, Daniel, was born with Down's syndrome on my twenty-ninth birthday. It was totally unexpected – and devastating because he was one of the children with Down's syndrome who suffers with very severe heart problems. He died when he was fourteen weeks old, having never come home from hospital.

I couldn't bear to go through the same sad experience again. When I was expecting Michael the following year, I had the CVS test and also fetal heart screening – in case our oldest boy Andrew, nine, was the fluke in being healthy and all our other children would have problems. Michael was fine, though, and so was our daughter Sarah, who's now four. I don't think I would have terminated either pregnancy if I'd discovered they had Down's syndrome. But I needed to know, and prepare myself for what was to come.

Down's Syndrome and Health Implications

Down's syndrome is the largest single cause of learning difficulties and is due to a chromosomal disorder named after John Langdon Down, the Victorian doctor who identified the condition. Normally, we have 23 pairs of chromosomes, but children with Down's syndrome are born with an extra chromosome or an abnormal rearrangement of chromosomes.

The health difficulties faced by Down's syndrome children fall into three categories: nuisance problems, potential disabilities and critical heart conditions. Most of the problems experienced by children are of the niggling, nuisance variety: runny noses, earache and sticky eyes, and modern medicine is making a really big effort to alleviate these, for example with dietary changes, antibiotics, drops and sprays.

The main priority is to prevent secondary disability. Hearing and visual problems are common, so parents are encouraged to have their children screened regularly and to get hearing aids and glasses as soon as they need them.

An underactive thyroid is also quite common, and it can be hard to spot. The symptoms – slowness, weight gain and duller than usual intellect – can be confused with features of Down's syndrome, even in those who, without the underactive thyroid, wouldn't have these problems. But screening can pick up the condition, and, with treatment, the improvements are remarkable.

By far the most serious condition is what is known as an AV canal defect of the heart, which affects 15–20 per cent of Down's children. It means that the four chambers of the heart, which are normally more or less cut off from one another, are in communication, which can wreak havoc with the circulation. It is very important to diagnose this problem in the first months of life before any lung damage occurs and surgery is now offered to children when they are very young, and has a good success rate.

Most people with Down's syndrome can now look forward to a long and healthy life – many remain in good health right through to their seventies. However, doctors have recently identified a susceptibility to Alzheimer's disease. Although fewer than half develop it, it starts earlier in life than in a normal person, and the progress is much more rapid.

But overall, parents of children with Down's syndrome have no need to expect them to be sickly and prone to problems. Some say that their Down's child is the healthiest of all their offspring, while others have to contend with terrible problems. As with all children, there is an enormous variation in both health and intellect.

ANYA'S STORY

Anya was just a few hours old when two grim-faced doctors informed her mother that she would be 'physically and mentally handicapped for life'. 'She was still reeling from the shock when a nurse came in and said, "Take no notice – your daughter will give you great pleasure!"' Anya says.

The image of a forty-five-year-old with Down's syndrome, wearing a pudding basin haircut and crimplene trousers and clinging to his mother's hand, is finally fading. More and more families now realize that it is reasonable to expect their children with Down's syndrome to grow up, leave home and lead a relatively independent though sheltered life – in much the same way as their other adult children. Quite a few people with Down's syndrome work, and some even gain driving licences and drive their own cars.

For Anya, who lives alone in London and works as a stained glass artist, nothing is more irritating than seeing adults with Down's syndrome being mollycoddled like babies. 'My mother was very tough,' she says. 'She was as strict with me as she was with my two older sisters, and she made sure I became independent.'

As well as having a mother who brought out the best in her, Anya is naturally bright. Reading and writing came easily to her as a child, and as an adult she expresses herself exceptionally well. She admits that her main problems have been to do with other people's attitudes. Even at the special needs schools she attended as a child, she was badly bullied.

'But I've been lucky in that I haven't had any ill health,' she says. 'Certain health problems are common in people with Down's syndrome. But, apart from needing to wear glasses for both long- and short-sightedness, I have very little wrong with me.'

THE ULTRASOUND SCAN

What It Is

Ultrasound scanning was introduced in 1958 and has been in widespread use since the early 1970s. The test gives a two-dimensional picture of the developing baby, using high-frequency sound waves.

When It's Done

You may be offered two tests, the first around weeks 10–12 of your pregnancy to 'date' it. At this stage you will not look pregnant, and may not even feel it. But the baby is clearly visible, swimming around on the scan picture. A further test is normally offered around weeks 18–20, and this one is used to detect abnormalities in the baby. Subsequent scans may be advised by your doctor if there's a worry about the baby's growth or the location of the placenta, and some women (with problems already mentioned) are offered regular scans throughout their pregnancy.

How It Works

A device called a transducer is placed on the abdomen. Sound waves projected from it travel through the abdomen, bouncing off tissues back to the transducer. The reflected sound waves are translated into a rough picture of your baby.

The procedure is quick and painless – although you usually have to have a full bladder to enable the scan to work, and this can be quite uncomfortable.

Why It's Done

- to confirm your EDD.
- to determine whether there is more than one baby.
- to check that the baby's physical characteristics are normal.

It can also

- identify an early pregnancy.
- show the size and growth of the baby.
- measure the baby's head, abdomen and thighbone.
- identify Down's syndrome in some cases.
- identify abnormalities such as hydrocephalus.
- measure the amount of amniotic fluid.
- locate and measure the placenta.
- identify placental abnormalities.

- detect and locate an IUD if you got pregnant while using this form of contraception.
- identify an ectopic pregnancy.
- check whether a miscarriage has or has not taken place.
- help to locate the safest place to perform an amniocentesis test.

Not all abnormalities can be detected by ultrasound. The scan shows structure, and while the structure of an organ may appear normal there may be an undetectable functional disorder. For example, the brain may look perfectly normal – but intellectual disabilities commonly occur in infants who have normally structured brains. Likewise, the structure of an organ may appear grossly abnormal on a scan but may produce only minor difficulties for the baby after birth.

The test at 18–20 weeks enables most normal structures of the fetus to be seen, and if an abnormality is detected it's still early enough for the pregnancy to be terminated if that's your wish. The main advantage in having a scan is to reassure you that your baby is healthy.

What Your Scan Operator Is Looking For

Your scan checks a series of sections through the fetus.

Head and Spine

This section is examined for three important abnormalities.

Anencephaly: a condition in which the bony skull and most of the brain is absent. This is easily identified, as the structures normally seen in the section through the head and brain are all missing. There is unfortunately no treatment, and the baby dies before or immediately after birth. However, the incidence of anencephaly is rare, ranging from 0.5 to 2 per 1000 births.

Hydrocephaly: an increase of cerebrospinal fluid in the chambers of the brain, which is present at birth in nearly all babies with spina bifida. The condition can be treated by a drainage procedure before or after birth, and although severe hydrocephaly has a very poor outlook it is not always bad news. The incidence of hydrocephaly is 0.5–3 births per 1000, and on the scan it is diagnosed when the size of the ventricles is larger than expected.

Choroid plexus cysts: tiny cysts which are seen in at least 1 in 100 fetuses scanned at 18–20 weeks, and which usually disappear by around week 24. The cysts do not cause any problems, but they need to be noted as they often occur in fetuses with an extra chromosome 18 – an abnormality known as Trisomy 18, which normally causes death soon after birth. If a choroid plexus cyst is detected, other abnormalities will

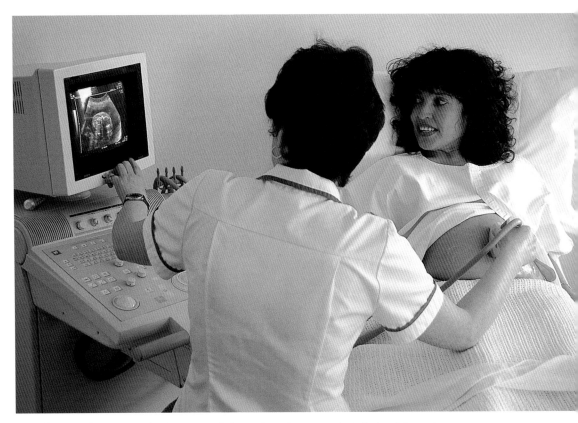

The ultrasound scan provides important information about your baby's development.

be looked for – particularly in the heart and lungs. If there are no other abnormalities, it's unlikely your baby has Trisomy 18. So finding one of these cysts is not a reason for concern, but a reason to look for, and in most cases rule out, other abnormalities.

Face and Neck

On the face the scan operator is looking for signs of clefts and cystic swellings.

Facial clefts occur in around 1 per 1000 births. Most involve the lip alone, or the lip and the underlying palate. The abnormality can be corrected with surgery in childhood.

Cystic swellings occur in around 1 per 200 pregnancies that miscarry, but are uncommon in liveborn babies. The outlook for the fetus depends on the degree of swelling of the neck, and whether there is swelling elsewhere in the body. The condition may be a sign of a chromosomal abnormality – usually Turner's syndrome (see p.128).

ELLEN'S STORY

I was fifteen when I discovered I had Turner's syndrome. My mother had taken me to the doctor because my periods hadn't started, and I was also very short for my age: four feet nine inches – and I'm still the same height now.

Our doctor referred me to an endocrinologist who took one look at me and diagnosed Turner's, because shortness and late menstruation are classic signs. He ran a blood test to confirm the diagnosis, and explained that the condition is caused by a chromosomal abnormality which only affects girls. Its main feature is that our ovaries don't function properly, so he prescribed hormonal treatment to bring about all the normal changes that happen at puberty – breasts, pubic hair and a monthly bleed. The hormones are important because they protect bone density. Without them, I'd be a high-risk case for osteoporosis.

But at just fifteen I wasn't ready to take on board the fact that, because my ovaries didn't function (even with the hormone treatment), I'd never be able to have a baby of my own.

Then three years later I changed to a new consultant, who explained it all over again. And I was so shocked that, as I travelled home that night, I was convinced I was walking past every single pregnant woman in London. It took me a while to come to terms with the fact that I may never be a mother.

Looking back, though, I'm pleased I knew so young that I had this problem. I was able to tell my husband, Jeff, before we married. We decided we'd adopt children instead, and we now have Emma, nineteen, and Thomas, fourteen.

These days some women are told when they're pregnant that the baby girl they're carrying has Turner's, and others discover soon after the birth. It's great that medical science has moved on so far – but sadly a lot of medical encyclopedias have never been updated and doctors often think that having Turner's is some kind of handicap. I feel so sorry for any mother who gets this message as an introduction to Turner's.

Certainly there are problems – but nothing that can't be overcome. Girls are now given a synthetic growth hormone which it's hoped will increase their final height. They'll never be amazons, but they're more likely now to go over the five foot mark, whereas, until recently, four feet six inches has been the average height for a girl with Turner's. And it's even possible – although not straightforward – for Turner women, to have babies, using a donor egg and IVF.

The major misconception, though, is that we have a low IQ. That's simply not true. Although, like a lot of Turner women, I have a problem with maths, I have a BA degree and I'm also qualified as an occupational therapist and drama teacher.

To me the main problem is the nuisance of trying to buy nice clothes that fit. But even that's improving with all the 'Petite' ranges high street shops are offering. I can now go wild in Principles and Next, just like anyone else!

Heart and Lungs

Structural heart abnormalities occur in at least 1 in 125 births. Almost half are now detectable on the scan – if one is detected in your baby you may also be recommended to undergo a chromosome test. Abnormalities of the lungs are rare prior to birth – the most common problem detected is that of cysts on one lung. But these can usually be removed after birth, although they may need to be drained while the baby's still in the womb.

Abdomen and Abdominal Wall

This is the most important section for checking the fetus's growth. The operator will also be looking for deficiencies in the skin and muscle, which may lead to some of the contents of the abdomen growing on the outside of the baby. If such a problem is detected (it occurs in about 1 in 5000 births) the baby can be treated, usually successfully, after birth. But one condition causing this kind of abnormality, exomphalos, may be linked to other abnormalities requiring further diagnosis with chromosome tests.

Also detectable from this section of the scan are:

Diaphragmatic hernia: this causes some of the contents of the abdomen to ride up into the chest. The hernia can be operated on after birth, but lung development may sometimes have been so badly affected that the baby cannot survive.

Kidney abnormalities: if very serious (for instance, the absence of both kidneys), the baby may die before birth or immediately after. Some cases, for example fetuses whose outflow of urine is blocked, may be suitable candidates for treatment in the womb.

Limbs

Calcium starts to form in the bones by the end of the first trimester, and by the time you're scanned at 18–20 weeks the bones will stand out as dense white lines. The femur (thigh bone) is usually measured on the scan to detect problems such as dwarfism. Markedly bent bones may indicate a condition known as osteogenesis imperfecta (brittle bones which break very easily). In severe cases the baby would be unable to survive the trauma of birth (see p.131).

Hands and Feet

The baby's fingers are counted, where possible, but the positioning of the hand may make this difficult. Club feet may be detected before birth. Treatment of a club foot should start soon after birth and involves repeated manipulation of the foot and ankle, sometimes using a plaster cast or splint to hold the foot in the corrected position.

TERMINATING A PREGNANCY FOR ABNORMALITY

You can have your pregnancy terminated at any time from the confirmation of your pregnancy to the 24th week. But two doctors will have to state that they believe continuing with the pregnancy involves a greater risk to your life, physical or mental health, or to that of your child, than terminating it. In practice, the law allows the doctor to consider 'the actual and reasonably foreseeable environment' of the woman – in other words if he or she feels that the woman requesting an abortion would become seriously depressed as a result of having the child, or that her circumstances would cause stress which would damage her health, these are grounds for allowing the abortion to go ahead.

Vacuum Aspiration or Suction

This method can be used up to the 12th week of pregnancy, under general, local or augmented local anaesthetic. The opening in your cervix is stretched to the same number of millimetres as there are weeks in your pregnancy. Then a tube is passed into your womb and its contents are sucked out with an electric pump or syringe.

Dilatation and Evacuation (D and E)

D and E can be carried out under general anaesthetic up to 14 weeks. The process is similar to the suction method, but after the fetus has been removed any remaining contents of the womb are scraped out (curettage).

If you need an abortion after 18 weeks your surgeon will examine you and look into your obstetric history before deciding on your best course of action. In some cases, it may be necessary to perform a two-stage abortion which involves staying in hospital for two nights and usually involves a mini labour.

Abortion Pill

Treatment with a drug called RU-486 (mifepristone) is used to induce a miscarriage, providing you are less than nine weeks pregnant.

After a preliminary consultation, you will have to make three visits to the clinic. On the first visit you are given three tablets to take. On the second, two days later, a hormonal pessary is inserted high up in your vagina. The abortion takes place on this visit and usually lasts about six hours, during which you will experience cramps like strong period pains. The pill works by blocking the action of the hormone which keeps the embryo in the womb. The womb lining breaks down and the embryo is

PHILIPPA'S STORY

My first baby, Hannah, now seven, was perfect, and it didn't occur to me that anything would go wrong with my second pregnancy. My routine blood test had been normal. And, at eighteen weeks, I went along for my anomaly scan, all excited about getting my first picture of the baby.

When the scan showed that Laura had short limbs, I felt my world collapse. I'd always thought I'd make a good mother to a disabled child. But suddenly the prospect of having a child of normal intelligence trapped inside a body which wouldn't work for her seemed terrible. My husband and I decided to have the pregnancy terminated, and, a week later, I went through the devastating process of giving birth to tiny Laura. I was too scared to look at her – and that's my biggest regret. But the midwife took pictures of her, and, eighteen months later, when I'd had another baby, Michael, now three, I got the strength to collect those photos and cherish them.

The post mortem on Laura revealed she had brittle bones and, if she'd survived the pregnancy, she could have died during her delivery.

People think we took the easy option in aborting our baby – but it was the most difficult thing Gary and I have ever had to do. We did it out of love – but living with our decision has been very hard.

lost in the bleeding which follows. The pessary speeds up the process. A week later you will return to the clinic for your third visit, which is to check that treatment has been effective and no infection has set in.

Possible Complications

Incomplete abortion: a small piece of tissue remaining in your womb can cause prolonged bleeding and increase the risk of infection developing. If your bleeding is heavy or you are still experiencing cramping after your second visit, you may require a D and C to complete the abortion. D and C (dilation and curettage) is a routine gynaecological procedure carried out under general anaesthetic. The cervix is dilated so that a spoon-shaped instrument can be inserted to scrape away the uterus lining, which soon grows back during the menstrual cycle. It may also be used for the following: blighted ovum (p.222); hydatiform mole (p.230); miscarriage (p.235); and retained placenta (p.239).

Continuing pregnancy: if you have not miscarried before leaving the clinic it is possible that the treatment has been ineffective – in which case again a D and C may be necessary.

Prostaglandin Induction

This method, used for late abortions, causes labour pains and the delivery of the fetus, and is still used in many hospitals. It can be very upsetting for anyone having to go through it, and particularly so if the reason you are having a late termination is that your baby has been discovered to have abnormalities. However, it is not the only option, whatever you may be told to the contrary. At Marie Stopes and other forward-thinking clinics a D and E (see p.130) is available up to 24 weeks. It means that you can have the operation done under general anaesthetic, with none of the labour pains associated with induction.

Counselling is available to couples who go through the trauma of terminating a pregnancy for abnormality. For details contact Support around Termination for Abnormality (see Address Book on p.252).

JUDITH'S STORY

'I'm very preoccupied with the thought that my baby has Down's syndrome,' I said to my doctor at my first and last antenatal consultation with him. He said it was highly unlikely, despite my worries about my age (37), but I wanted to know for sure – and the sooner the better. So I asked for a CVS test which can detect Down's syndrome much earlier than amniocentesis. If my fears were realized, a decision to terminate the pregnancy would be so hard. I'd spent most of my working life with people with learning difficulties and their families, and over the years I'd known many children and adults with Down's syndrome.

All arrangements from then on were made over the phone. I did not meet the registrar who terminated my pregnancy until the operation.

The CVS had been performed by another consultant in a hospital thirty miles away. Perhaps because it was a relatively new test – and who knows, perhaps I was the first to have a positive result – there were no arrangements for letting me know the result. I was left to ring around for a couple of days trying to find someone who could give me the information, until I eventually contacted a sister in the second hospital who told me that my baby was a boy with Down's syndrome. I later discovered that the results came only twenty-four hours after the CVS, but it was nine days before I was told.

I was thirteen weeks pregnant, and it seemed that if I was to have a surgical termination under general anaesthetic there was no time to lose. I had done my own thinking about the options before electing to have a CVS, so I went to hospital the day after receiving the results. I still wished I'd been given some opportunity to talk about my decision to my doctor or the registrar or the nurses. I badly needed to explain my experience of people with Down's syndrome – the positive qualities as well as the overwhelming difficulties they face in their lives. I didn't want approval of what I was doing, any more than condemnation – there is no black or white in this situation.

Once in hospital, I was left alone for most of the day. I persuaded the registrar to let me go home that evening and had one follow-up appointment with the consultant seven weeks later, meeting him for the first time. But I needed professional support. Perhaps it was not recognized that the feelings involved in an early termination of a wanted pregnancy are very different from those in an unwanted pregnancy.

The grief over the loss of a baby which has not gone full term is rarely understood by those who haven't experienced it. Perhaps this is even more the case when the baby is lost as early as thirteen weeks. The sense that the baby was unacknowledged by anyone except his parents was hellishly lonely. I had absolutely nothing to show he ever existed. The unfulfilled dreams and loss of hope for the future were hard to bear. It took another three years before I could begin to take tentative risks with contraception which resulted in my fourth pregnancy.

This time, in spite of growing anxiety, I tried to be more optimistic about a happy outcome. I chose not to have CVS because of the risks to the baby, but when I got the grim results from the triple test I had an amnio, from which I learned that my longed-for daughter also had Down's syndrome. This time I had the opportunity to discuss my situation with the consultant and a paediatrician. I recognized that, for the baby's sake, I was going to have to make the same decision all over again. This time I involved my two sons, telling them about their sister and the problems she would face in her life if she survived the birth. They responded sensitively and maturely, with sorrow and understanding. We named our baby Ceri, and after the cremation the four of us had a funeral ceremony in the garden.

The attitudes of hospital staff, this time, helped me a great deal. They demonstrated great sympathy and acceptance. Their openness and honesty helped me to feel respected and valued, in contrast to my previous experience. I was glad to be able to see and hold my daughter and for my husband to take many photos. We had as much time as we wanted on our own with her to make our farewell. Being together throughout made me feel less lonely, and we felt very close in our suffering.

The greatest gift has been from Ceri herself. It seems to me there is extraordinary significance in the fact that what should have been her birthday in November was exactly the same date as her brother's three years earlier. At her birth and death I felt calm and peaceful, and at last released from the sense of horror and guilt of the last three years. Of course, the feelings of deep grief which have followed are only too familiar – but I have more faith that this time I will come through it, eventually.

YOUR QUESTIONS ANSWERED

Q: ***How safe is the ultrasound scan?***

A: The scan's been used routinely for over a quarter of a century and while it is unlikely that major problems are caused by scanning, we do not know that it's 100 per cent safe.

Q: ***Will I be told the sex of my baby during a scan?***

A: The sex is identifiable at 18–20 weeks, but the baby's position may make it difficult or impossible for the operator to see the genitals. And some hospitals will not, as a matter of policy, tell the mother the gender of her child.

Q: ***I've heard of ultrasound scans through the vagina. Is this dangerous?***

A: Vaginal ultrasound may be recommended in early pregnancy when it can give more information than an abdominal scan, especially if a suspected miscarriage or ectopic pregnancy needs to be diagnosed. The probe is put just inside the opening of the vagina and does not touch the cervix, so there's no risk of bleeding or miscarriage.

Q: ***Why do I need to drink so much water before a scan?***

A: Your bladder lies in front of your uterus. When the bladder's full, the uterus rises out of the pelvis and so can be seen more easily on an abdominal scan.

Part 2

BIRTH AND AFTERWARDS

6 *Preparing for Childbirth*

The birth of your baby should be a happy experience that you will cherish forever – and this should be the case whether you plan to have your baby at home, surrounded by personal comforts, or in hospital, where you have easy access to high-tech help. Take time to consider the options available to you. Doctors and midwives no longer make decisions without your having a say – and doing things your own way should not be a struggle.

YOUR OPTIONS

Some doctors don't offer their patients the choice of having a baby at home. In this case you may have to sign up with another practice for the duration of your pregnancy. You may even find yourself struck off for insisting on a home birth. So find out from your own doctor's practice, as early as possible, what your options are.

In labour, too, there are alternatives. You don't have to have conventional pain relief though you may need it. Some women enlist the help of a reflexologist to help them through labour. Like acupuncturists reflexologists believe in an energy force which flows through the body, bringing health to every part. They see the feet as a barometer of an individual's general wellbeing. Massaging the point on the foot which relates to a problem area encourages energy to flow to the affected area and assist its recovery. If you enjoy being touched and are already accustomed to having reflexology treatment, this could be an attractive pain relief option for you. If you prefer the alternative approach, try to plan well ahead so you stand the best chance of having the kind of labour and delivery you want. But keep your options open because you don't know how your labour will go, or what you may need, until it happens.

TRACY'S STORY

I'd been seeing my reflexologist about my high blood pressure since early in the pregnancy. Reflexology is safe to use alongside traditional medicine – although some therapists won't treat people with acute infection or fever, or those who've had thrombosis, a heart condition, or epilepsy. Some also say that women with a 'risky' pregnancy should avoid reflexology. But Beryl is experienced, and has treated a lot of pregnant women and she didn't see my high blood pressure as a problem – in fact, she kept it under control and I didn't need any extra treatment. All along, she explained that she'd have to avoid the part of my foot relating to the reproductive area, as that could bring on a miscarriage. But I trusted her completely and she soon had my blood pressure at a safe level.

I had a wonderful pregnancy, but Chloe was nearly two weeks late and I was going to be induced. Beryl knew I was worried and said it would speed things up if she worked on the part of my foot she'd so far been avoiding.

I gave her the go-ahead, and the next morning I had a show and knew Chloe was finally on her way. By the time I got to the hospital I was already 6 cm dilated – and in very little pain. When the contractions got worse, a midwife asked if I wanted anything. 'Just my reflexologist!' I said.

Beryl massaged my feet and legs and I had no other pain relief. The midwives couldn't get over it.

COPING WITH FEAR OF CHILDBIRTH

Many women fear the pain, unpredictability and emotional upheaval of childbirth. This fear may also be compounded by a phobia about hospitals (see pp.140–41).

Labour

If your overwhelming fear is of the pain of labour, there's little point in dreading it but a lot to be said for preparing yourself for it. Labour is painful, and you must come to terms with that. If you're prepared, you may find that, in the event, it wasn't as bad as you'd anticipated. If, on the other hand, you try to switch off from the thought of pain and concentrate on making this a happy experience, you may be unlucky and end up with a long and excruciating back labour (see p.167) which you are unable to deal with.

In general, both women who fear pain the most and those who expect it least have a harder time during labour and delivery than those who are realistic and ready for any eventuality. So it's important to prepare your-

If you have previously enjoyed relaxing in the bath to overcome period pain or painful cystitis, you may benefit from being in water for part of your labour.

self, emotionally and physically, in order to reduce your anxiety and make your labour more tolerable.

Make sure you understand what's happening – a childbirth class will give you the education you need. In the past women suffered more in labour because they didn't understand what was happening to their bodies.

Keep fit. Prepare your body for childbirth with the exercises your class teaches you, or those on pp.82–86.

Put pain in perspective. If you're worried, think to yourself, 'yes, childbirth is going to be a painful experience – but it will end, and when it does I'll have my baby.' If you're concerned about timing, the average labour with a first baby is 12–24+ hours, and only a few of those hours will be uncomfortable. Few labours are allowed to progress beyond 24 hours (at which point the doctor's likely to advise a caesarean), and many last just a few hours from start to finish.

Line up a birth partner. Having your partner, best friend or mum with you is a must, however independent you like to think you are!

Don't be too rigid about not accepting pain relief. You won't gain any points for being a martyr, and asking for medication is no sign of failure.

Don't worry about making a fool of yourself – midwives have seen it all, and what seems embarrassing now (involuntarily emptying your bladder or bowel, or squealing like a pig) will not be a problem for you, or anyone else, when you're giving birth. Labour and delivery are the best excuse there ever was to be yourself and let it all hang out!

If you're concerned about losing control, working harder at your exercises, and even making a birth plan (see p.161), can help things go roughly the way you want. But do try to be open-minded to avoid disappointment and remember, yelling and screaming are forms of pain relief for some women.

Hospital Phobia

First, realize that you are not alone. A phobia of hospitals, medical procedures, blood or injury is extremely common. Many people go years without seeing a dentist or doctor for this reason. A fear of needles and injections is also very common, and many sufferers refuse major surgery and lifesaving antibiotics rather than have an injection. And a phobia of blood can be so intense that it puts women off becoming pregnant.

Accept the need to help yourself or to be helped. It may seem easy to avoid the things which frighten you, but consider the impact this is having on your life. Even if you don't need to go into hospital for this baby, there may be some time in the future when you do – and then you'll have to cope, somehow.

Try to familiarize yourself with the object of your fear. If it's the sight of a needle which sends shivers down your spine, start by looking at pictures of needles and build up to seeing and even touching the real thing (with the help of a sympathetic professional).

If you start to panic when you enter a hospital, ask the staff to show you around so the environment feels less hostile. Many maternity hospitals arrange days when their antenatal patients can tour the wards. Take the opportunity if it's offered, so you know what to expect.

People who faint at the sight of blood have been helped by looking at scenes of blood and injury while lying down, so that they cannot faint. You may start by watching blood taken from someone else, then move on to having blood taken from yourself while you're lying down. Taking a small sample of this blood home with you is like having a trophy, and a reminder of how well you're doing.

Eventually you may be able to do the unimaginable and watch films about blood transfusions and open heart surgery to the point where they bore you. And, by this time, going to the haemotology unit to have blood taken will no longer be an ordeal. Some former phobics have even gone on to enrol in first aid classes.

Talk through any underlying causes of your phobia. A hospital phobia may have been triggered by a visit to a sick relative when you were a child, or even a white-coated doctor shouting at you when you were small. It may be difficult to recall this incident without the help of a counsellor, but, once you have, you'll be able to put it in perspective and realize it's no longer a threat to you.

Give yourself lots of praise. Keep a diary of the steps you've taken to overcome your phobia and build up your self-esteem. If you've sat through an episode of *Casualty* or *ER* without hiding behind a cushion, give yourself a gold star!

Try not to think about your fear too much before you actually face it. Dwelling on what's to come can get your anxiety out of control. Imagine you're putting the phobia in a box and shutting the lid on it, till the day you have to go into hospital.

Learn to cope with panic. Deep breathing exercises are a useful tool when you feel your heart begin to race. Breathe gently from the diaphragm to stop the adrenalin reaching a peak.

Concentrate on making your experience a happy one. A good hospital should make you feel as comfortable as you would be in your own home, and taking in things like taped music will also help considerably.

A SIMPLE BREATHING EXERCISE

Breathe slowly in through one nostril (close the other one by pressing your finger against it), and as you do so feel your diaphragm gently rise to your chest. Then breathe out, very slowly, through the other nostril, imagining as you do so that you're directing your breath through every part of your body. Continue until you feel calmer and more relaxed.

CHOOSING A CHILDBIRTH CLASS

Your doctor or hospital should be able to give you details of local childbirth classes, and most maternity hospitals offer parentcraft classes. Alternatively you could contact the National Childbirth Trust or Active Birth Centre (See Address Book) who run classes all over Britain.

If you are planning to squat in labour, practise in advance – try to keep your heels on the floor and balance your weight evenly between the balls of your feet and your heels.

Active Birth concentrates on yoga and breathing. For those who enjoy yoga it can provide the key to a relaxed and enjoyable pregnancy, and many of the gentle positions taught by Active Birth teachers are similar to birthing positions. If you go to one of these classes your body will slowly absorb this knowledge so that you will move freely and instinctively in labour and be able to use squatting positions when giving birth.

You'll also learn to focus on the rhythm of your breathing, which will make you more comfortable in pregnancy and better able to cope with the intensity of labour.

The best time to start this class is in the third month of pregnancy, and no previous experience of yoga is necessary.

The National Childbirth Trust provides breastfeeding and postnatal support as well as antenatal courses which are designed to cover all aspects of birth preparation. Classes usually start when you're between 28 and 32 weeks pregnant.

Enrolling in an antenatal exercise class will give you the opportunity to meet other pregnant women in your area.

Parentcraft classes are usually run by midwives and health visitors at the hospital where you plan to deliver. They will be tailored to the hospital's particular routines and can be a useful introduction to your hospital, even if you attend another class too.

Childbirth Education Philosophies

There are three main schools of thought about childbirth education, and your teacher may combine elements of all three.

Deep Breathing (Bradley)

The emphasis is on good diet and exercise to prepare the muscles for birth and the breasts for feeding. You'll learn to imitate your sleeping position and breathing and to use relaxation to make the first stage of labour more comfortable. Instead of trying to keep your mind off the pain, the Bradley approach uses deep abdominal breathing to help you concentrate hard on working with your body.

SHOPPING LIST OF BABY BASICS

During pregnancy mums-to-be can be inundated with catalogues detailing all the equipment their baby is claimed to need. In fact, in the first few weeks you need very little. Starting with just the basics will prevent you wasting money and give you a chance to work out over the early months what else you really do want to buy. And remember, you don't have to brave the high street shopping crowds – most items can be obtained by mail order. For addresses, look in any pregnancy magazine.

At the very least, you will want most of the following:

- 4 vests: choose the front-tie style if you're worried about getting the vest over the baby's head.
- 4 stretch suits for day and night wear or nighties, which make changing easier.
- Cardigans and outerwear (e.g. fleecy bodysuit), depending on the weather and the time of year.

- 1 packet first-size nappies.
- Cotton wool (in the first few weeks, you can wash your baby's bottom with water and cotton wool).
- A small cradle, carrycot or moses basket. When buying, think about practicalities. If you want to move your baby around the house with you, it will be easier to transfer a moses basket (with or without a stand) or carrycot.
- Buggy: buy the sort that reclines and can therefore be used right from birth.
- 2 sets of cotton sheets for the cot.
- Cotton cellular blankets.
- Wipeable baby changing mat, which you can use on the floor, bed or baby changing unit.
- Baby bath.
- Sterilizer, if you plan to use bottles or soothers.
- Baby car seat – essential for the baby's journey home from hospital.

Psychophysical (Grantly Dick-Read)

This approach dates back to the 1940s and 1950s. It uses relaxation techniques to break the fear-tension-pain cycle of labour and delivery.

Psychoprophylactic (Lamaze)

This is a similar idea to the psychophysical one above, using relaxation techniques to fight pain. But Dr Lamaze also introduced an element of conditioning, so that you respond to contractions in a way that will help rather than hinder your labour.

WHERE'S THE BEST PLACE TO HAVE YOUR BABY?

Most doctors still see pregnancy as a medical condition, and childbirth as a procedure which should take place in the safety of a hospital. But more and more mums-to-be are turning to home birth. Where would you rather be?

Having Your Baby in Hospital

Most women still choose to have their babies in hospital, although there is a growing trend of giving birth at home. The advantage of being in hospital is that emergency care is on site in case you need it, and it's possible to be in and out with only a short stop-over, so that most of your labour and postnatal recovery takes place at home.

HOSPITAL BIRTH

For:
- Complications can't always be predicted. If something goes wrong with you or the baby, help is immediately at hand.
- If you need the help of forceps, ventouse (vacuum) or an episiotomy, this must be done in hospital.
- The labour may be more painful than you anticipate. At home you can be given gas and air, but drugs and epidurals are only available in hospital.
- Many maternity hospitals now have single rooms with en suite bathrooms and TVs.
- Your partner can usually stay with you.

Against:
- You're one of many patients.
- Other women may be giving birth on the same corridor and you could hear them.
- You don't start your baby's life in the comfort of your own home.
- You'll need to make babysitting arrangements for your other children.
- You might get an infection.
- It is slightly *less* safe, statistically.
- You are more likely to need an epidural.
- You are less likely to have a midwife looking after only you.

KATRINA'S STORY

I'd never been under any illusions about having my baby at home. I'm an acquiescent patient and I was happy to go along with whatever my doctor suggested. With hindsight this was just as well, because when I was six months pregnant I suddenly developed complications.

I'd gone to my doctor for my routine antenatal check-up. All previous checks had been entirely problem-free. But this time I saw a different doctor, who felt my tummy and immediately reached for the phone. While he was waiting for the hospital to answer, he explained that the 'height of fundus' measurements were indicating that my baby was 'small for dates'.

He crossed his fingers and wished me good luck as I left for the hospital. I felt that, from that day on, all the monitoring my baby and I went through was vital – and I felt well looked after rather than bullied by the hospital.

The pregnancy progressed with increasingly more regular visits to my consultant. Finally, when I was 38 weeks pregnant, she decided to admit me. The baby's heartbeat had been 'funny' when she was listening to it. It had swiftly returned to normal, but she didn't want to take any chances – and that pleased me.

I sat in bed on the antenatal ward for four days over the bank holiday weekend, until, just after midnight on the Tuesday morning, the nurse woke me up for my now three-hourly check on the fetal heart monitor.

When she came to unplug me, half an hour later, I explained that the read-out might be a bit odd-looking because I'd been having fairly strong contractions. It still didn't occur to me that I was actually in labour But when a doctor appeared with a torch to examine me, I was amazed to learn that my cervix was already 4 cm dilated.

A midwife walked me down to the delivery suite, and I could tell immediately that walking would help ease the pains, which were now like very heavy period cramps. But when I asked if I could be mobile she said, 'No way!' I knew that, for my baby's sake, I had to comply. She rigged me up to a fetal heart monitor and prepared me for a drip, in case I needed one. I had a low platelet count in my blood, so supplies had to be ordered in case I lost a lot of blood. Then she gave me a sleeping tablet and told me she'd call my husband at 4 a.m.

I woke on the dot of four, pressed my alarm button and asked for Paul to be fetched. By the time he arrived I'd been given Pethidine and was completely out of it. I hadn't a clue what was going on until around 6 a.m., when I felt the urge to push.

Our baby girl was born twenty minutes later, extremely tiny – only 4 lb 12 oz. She was immediately rushed off to be dressed in premature baby clothes to keep her warm.

Then another problem arose – the placenta did not come away. Suddenly I had what seemed like Uncle Tom Cobley and all sticking their hands inside me to try and get it out. It was undignified and painful – but I felt I could have been in great danger if this had happened and I'd been at home. I was given a general anaesthetic for a D and C.

So much happened to me that could have been very serious if I hadn't been in hospital that I'll never regret having been such a compliant patient. As much as I admire any woman who's determined to have her baby at home, I can never help worrying about her safety in taking that decision.

Although giving birth is a natural event, there can be unexpected complications. For instance, the labour may be slow to progress, the baby may become distressed, or the umbilical cord may wrap around his neck. Finally the placenta may be delivered incomplete, or retained, in which case you may need an emergency D and C (see p.131).

Having Your Baby at Home

Providing you have a low-risk pregnancy, and there's no reason to think that anything will go wrong in labour, you may wish to have your baby at home. Most women who have a baby at home after a previous hospital delivery say they enjoyed it much more and also felt it was a better experience for the baby. The whole family can be present for the arrival; you are not tied to hospital rules and regulations; and you won't have to change room between labour and delivery. In your own home you are in charge and the midwife or doctor are your guests – and this makes a big difference to women who find it difficult to assert themselves in a hospital environment.

Many doctors worry about the growing vogue for home births, but it's possible to bypass him and use an independent group of midwives for all your antenatal care. You will then get to know your allocated midwife very well, and over nine months have the opportunity to build up your trust in her judgement. She will be able to tell you if there's any cause for concern which may mean a hospital birth is safer after all, and she will also be able to help and supervise your labour at home.

HOME BIRTH

For:
- ◆ As in a good hospital, you can do things your own way, using posture and breathing to get through problems, while still being supervised by a midwife.
- ◆ You can enjoy and celebrate the birth with your family.
- ◆ Your partner can participate fully.
- ◆ You can eat and drink when you want.
- ◆ You're more relaxed and the baby will be less traumatized.
- ◆ You don't have to have any medical intervention you don't want.

Against:
- ◆ Home birth is not appropriate for everyone. Any indication that your labour may need help – for example, if you develop high blood pressure or anaemia – will mean you may have to give birth in hospital after all.
- ◆ Transfer to hospital may become necessary if your labour needs help.
- ◆ If you need an epidural you'll have to go to hospital.
- ◆ If things don't go as you plan, this may trigger some degree of postnatal depression – but this is very rare.

THERESA'S STORY

My doctor wasn't at all impressed when I told him I wanted to have my first baby at home. He went on and on about the risks, and eventually I decided to go to an independent midwife for all my antenatal care. In fact the midwife who delivered both my babies is my sister-in-law, and having someone I knew so well made my experience an even happier one!

I knew I was a low-risk pregnancy, and didn't see why I should be treated like an ill person by doctors in white coats who didn't know me from Adam.

I also knew that most problems are indicated before labour starts, and it was reassuring to know that I really wasn't putting myself or my baby in danger by opting to stay at home.

My midwife gave me a list of things I'd need for the birth – and it read more like a painting and decorating memo. We needed a bucket, plastic bags and so on. The whole business started to sound very messy, though in the event not a drop of blood fell on to our bedroom carpet!

I went into labour with Tom at about 2 a.m. and he was born six hours later. I found the most comfortable place of all was sitting on the loo. But my midwife was worried because our loo is very small, and she thought we ought to take the door off so my husband Michael could sit with me. It was hilarious – there I was in labour on the loo, and there was Michael with his Black and Decker drill pulling the door off its hinges. In fact, by the time he got it off Tom's crown was beginning to show and I was ready to give birth!

I went back into the bedroom, and he came almost straightaway while I was in a standing position. It makes sense to stand up because the force of gravity helps the baby on its way – in hospital I would probably have been stuck on my back, pushing uphill.

VAGINAL BIRTH AFTER CAESAREAN

Not so long ago any woman having a caesarean for her first baby would expect caesareans for all her subsequent babies – up to a total maximum of three. It was naturally disappointing for any woman planning a big family to end up on the operating table for her first child. But now the theory has been turned upside down and the new norm is 'vaginal birth after caesarean' (vbac) as far as possible.

Although a lot of repeat caesareans are performed at the request of the mother, who naturally wishes to avoid any unnecessary pain, a vaginal delivery is actually safer (but the risks attendant on any birth are minute these days). The risk of dying in a vaginal delivery is 1 in 10,000; that of dying during a surgical delivery is 4 in 10,000.

JULIETTE'S STORY

I'm a total wimp about doctors and hospitals. The minute I'm in that clinical environment I give up emotionally and physically and let the professionals take over.

It must make me a good patient. But it wasn't what I wanted for the births of my two children, three-year-old Cyan, and Cal, three months. And I knew I stood a better chance of being in control if I stayed at home.

Everything went quite well with Cyan until the last half-hour, when she got stuck and we all had to be transferred to hospital so she could be pulled out with forceps. I was really disappointed that things hadn't gone to plan, and I became quite depressed and angry afterwards. But my midwives were convinced I'd succeed next time round. They were right, and giving birth to Cal was one of the most wonderful experiences of my life.

I woke up in labour at around 3 a.m., and within minutes my lovely midwife Margaret arrived to help out. My husband Alan had the water bath we'd hired all set up in the sitting room, and my mum whizzed over to help out with Cyan.

Her birthday party was planned for the following afternoon, so there were plenty of presents to distract her when she got worried about the strange animal noises I was making.

I found that being in the water bath halved the pain, and I didn't need any other form of pain relief. Margaret is trained in complementary medicine so she knew all the best positions for me to get into, and she encouraged me to open my eyes wide and roar like a lion as I pushed. Within three hours of going into labour, little Cal was safely out in my arms. It had taken just three pushes to get him out – and even though he weighed 10 lb 5 oz I didn't tear at all.

Mum brought Cyan in to see Cal minutes after he was born, and she looked completely dumbstruck as she reached out and held his little hand. Margaret said that children who are in the house when a sibling is born will bond more easily with the new baby, and we've certainly had no problems.

Being at home, Alan and I felt in control of everything that happened. We could eat and drink when we wanted to, and we were hosts to our midwife, rather than feeling like guests of a hospital. We were aware of the complications that can arise – but felt that, with the hospital just five minutes down the road, we'd be OK come what may.

Another good reason for having a vaginal delivery, if you can, is that you will save yourself the days of abdominal pain which follow a caesarean, and weeks of slow recovery.

The majority of women who've had previous caesareans can now expect to deliver vaginally and go through a normal labour. Whether or

Even if you decide on a hospital birth, the first stage of labour may start at home, when your partner can help you through painful contractions.

not this will apply to you depends on the type of uterine incision you had with your caesarean and the reason your baby was delivered surgically.

If it was a low-transverse incision (across the lower part of the uterus), a vaginal delivery should be OK. This is the type of incision 95 per cent of women have today, and their chances of a successful vbac are very good. But if you had the old-fashioned vertical incision in the uterus, which is still sometimes necessary, you will be advised not to attempt a vaginal delivery because of the risk of rupturing your uterus.

If the reason for your previous caesarean was an uncorrectable problem (your pelvis is too small or badly contracted), vaginal delivery is not going to be an option. But if you had surgery because of a problem that is unlikely to be repeated, a vaginal delivery should be an option this time round.

Some doctors are still quite rigid in their views about vbac – so, if you feel strongly about wanting a vaginal delivery, broach the subject early. Remember:

◆ The risk in vbac is that the previous uterine incision will rupture under the stress of labour. This is unlikely if you've had a low-transverse incision. But take your childbirth classes seriously and use what you learn to keep the stress on your body to a minimum.
◆ Don't delay contacting your midwife when labour begins.
◆ Tell your doctor or midwife immediately if you notice any unusual abdominal pain or tenderness between contractions.
◆ Make sure you're delivering in a hospital fully equipped for an emergency caesarean – a home birth is unlikely to be an option for you, although it may not be impossible – talk to your doctor.

PREPARING YOUR BODY THE NATURAL WAY

You've looked after your diet, learned to relax, and done all the exercises outlined in Chapter 4. What more can you do to prepare your body for childbirth?

Drinking raspberry leaf tea is recommended to tone the uterus for labour and birth. One teaspoon of tea infused in a cup of boiling water, up to three times a day, is the suggested dosage. Raspberry leaf tea is available by mail order from Neal's Yard (see Address Book).

Massaging the perineum (the area between the pubic bone and the coccyx, which takes in the urethra, vagina and anus) is a good way to increase suppleness in preparation for labour and birth. Massage the area daily with wheatgerm or almond oil, or calendula.

The homeopathic remedy Caulophyllum (blue cohosh) taken at 37 weeks may strengthen contractions and soften the cervix for an easier delivery.

If your baby's overdue and you want to help her on her way, you can try to bring labour on by making love – semen contains small amounts of prostaglandins which help to soften the cervix in preparation for childbirth. Having your nipples stimulated may release the hormone prolactin, which also softens the cervix.

PAIN RELIEF: WHAT'S AVAILABLE?

For some women labour is short and straightforward, and the level of pain is quite manageable. For others it's a long and difficult process, and the pain is beyond a level they can cope with. If you approach labour feeling confident and well informed, with an open mind about the kind of pain relief you may need, you stand a much better chance of a happy experience.

The uterus uses a lot of energy, which it makes from glucose and oxygen in the bloodstream. Strong contractions can cut down the blood supply and energy to the uterus muscle. As a result waste products such as lactic acid are not cleared and can build up, causing contractions to feel more painful.

Keeping fit during your pregnancy will give you more flexibility and stamina in labour. Remaining upright and mobile during contractions will also help.

TIPS TO HELP YOU COPE

What makes pain worse	Solution
◆ Fatigue	Take plenty of rest during your ninth month
◆ Expecting pain	Try to distract yourself
◆ Being alone	Make sure you have a birth partner lined up
◆ Being hungry or thirsty	Have light snacks during early labour, and sip water throughout
◆ Stress or anxiety	Remember your relaxation and breathing exercises
◆ Fear	Read up about childbirth before the event, so you know what to expect
◆ Feeling sorry for yourself	Concentrate on the reward at the end
◆ Lack of control	Educating yourself about childbirth will give you more confidence to cope with the event

As labour builds up, your body produces natural pain relievers called endorphins, which are also produced during exercise. These act on the brain like an anaesthetic, reducing the sensation and perception of pain. However, endorphins are rarely enough to see you through labour without additional pain relief, be it self-help, or a complementary or orthodox remedy.

Natural Pain Relief

Breathing: mothers-to-be have been taught breathing exercises at antenatal classes for years, and they are one of the most basic but effective ways of dealing with pain. During your preparation for childbirth, practise breathing out slowly and deeply with your partner. In labour, deep, slow breathing will help you cope with contractions. If your partner knows the routine, he can help you slow down if you start to panic-breathe (which can cause hyperventilation – abnormally rapid, shallow breathing – and dizziness).

Distraction: keeping yourself busy, as far as possible, will take your mind off the early stage of labour. When labour is well established, singing or listening to your favourite music can help. Visualizing yourself in a special place can also work wonders. Get to know in advance what works best for you.

Hot and cold compresses: a cold compress (a wrung out towel or an ice pack) can help pain in the lower back. Warm towels or flannels on your perineum, or a hot water bottle on your lower back, are comforting and relaxing.

Massage: having your scalp, shoulders, arms and lower back massaged by your partner is very comforting in labour. Practise in advance, so your partner knows what you like him to do. If you're new to massage, the basic rules are to keep warm, and use oil or talcum powder to enable the massager's hands to move smoothly. Your partner should use a firm, steady pressure and emphasize each downward stroke.

Relaxation: the kind of relaxation exercises learned during pregnancy will, if practised in labour, enable oxygen to flow to your muscles, cutting down on muscle tension and making your contractions less painful.

Water: sitting on a stool or chair under the shower can feel wonderfully relaxing, especially if you direct the jet towards the part of you that's hurting most. Many hospitals have large baths which you can soak in once your cervix is dilated beyond 4–5 cm, and a birthing pool, if you have access to one, is fantastic for pain relief – even if you don't plan to give birth in it.

Complementary Therapies

Aromatherapy, homeopathy, acupuncture, hypnosis and reflexology can all help in labour. If you want complementary medicine for childbirth explore all your options early on, and always seek the advice of an experienced practitioner.

Acupuncture triggers the release of endorphins, the body's natural painkillers. The downside is that it may immobilize you. If you are contemplating this option you'll need to consult a qualified practitioner, preferably well in advance of your anticipated delivery date.

Aromatherapy is great as long as you're not one of those women who hate being touched once contractions start. The combination of essential oils and massage is an excellent way to ease back pain and relax you generally, but you will need a willing partner or midwife to massage you. The Active Birth Centre (see Address Book) makes a labour oil containing geranium, marjoram, clary sage and lavender.

Bach Flower Remedies may also relax you and lift your mood. They may be useful combined with other forms of pain relief.

Homeopathy stimulates the body to heal itself and may help relax you.

Hypnotherapy: researchers have shown that hypnotherapy can be more effective in relieving pain than some of the strongest drugs, including Pethidine. It involves visualization, which allows you mentally to turn down the intensity of the pain, like turning down the heat of a

KATIE'S STORY

As soon as I was pregnant with my first baby, Joshua, all my friends started telling me their birth horror stories. How much pain they'd been in, how they'd torn, the number of stitches they'd had . . . I got all the gory details.

I started to dread my own labour and delivery. When I happened to mention this to a friend who's a practising hypnotist, he said, 'You don't have to go through all that – have you considered hypnosis?'

I was willing to try anything and spent four sessions with John, during which he 'programmed' me to cope well with the pain of childbirth, and recovery after it.

As my expected delivery date drew near I began to feel more relaxed, and when I went into labour I felt totally in control. I used gas and air pain relief, but more for something to do with myself – and at no time did I feel as if I couldn't cope.

Out of all my friends who delivered around the same time, I had by far the best experience – with no tearing or stitching, and a great recovery.

It is a good idea to learn a bit about the various forms of pain relief before going into hospital. If you feel strongly that you want one form and not another, or that you would like to try gas and air before accepting something stronger, you may like to include this in a birth plan (see p.161).

cooker. Some women can even switch off the pain completely. A good hypnotherapist should be able to write you an individual programme during pregnancy which will be automatically triggered once labour starts. However, not everybody is good at self-hypnosis and you may find it difficult to concentrate.

Orthodox Pain Relief

Entonox (gas and oxygen) is a 50/50 mixture of nitrous oxide (laughing gas) and oxygen which you inhale through a mask or a spout you can bite on. It works by altering your perception of the pain rather than by anaesthetizing the actual pain. It may make you feel woozy, but has no adverse effect on the baby.

Hospitals supply Entonox on tap, but portable cylinders are used for home deliveries. It tends to be more popular with mothers who've already had one baby than with first-time mums.

The main advantage is that you're in control and can use it as and when you want to. However, it may make your mouth very dry, so take plenty of sips of water.

To make best use of Entonox while you are in labour, inhale at the beginning of a contraction.

Epidural anaesthesia is an injection of anaesthetizing drug between two of the spinal vertebrae. It removes pain from the lower half of your body but can sometimes numb the entire lower abdomen, and you may need a catheter to drain your bladder. You may not be able to control your pushing, and there is a higher likelihood of having to have the baby delivered by forceps or vacuum extractor. As with Pethidine, the baby may be sleepy and difficult to feed. Some babies also cry a lot for several weeks after a birth involving an epidural.

Ask your midwife about the kind of epidural drug being administered. Newer ones have the advantage of leaving you free to move your body during the pushing stage. See Brenda's Story opposite.

An epidural is always given by a qualified anaesthetist. You will be asked to curl up on your side or sit leaning forward, and must keep very still. You are given a local anaesthetic first, then a hollow needle is used to put a fine tube (catheter) in your lower back. A test dose is given before the full amount. You may be turned from side to side to even up the effect as your legs start to feel numb. The epidural takes twenty to thirty minutes to set up, but pain relief can be instantaneous for some women. Relief lasts for two to four hours, but the dose can be topped up if necessary. A good epidural can be tailed off for the second stage of labour so that you can push. If you have had an epidural in the past, you're likely to notice the difference with the newer ones now available. Many women are delighted with the type of relief they offer.

About 90 per cent of women have total pain relief from an epidural, but sometimes it only works on one side of the body, or leaves a patch which is not numb.

The advantages are that you can stay alert, and, if you need a caesarean, this can also be performed with the epidural so you can stay awake and greet your baby. There are also few side-effects to the baby.

However, an epidural is a surgical procedure and you will be in bed, attached to a drip and contraction monitor. There's also a slight risk of severe headache and long-term backache.

Other local and regional anaesthetics include:

Spinal anaesthesia, which takes about five minutes to work and numbs you from the waist to the knees. It gives effective pain relief, but can be dangerous because your blood pressure drops so that the oxygen supply to the baby is reduced.

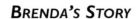

BRENDA'S STORY

My first baby, Eoin was delivered by emergency caesarean, so I had no experience of labour or childbirth when I was expecting my second, Ryan. I'd heard millions of horror stories about the pain, and frankly I was dreading it. A lot of my friends had had epidurals to help them through the labour. But my sister-in-law told me she'd been unable to move from the waist down with her epidural, and that sounded horrendous too.

I decided I'd let the labour take its natural course as long as I could, but I wouldn't rule out having an epidural. When I got to hospital the anaesthetist explained that she would use a new style of drug, Naropin, if I had an epidural, and that it would allow me to move as much as I liked – so I said yes. All I felt was a scratch on my back, and suddenly the pain was gone. I was still able to move my body, and I knew I'd be able to push too – the great advantage of this drug is that it lessens the likelihood of having a forceps birth. In the event, I had to have a last-minute caesarean. But that was done using the epidural too – and although I was awake it was totally painless. My husband Sean and I were able to hold Ryan straightaway – and my recovery was much quicker than when I had Eoin, under general anaesthetic.

Pudendal block, an injection numbing the nerves in the perineum after full dilation, and usually given before an episiotomy or a forceps or vacuum extraction.

Caudal anaesthesia, which is similar to an epidural but needs a stronger dose of anaesthetic, and tends to be used for a very difficult second stage of labour.

Again, it's a good idea to find out in advance of going into labour whether these options are likely to be open to you, and whether your doctor or midwife recommends them.

Meptid is a similar drug to Pethidine, with the same kinds of side-effects (see below).

Pethidine is a synthetic drug derived from morphine. It is usually administered by injection and the effects last for up to four hours. Like Entonox, it works by altering your perception of the pain rather than taking away the pain itself. If possible it should not be given within one to four hours of delivery, but this is difficult to assess. It does help you relax during your labour and you will be less aware of the timing and anxiety surrounding the birth, but the drug crosses the placenta and may make the baby very sleepy after the birth. It can also suppress the baby's sucking instinct and interfere with early breastfeeding.

The main advantages are that it can help relax you if you've been very anxious or tense, and allows you to rest between contractions. However, you don't know how your body will react to the drug, and once it's been administered you're stuck with the effects for two to three hours whether you like it or not. Depending on the dose, you may have to stay in bed if you've taken Pethidine, which may interfere with your plans for an active birth.

Transcutaneous electrical nerve stimulation (TENS) relieves pain via four electrode pads on your back which discharge an electrical current. The idea is that these currents block the pain you would otherwise be experiencing. The method takes some getting used to, and should be practised from early pregnancy if you're planning to use it. It has no known ill-effects on the baby, but the main drawback is that, for some women, the method is totally ineffectual.

WHAT TO TAKE TO HOSPITAL WITH YOU

Suggestions for Labour

- a baggy T-shirt or short nightie.
- a face flannel.
- two natural sponges which you can dip in cold water and suck on.
- a spray bottle of water.
- vaseline or lip salve for dry lips – your lips will become very dry from panting and breathing in labour.
- oil for massage.
- snacks for your partner.
- fruit drinks with bendy straws.
- a distraction – e.g. a beautiful picture to look at.
- something to keep you busy in the early stages or if everything comes to a standstill – e.g. crosswords, jigsaw puzzles, magazines.
- candles, if allowed, for softer lighting.
- music can be soothing in labour – ask if there is a CD/tape machine available for use.
- small change for the telephone (or ask if you can take your own mobile if you have one).
- camera and fast-speed film.

It is best to be prepared for labour from 37 weeks onwards. Although your EDD is at 40 weeks, you are 'at term' from 37 to 42 weeks. Having your bag ready packed will mean you don't have to worry about pulling things together at the last minute.

Suggestions for After the Birth

- maternity pads – the old-fashioned, cotton style is best. Avoid plastic as this will make your perineum hot and sweaty and increase the likelihood of infection.
- paper pants.
- witch-hazel – you can use it to soak your pads to make a soothing compress for stitches.
- a button-through nightie or pyjamas for easy breastfeeding.
- a smarter nightie for photo-opportunities!
- dressing gown and slippers for walking around the ward.
- sports bras to make your breasts more comfortable.
- nursing bra and breast pads.
- soft loo roll.
- ear plugs and a sleep mask if you're on a noisy ward.
- wash bag with brush, comb, make-up and deodorant.
- writing paper, pens and address book.
- small radio/CD player.
- something to read.
- arnica to soothe bruising.
- lavender oil for your bath – it's calming and mildly antiseptic.

Suggestions for Your Baby

- several vests.
- several babygro suits or gowns.
- hat.
- oversuit or cardigan for travelling home in.
- a small packet of first-size nappies.
- muslin wipes – useful for mopping up dribbles and possets (see p.194).

HOW THE FATHER-TO-BE CAN HELP YOU IN LABOUR

Many midwives complain that the partner is no use at all unless he's actively involved with encouraging your breathing and reminding you of the exercises you've taught yourself to get through the pain.

But you may want your partner there purely for moral support – to you he's a help if he's by your side, holding your hand, helping you stick to the birth plan and, of course, sharing the wonderful experience of seeing your new child for the first time.

He may also have a vital role to play in helping clean and weigh the baby after the birth, and even in caring for the baby in the unlikely event that you are taken away for treatment after the birth.

DO YOU WANT A BIRTH PLAN?

A birth plan is a record of what you would like to happen during your labour and after the birth. The idea is that you and your midwife know from the outset what your intentions are. If things change during labour – for example you'd hoped to resist taking drugs or having an epidural, but find you're in more pain than you'd anticipated – your midwife will discuss your options and refer you to your birth plan. It's important, however, to remain flexible about your plan, as your condition or your baby's may change unexpectedly and your midwife or doctor may no longer find it practicable to stick to your original wishes.

When making a birth plan, think about the following questions:

- Who would you like to be with you during the labour and delivery?
- Do you want your birthing partner to stay with you in the event of a caesarean or forceps delivery?
- Do you want to bring in any special equipment such as a beanbag or a birthing chair?
- Can you choose the way your baby's heart is monitored (see pp.162–63)?
- Do you want to be treated by women only?
- Do you mind if medical students are present?
- Do you want the freedom to move around in labour?
- Is there a special position you'd like to use for delivery?
- Do you plan to manage without pain relief?
- If you need pain relief, do you have any preferences?
- Are you planning to use massage/alternative therapies for labour?
- Do you want your baby cleaned (see p.173) before he or she's handed to you?
- Do you want to feed your baby straightaway?
- Are there any special religious customs you want to be observed?

YOUR QUESTIONS ANSWERED

Q: *What's an episiotomy and why is it done?*

A: An episiotomy is a small cut made in the perineum to enlarge the vaginal entrance just before the baby is born. The procedure used to be performed routinely by many hospitals, but there's now a growing movement against it. Midwives claim that:

- small tears mend and heal better and with less discomfort than an episiotomy.
- many episiotomies extend into ragged tears anyway.

However, in special circumstances an episiotomy may still be required, often alongside forceps. For example:

◆ your baby may be in distress, in which case he will need to be delivered quickly. Forceps will protect his head so he's not subjected to pressure during the birth – and an episiotomy is almost invariably used alongside forceps.
◆ you may have high blood pressure and be advised by the midwife not to push too much.

It's better not to tear or be cut, and good midwives can help you avoid either – usually by helping your baby slide out gently and slowly, with you blowing rather than pushing. If you do have an episiotomy – or a tear – it should be sewn up as soon as possible after the baby's born, with plenty of local anaesthetic. (When you are given the episiotomy your pain relief drugs should be already up and running – if not, ask for some.) The stitching may be done by a doctor, although midwives tend to stitch the mothers they've delivered. The layers of the vagina, the muscles of the perineum and the skin all have to be closed separately – but usually with thread that dissolves rather than the kind that has to be taken out later.

Q: ***Is fetal heart monitoring really necessary in labour, or can I refuse it ?***

A: Fetal heart monitoring is routine throughout labour in many hospitals, and allows problems to be detected early so they can be resolved. See Chapter 5 for details of the tests, and talk to your doctor or midwife about whether you really need the monitoring. Depending on your own circumstances, you may wish to refuse it, or to have it intermittently instead of continuously.

There are two types of electronic fetal monitor:

The external monitor, which straps round your abdomen holding in place the tocodynamometer (the pressure gauge which records contractions) and the ultrasound transducer (which registers the baby's heartbeats).

The internal monitor, which is more accurate than the external monitor, and is inserted through the vagina and cervix and attached to the skin of the baby's head. This of course can only be done if the membranes have been ruptured.

If there's any reason to anticipate problems in your labour – such as difficulties with a previous birth or baby or induction (which makes it essential because the drugs used can produce powerful contractions

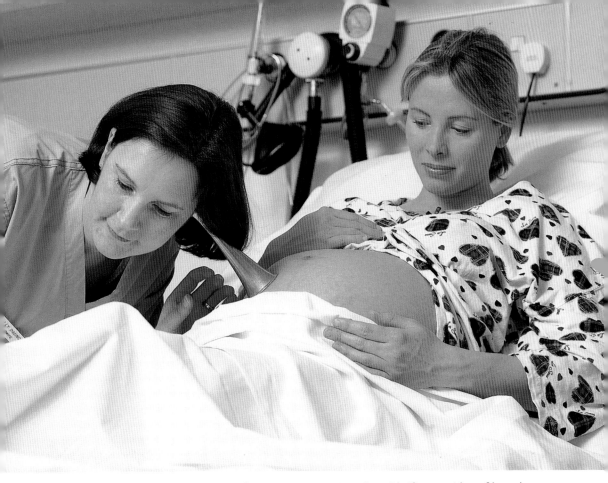

Listening to the baby's heartbeat just after a contraction gives the midwife some idea of how the baby is reacting to labour.

which may occasionally cause the baby some stress) – then your care-givers may monitor you continuously. Electronic fetal monitoring allows them to do this. It's also reassuring for you to see that the baby is safe, despite your own immense pain and stress. And, as the monitor also shows you when the next contraction is starting, you have time to pre-pare yourself.

The main drawbacks are the discomfort and awkwardness of being strapped to a machine. You can move around, but you'll be restricted by the wires. And, providing all is well, you may want to ask for intermit-tent monitoring; or monitoring with a hand-held Doppler machine, which the midwife can use to listen to the baby's heartbeat just after a contraction to see how it has affected the baby.

If you know in advance that electronic fetal monitoring is a matter of routine in your hospital, you can talk to your midwife, before the frenzy of labour, about the alternatives.

7 Labour and Delivery – What to Expect

Chapter 4 outlined the symptoms of false labour and prelabour. Sooner or later you'll be embarking on the real labour, and it's best to be as well informed as possible.

RECOGNIZING THE REAL THING

Once the contractions of prelabour are replaced by stronger, more painful and more frequent ones, the labour is probably for real if:

- the contractions intensify and aren't relieved by a change of position.
- they become progressively more frequent and painful.
- you have a pink or blood-tinged show.
- your waters break.

If you're in any doubt call your doctor or midwife, and in any case call them if you know you're in labour. They'll tell you what to do next, be it staying at home a while longer, or (for example if your waters have broken) coming into hospital. Don't be put off by fear of embarrassment in case it's not labour, and don't delay too long unless you're planning a home birth, everything is ready and your midwife lives extremely close by. Even though the start of labour may herald a long wait, it's an unpredictable process and you must be prepared for a short labour too.

THE STAGES OF LABOUR

First Stage: Early Labour (up to 4 cm Dilated)

The cervix at the bottom of the womb has softened and ripened during prelabour. Now it's starting to open. As it does so, the mucous plug inside the cervix comes away – you experience this as a pink or bloody

TARA'S STORY

My waters broke when I was standing outside an art gallery in central London. I had two friends with me and they hailed a taxi and bundled me in. I kept apologizing to the midwives at the hospital, because I didn't feel as if I was in labour. One of them suggested I have a bath for something to do, and when I got out I said, rather sheepishly, 'I seem to have a bit of a tummy ache – do you have any paracetamol?' She said, 'OK, dear, let's check you over first.' Minutes later she informed me I was 10 cm dilated and ready to push! Everyone hates me for having such a quick and easy delivery – I guess I was extremely lucky.

'show'. Sometimes labour begins with a sudden breaking of your waters as the amniotic fluid pours out, or a slow trickle.

Try to stay relaxed now – it will help the delivery. Eat high-energy foods such as pasta, bananas, toast and honey, but check with your midwife as labour progresses that she's happy for you to continue eating and drinking.

First Stage: Active Labour (4–10 cm)

As your uterus contracts to pull the cervix open over the baby's head, it also moves forward to push your baby down hard on to the cervix, where the pressure of his or her head helps it to open.

The more relaxed you are, the better your uterus will work. Active labour lasts on average between two and three and a half hours, but there are many variations. For instance, the uterus can achieve more in less time if contractions become stronger, longer and more frequent (three to four minutes apart and lasting 40–60 seconds). Each contraction should have a distinct peak – but they may not be as regular as you'd expected.

Stay as upright as you can and lean forwards, never backwards. Kneel forwards on the floor or on the bed, over a beanbag or a pile of pillows. Or lean into your partner's arms. The all-fours position is very popular and allows you to rock from side to side during a contraction. Your partner can also reach your back easily if you want it stroked or massaged.

Now's the time to focus on your breathing to stop yourself tensing against the pain. Breathe out through your mouth – sighing or groaning deeply helps a lot.

Stretch whichever part of your body you find yourself tensing. If your hands are clenched in tight fists, stretch out your fingers and sigh out through your mouth at the same time. If you can't remember to do this during a contraction, take the opportunity in the space before the next one comes along.

INDUCTION

About one in three deliveries need a kick start. As long as vaginal delivery is going to be safe, induction is usually the first choice for getting a baby out before he does so out of his own accord.

Most inductions take place because the pregnancy has continued past term and the placenta is beginning to deteriorate (see pp.239–40). In mothers over 35 an inadequate placenta is more common after 40 weeks – so induction may be recommended earlier for you than for younger women, who may be allowed to go to 42 weeks.

Other reasons for induction include:

◆ high blood pressure.
◆ a labour that hasn't progressed more than 24 hours after your waters have broken.
◆ a weak or erratic labour

Your labour may be induced in one of the following ways, depending on your informed consent:

◆ Prostaglandin pessaries may be administered to ripen the cervix enough to start labour off. They can take several hours to work and usually contractions start gently and build up over time.
◆ Artificial Rupture of Membrane (ARM) is performed by a vaginal examination. If the cervix is open enough, a small plastic instrument with a sharp hook on the end is passed through the cervix and the bag of waters is punctured. It shouldn't hurt. If it does, tell the doctor to stop at once.
◆ You may be given an injection of syntocinon (a synthetic hormone) to stimulate contractions.

Transition (Preparing to Push)

You've reached the end of the first stage of labour when you feel an irresistible urge to push down. The intensity of contractions picks up, with peaks that last almost the entire 60–90-second duration of the contraction. Some women experience multiple peaks, and you may feel as if the contractions never completely disappear.

You're likely to have a lot of pressure in your lower back or rectum and may feel as if you want to move your bowels. You may be grunting involuntarily and your body temperature may change, making you warm and sweaty or chilly and shivery. More capillaries in the cervix will rupture, increasing your bloody vaginal show, and you will probably feel exhausted.

When you reach this stage, your midwife will give you a vaginal examination to check that you're almost 10 cm dilated. As soon as you are, you'll be allowed to start pushing (also known as bearing down).

Although some women want to be alone during labour, most welcome the support of their partner, or another birth companion, with whom they can be themselves and do what comes naturally.

BACK LABOUR

So-called 'back labour' means the baby has the back of his head pressing against your sacrum. This is very painful, and the pain often doesn't let up between contractions. Epidurals are made for this type of labour, but unfortunately they can make a caesarean more likely.

Try changing your position to take the pressure off your back. Crouch, squat or get on all fours to make yourself more comfortable. If you don't feel up to moving, or have to stay in bed because you've been given Pethidine or you're attached to monitors, try to lie on your side with your back well rounded.

Press a hot water bottle or even an ice-pack against the painful area to soothe the pain.

If your midwife says you're not ready to start pushing, pant or blow instead. My antenatal teacher taught me to chant out loud, 'Hoo, hoo, ha!' Pushing against a cervix that isn't completely dilated can cause it to swell, delaying delivery.

Second Stage: Pushing

Now, when you have a contraction, the baby is being squeezed by your uterus down the elastic tunnel of your vagina, between the bony passage of your pelvis. With luck, you'll get a second wind for this stage of labour.

Get into a pushing position. Semi-sitting, squatting or going on all fours is best, because gravity will be on your side to give you more pushing power. The more efficiently you push, the more quickly your baby will get through the birth canal, so listen carefully to your body and when you feel like pushing give it your all. Midwives should not tell you when to push but ask you when you feel like it.

LONG LABOUR

Your labour will progress well if you have strong uterine contractions which open the cervix, and a baby who can fit through your pelvis. If the contractions are too weak, or your baby is too large or your pelvis too tight, you may be in for a long labour.

It's considered a long labour if there's little or no dilatation after 20 hours if you're a first-time mum, or after 14 hours if this isn't your first child. Sometimes the delay comes about because the contractions you've felt are those of a false labour. But there's also a theory that some women panic at the onset of labour, triggering the release of chemicals in the nervous system which interfere with the contraction of the uterus.

If contractions stop for about two hours during active labour, there's a 50:50 chance it's because of dispropor-tion between the size of the pelvis and that of the baby's head. But the labour may slow down purely because of exhaustion.

The baby may move very slowly down the birth canal (at less than 1cm per hour in women having their first babies) but the birth may be otherwise uneventful. You may have your waters broken, or be administered oxytocin, to speed things up.

If the pushing stage lasts longer than two hours, your doctor may want to use forceps or perform a caesarean (see Chapter 8). But if steady, though slow, progress is being made, and both you and your baby are doing well, the natural vaginal delivery will go ahead, possibly with gentle easing of the head with forceps. Maybe you should do what your body is telling you and have a rest and be thankful.

Second Stage: Birth

Your baby's head will stretch the skin of your perineum and emerge, followed by the shoulders and the rest of the body. This may take several contractions, but the midwife's hands will be near to ensure that your baby comes out safely. If you're able to stay on all fours for the delivery, your baby's head will stretch the tissues at the back of the vagina more gently and you're less likely to tear. If you need an episiotomy, this will most likely be done at the height of a contraction – when the pressure of the baby's head numbs the area.

The umbilical cord will be cut and clamped at once, unless you instruct otherwise, and your baby will be handed to you. You may feel a surge of love for him or her – but don't worry if you don't. For many women the main feeling is overwhelming relief that labour is over.

Third Stage: Delivering the Placenta

After the birth of your baby, your uterus continues to contract strongly to expel the placenta. You may be asked to push against the midwife's hand, placed on your lower abdomen, while she gently pulls on the cord with the other hand.

EMERGENCY DELIVERY

If you find yourself having an emergency delivery the first rule is to stay calm – your body and your baby can do most of the job on their own. Try to get hold of your partner or a friend to assist.

Call for an ambulance and ask the emergency controller to contact a midwife. Then explain that you're having a baby – the controller will be able to give you advice over the phone. Start panting to prevent yourself from bearing down. If you're lucky enough to have someone with you, it's their job to comfort and reassure you. Wash your vaginal area, then get on your hands and knees or on your bed.

As the top of the baby's head appears, pant ('hoo, hoo, ha') instead of pushing. Your companion should press the baby's head very gently to stop it flying out. Let the head emerge gradually – never pull it out. If there's a loop of umbilical cord around the baby's neck, your companion should hook a finger under it and gently work it over the baby's head.

When the head has been delivered, gently stroke the sides of the nose downward, the neck and under the chin upward, to help expel mucus and amniotic fluid from the nose and mouth.

Next, your companion should take the head gently in two hands and press it very slightly downward (without pulling). You should push now

SHARON'S STORY

The birth of our second child became a family occasion when I woke up at 7 a.m. feeling slightly uncomfortable, three days after the baby's due date. I ran myself a bath, which my three-year-old promptly jumped into, and by 7.20 the contractions were becoming so painful that I had to get on all fours and practise my breathing exercises. My husband came into the bathroom, saw what I was doing and disappeared to call 999. He was still talking to them when I shouted, 'The head's out!' Hearing this, the operator instructed him to get back to me and make sure the baby's airway was clear. My husband got back to the bathroom just in time to catch Gemma as she plopped out, and the ambulance crew arrived five minutes later to cut the cord for us. My daughter Jody had watched the whole thing and stayed remarkably calm. All she said afterwards was, 'It's a baby, but it hasn't got any clothes on!'

to deliver the front shoulder. As the upper arm appears your companion should lift the head out, watching for the rear shoulder to deliver. Once the shoulders are free, the rest of the baby should slip out easily.

Quickly wrap the baby in clean blankets or towels. You can hold the baby on your abdomen or breast. Don't try to pull the placenta out, but if you deliver it before help arrives, wrap it in towels or paper and keep it lifted above the baby. There's no need to try to cut the cord. The doctor or midwife will do that when they arrive. While you wait, you and your baby should be kept warm and comfortable.

An Emergency Delivery on Your Own

If you're alone, first ring the emergency services. Then try to get comfortable, and use your hands to ease the baby out while you gently push. Don't pull the umbilical cord, or cut it. Concentrate on keeping yourself and your baby warm until medical help comes.

If you live in a remote area and you know an ambulance would take some time to get through to you, try to make sure you're never alone right at the end of your pregnancy.

Your newborn baby's skin may be coated with a thick creamy substance called vernix. This is produced by skin cells as they drop off into the amniotic fluid and forms a protective coating. It is gradually absorbed, so you don't have to wipe it off, except on the head, where it sticks in the hair, and in the groin and neck, and under the arms. He may also have dark hair (lanugo) covering parts of his body – especially if he's premature.

YOUR NEWBORN BABY

Although there's still work to be done by the midwives caring for you both, all you may want to do is cuddle and coo over your new baby. So, unless there's a problem, instruct them to wait while you welcome your baby.

The cord will be clamped – and you may want to ask your midwife or doctor to wait till it's stopped pulsating – but not if you've had syntometrine. Hold the baby at the same level as the placenta and wait for the cord to become flaccid, which means the flow of blood between baby and placenta has stopped. Then rest your fingers on the cord and wait for the throbbing to stop completely. There's usually no reason why you can't delay having the cord cut until after the placenta's delivered, as long as you hold the baby by your thigh, level with the placenta, until it's cut. Cutting the cord is a simple procedure and your partner may like to do it. Ask ahead of time if this is what you want.

A mucus extractor (a plastic tube inserted into the nostrils to suck out secretion) may be used on the baby, but only if his or her airways are blocked. Normally the mucus drains naturally.

The baby may be given vitamin K (see p.176), with your permission, and will always be given what is known as an Apgar score (see p.177). He will also be weighed and measured – although his recorded length when curled up may be nothing like the one recorded later in the week!

Many new parents fear that the baby will be taken away after the birth. This is unlikely unless there's a problem, which should be fully explained to you.

Don't worry about instantly putting your baby to your breast. Some are born ready to suck, but many need time and you'll have to be patient, letting the baby lie against your breast while he gets used to the idea. Sometimes midwives will try to force the baby on to the breast, as sucking the nipples stimulates contractions to release the placenta. If you don't like this method, ask if your nipples can be stimulated by some other means – perhaps manually, by you or your partner.

Some hospitals still offer newborns water, or sugar water. But this is unnecessary, as the baby needs milk, not water. As long as your baby is producing six or more wet nappies in the course of 24 hours and the urine is pale amber or colourless, he is getting enough milk from you – and any fluid other than milk can be harmful to a newborn. A very small number of babies may need supplementary bottles in the first days, if they're very underweight or have a low blood sugar level. But remember that once you start supplementing feeds the amount of milk you produce may diminish, as demand stimulates supply. So try to make breastmilk, rather than formula, the dominant feed if you intend to go back to fully breastfeeding your baby.

YOUR QUESTIONS ANSWERED

Q: *If the doctor wants to induce, do I have a choice?*

A: You have the right to refuse any procedure. But you also have a responsibility to your baby. So any choice you make depends on your doctor's reasons for advising induction (see p.166). If it is because your pregnancy is post-term, you need to be sure that the baby really is overdue. If you didn't have the 18–20 week dating scan, a careful review of your dates may be helpful. If you're in any doubt, ask for an ultrasound scan now. This will check the flow of blood to the baby and the volume of amniotic fluid (which is reduced if the baby is post-term). If your clothes are feeling looser, this may be a sign that amniotic fluid is decreasing.

Q: *My mother says she was shaved, had a catheter inserted and was given an enema at the time she was having me. Does this still happen?*

A: Life in the labour ward isn't like that any more! Shaving and emptying the mother's bowels are no longer regarded as necessary, though you may have your pubic hair shaved and a catheter inserted to drain your bladder under certain circumstances, such as a caesarean.

Q: *How safe is a water birth?*

A: Using a birthing pool is no longer considered an 'alternative' practice, and many hospitals encourage women to use water – for labour if not delivery – as it helps reduce pain. According to Sheila Kitzinger, who has campaigned to give women the choice of water birth, half of all women who use water in labour go on to give birth in the pool, too. And she reports that they often believe that the water provides a more gentle transition to life for the baby, who has been floating in amniotic fluid for nine months.

However, critics of water birth argue that there may be an increased risk of problems such as infection for both mother and baby, trauma to the baby, perineal trauma and postpartum haemorrhage.

If you are considering a water birth, go through an organization such as The Active Birth Centre (see p.251), who can put you in touch with a midwife who's familiar with water deliveries and the safety guidelines for using birthing pools.

Water birthing pools hold about 450 litres (100 gallons) of water, which weighs 450 kg (about 1000 lb). So if you're planning to hire a pool to use at home, make sure your floor can stand the weight, and that your water tank holds enough water to fill it (most domestic tanks hold a maximum of 320 litres/70 gallons).

Birthing pools are available for use at home, and in many hospitals. Even if you do not deliver your baby under water, you may want to use the pool in labour.

Many hospitals have birthing pools but these are not used routinely. However, you may be considered for a water birth in hospital if:

- you have had a problem- and risk-free pregnancy and no potential problems have been identified.
- your baby's size is compatible with your ability to deliver safely.
- you're at least 38 weeks pregnant when you go into labour.
- your baby is head down, not breech or transverse (see pp.96–102).
- there's no sign that your baby's distressed.
- your baby's heart has been monitored and found to be satisfactory.

Q: **What is syntometrine and why do I need it?**

A: Syntometrine (or syntocinon) is a combination of synthetic oxytocin (to promote strong contractions) and ergometrine (which ensures the contractions close the cervix). It is given, by injection, usually after the baby's first shoulder has been delivered, to speed up the delivery of the placenta after the birth before the cervix closes.

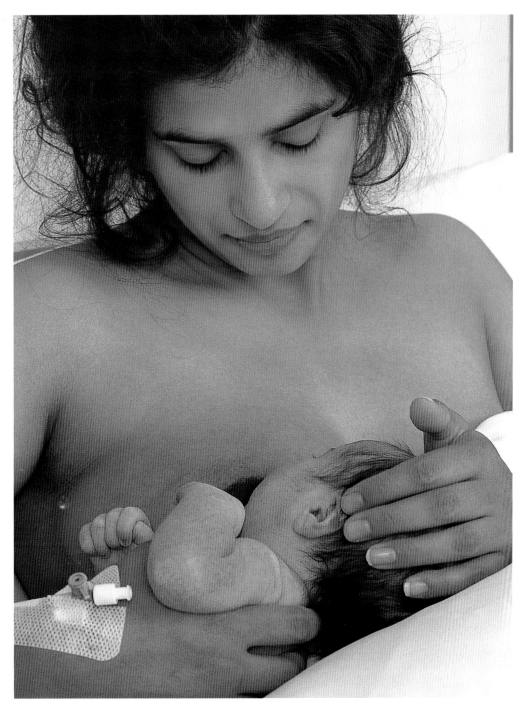

Whether at home, or in hospital, your first moments with your baby are precious. You should be given the choice of whether you want to hold him immediately or have him cleaned first.

It is thought to reduce the risk of haemorrhage after giving birth, but can cause complications of its own. If it takes effect before the placenta is delivered, the placenta can be trapped and need to be removed manually under general anaesthetic. Syntometrine can also make you feel nauseous, and it's been suggested that it can delay the production of breast milk.

You do have a choice about whether or not you receive syntometrine – and, if you've so far had a problem-free, drug-free, natural birth, there are good reasons to expect your third stage to follow the same pattern. But if you've had an epidural, delivering the placenta may not be so straightfoward and syntometrine may help you.

Q: *Will I be expected to stay in bed when delivering?*

A: The idea of trying to give birth while you lie flat on your back isn't appealing. Even if this is your first baby, it doesn't take too much imagination to see that pushing the baby out will be easier if you are upright and have gravity on your side. In fact, it was only at the end of the eighteenth century that the lying down position caught on. Before then, women walked around during much of their labour and sat up in bed or on horseshoe-shaped birthing stools to deliver.

If everything is going smoothly, and no problems are anticipated, you will be able to go on all fours, squat, or use a birthing stool (if available) to deliver your baby. But discuss this with your midwife first – she may have a preferred position that suits you both. The birthing stool, if required, will also have to be brought to your room. So don't wait till the last minute to ask for it.

The main reasons you may have to stay in bed are that you are attached to a blood pressure monitor or drip (which have wires with a limited stretch), or you've been given an epidural or Pethidine (which make it unsafe for you to be on the move). If your contractions are fast and furious, there may be little time even to think about getting up and walking around in between. And if the second stage (pushing the baby out) is equally rapid you may forget about getting on all fours. But most modern maternity units have beds which convert into birthing chairs so that you can keep your back well supported while you sit upright, with the midwife having easy access to the baby.

Q: *Will my baby be given an injection of vitamin K, and why?*

A: Vitamin K is given to newborn babies to help their blood clot efficiently. Giving it by mouth is considered better than an injection, but not all maternity units offer vitamin K in any form. It's usually most advisable for pre-term babies and those who've had a difficult birth.

Q: ***What is an Apgar score?***

A: The Apgar score is the result (out of 10) of a test on newborns for the following:

- ◆ heart rate.
- ◆ breathing.
- ◆ skin colour.
- ◆ muscle tone.
- ◆ reflex response.

Each is given up to 2 points, but a total of 7+ is considered fine. Anything below 7 will need intervention from the midwife or doctor, for example gentle suction to clear mucus from the baby's throat to make his breathing easier.

Q: ***How long will I have to stay in hospital?***

A: Your length of stay depends on your recovery and that of your baby. Although it may be irritating to be kept in longer than you want, no hospital would choose to keep you in for the fun of it. You can, of course, insist on discharging yourself. But this is unwise if the doctors have good reasons for asking you to stay in so that your progress can be monitored.

The best way to ensure you're in and out quickly is to book a Domino birth, if the scheme is available in your area. This means that a community midwife will bring you in and deliver you herself. As she then returns home with you, you may be able to leave just a few hours after the birth.

But, even on the Domino scheme, you're likely to need a longer stay if there are any complications such as:

- ◆ your baby's underweight.
- ◆ you have high blood pressure.
- ◆ either of you has an infection.
- ◆ you've had a caesarean.
- ◆ you've had a catheter.

Try to be flexible about your plans to stay in hospital. It can be upsetting and frustrating to be kept in when you expected to be back home, but since none of us knows exactly what will happen when we give birth we should all be prepared for the unexpected and to take things one step at a time.

8 Coping with a Complicated Delivery

Not all deliveries are straightforward. You may know during pregnancy that you're going to have a planned caesarean or a breech delivery. But even women who've enjoyed the easiest of pregnancies can run into complications in childbirth, which is why I urge all mothers to be prepared for the unexpected!

PROLONGED LABOUR

Some labours last 24 hours. And while gentle slowly progressing labours can be normal and don't require intervention, there are situations where help may be needed.

First Stage

Insufficient uterine contractions are the most likely cause of delay. The contractions may be weak because of what is known as hypotonic inertia, in which the uterus never seems to get going and so labour is never properly established. Nobody knows why some women develop this problem, but a very small dose of syntocinon given intravenously can convert hypotonic inertia into normal uterine activity.

Hypertonic action is the opposite to hypotonic inertia, and involves ferocious contractions of a few seconds each. The problem is often associated with a baby in a posterior position, and you may have severe backache too. These contractions, although strong, are not as efficient as normal ones, and lead to prolonged labour. Fear is thought to underlie many cases of hypertonic action, but better antenatal care and preparation for labour have made this problem less frequent than it used to be.

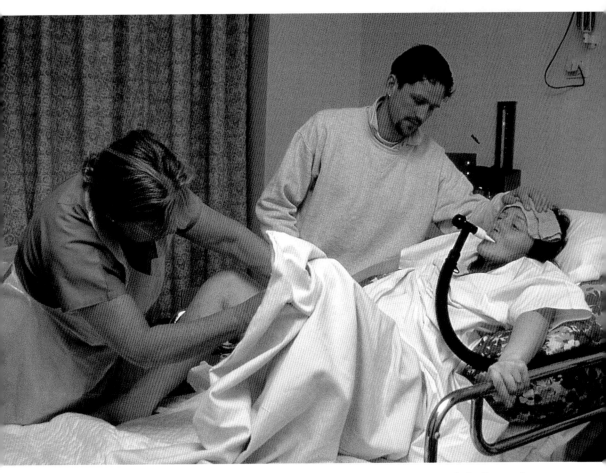

Handled sensitively, a complicated delivery shouldn't be traumatic for you, or your baby. Remember that what matters is that you are both healthy after the event.

Pethidine or epidural anaesthesia, combined with intravenous syntocinon, can restore normal contractions.

A big baby – especially if it's your first – can cause a delay. But even if she's not particularly oversized, her head, if not well flexed, can artificially increase the diameters which have to pass through your pelvis – again causing delay.

A posterior position baby also presents a larger diameter to go through the birth canal. In the majority of cases, the head rotates within the pelvis and a normal delivery can take place. In the few instances where the head fails to rotate, forceps or ventouse may be used to rotate it. If the head stays in the posterior position and doesn't descend through the pelvis, a caesarean may be necessary.

A small pelvis may delay labour, and although your obstetrician can have an X-ray taken if he suspects this is going to be a problem, many prefer to wait and see what happens in labour, then deliver the baby by caesarean if there's a hold-up. Afterwards an X-ray may be taken to determine the course of action for subsequent pregnancies.

The soft tissue of the pelvis can very occasionally cause delays in labour when, because of an abnormal amount of fibrous tissue in a rigid cervix, it is slow to dilate. Doctors don't know why this happens, but an epidural can help.

Second Stage

Again, inadequate contractions, a baby with a large head, or a mother's small pelvis can cause the delay. A caesarean may be advised, but is not inevitable. As long as the head (or breech) is descending or advancing, and you and your baby are in good condition, delivery should continue vaginally.

FETAL DISTRESS

A baby may become distressed – deprived of oxygen – because of a long-standing problem with placental insuffiency (see pp.239–40), because the cord is knotted or twisted around her neck, or because a haemorrhage has taken place behind the placenta.

The signs of fetal distress are:

Meconium – the baby's first stool – may be passed during labour. If your midwife sees this green-stained liquid draining out of your vagina, she will take it as a warning that the baby is becoming distressed – although some babies do pass meconium for no apparent reason. If the baby is distressed, his or her heart rate will also become irregular or slow. But even if the baby isn't distressed, and has simply passed meconium during labour, a paediatrician will normally be called to prevent any complications arising from the presence of meconium in the baby's airways.

A fast or slow fetal heartbeat (above 160 or below 120, which is the normal range for the baby), may suggest distress. Fetal heart monitoring may be used, enabling immediate action to be taken if there's obvious distress.

Violent movements of the baby, as if she's turning over, can also indicate distress in labour.

A severely distressed baby must be delivered as soon as possible, by caesarean (see pp.185–87) or using forceps or ventouse (see p.184).

BREECH DELIVERY

Carrying a breech baby (see pp.99–100) used to mean an automatic caesarean. Now vaginal delivery is more common, but bear in mind:

◆ Vaginal deliveries are safe in about a third to a half of breech births, but only if the doctor or midwife is experienced in the procedure.

◆ Some studies of vaginal breech deliveries suggest that the potential risk is not always from the delivery itself, but from the reason for the breech, such as a premature baby.

◆ A vaginal delivery is unlikely to be attempted if the baby is in the complete breech position (upside down vertex) or has one leg dangling down (footling breech) or is facing upwards. The easiest breech position to deliver is the frank breech, in which the baby has his legs folded straight up.

◆ The baby must be small enough for easy passage, but not so small that a vaginal delivery becomes risky – and premature babies presented by breech under 34 weeks are nearly always delivered by caesarean.

◆ Up until the second stage, a vaginal breech labour progresses in much the same way as a vertex (head down baby) labour, but it will be considered by your carers to be a 'trial labour'.

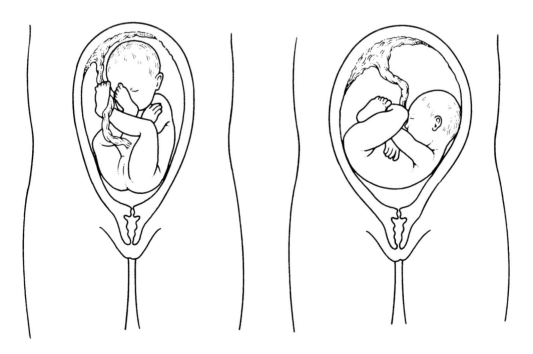

Breech presentation   Transverse presentation

♦ Be prepared for an epidural, which may be necessary to stop you bearing down too hard before you're fully dilated – this could trap and compress the cord between the baby and the pelvis.

♦ You're likely to be admitted to a delivery room at the end of the first stage, because there's always a risk that a caesarean will become necessary.

♦ You may be able to deliver the baby naturally until the legs and lower half of the body are out. Then a local anaesthetic is sometimes given before the shoulders and head are delivered.

♦ Delivery of the head and shoulders may need extra help with forceps and a wide episiotomy, but this isn't a foregone conclusion.

♦ Be prepared for an emergency caesarean. This advice applies to all expectant mums, but with a breech baby there's a higher chance of this eventuality. Remember, having a caesarean isn't the end of the world. What matters is that you and your baby are safe and well before and after the birth.

OTHER AWKWARD BABY POSITIONS

Transverse and Oblique Lie

With a transverse lie the baby's spine is at right-angles to the mother's spine, forming a cross. An oblique lie is anywhere between a longitudinal (spine to spine) lie and a transverse lie. Either the head or the breech lies in one or other groin, just above the crest of the hipbone.

Only about 1 in 300 babies are in a transverse or oblique lie at birth (compared with 3 per cent of babies being breech). These positions are more likely when:

♦ the muscular wall of the womb is slack, or stretched by previous pregnancies.

♦ there's excessive fluid around the baby.

♦ something such as a big fibroid in the lower part of the womb wall is blocking the entrance to the pelvis.

Unstable Lie

A baby is said to have an unstable lie when he or she seems reluctant to settle in one position, usually because of excessive amniotic fluid or a floppy, slack womb wall.

Attempts will usually be made to turn a baby into a longitudinal position before labour. If this cannot be done, a caesarean is usually recommended if the lies does not stabilize in early labour.

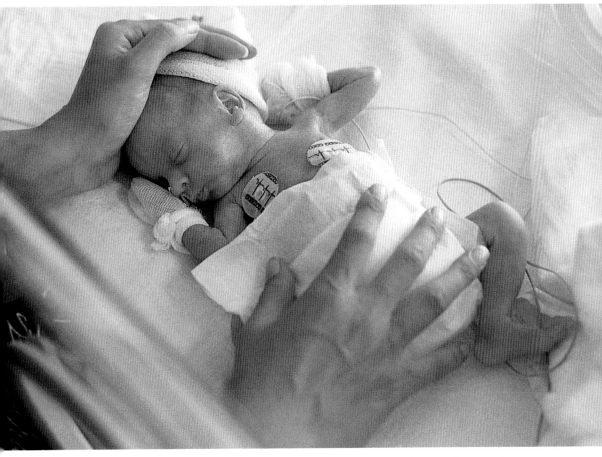

About six per cent of all babies are 'low birthweight – weighing 2.5 kg (5¹/₂ lb) or less – and many need intensive care. At least half these babies are born prematurely – before 37 weeks (see pp. 244–45), and although it's distressing to see your baby attached to tubes and wires in an incubator, you can still stroke and cuddle her through the portholes. Your love and affection may be just as important as the modern medical technology which has improved survival rates dramatically.

POTENTIAL DANGER

Occasionally it may not be realized that the baby is lying obliquely or transversely until labour starts. The force of the contractions may push the presenting part – shoulder, arm or leg – down into the birth canal and the umbilical cord may be the first thing to drop into the vagina once the waters have gone. This is a very dangerous situation and means the baby cannot be delivered vaginally, so an emergency caesarean will normally be advised.

FORCEPS AND VENTOUSE

A doctor who recommends the use of forceps should seek your consent and keep you fully informed about why the procedure is necessary in your particular case. Forceps may be required in the following circumstances:

♦ to turn a baby's head if the presenting part is too wide to descend through the birth canal.

♦ you're too tired to push hard enough to finish delivery without help.

♦ your baby's distressed.

♦ there's a delay in the second stage of labour and no progress with good contractions.

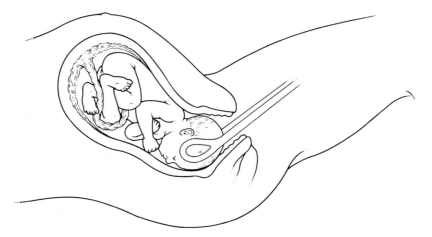

Forceps are like large salad servers, which cradle the baby's head.

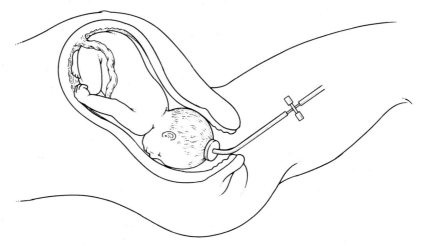

Ventouse can be used before the cervix is fully dilated.

SANDY'S STORY

My labour was induced because I was ten days past Sam's due date and the obstetrician thought this was for the best. I didn't mind too much because, having two other children, my husband and I could start to plan around them.

But I was aware that being induced would probably mean a long and painful labour – this had been my experience with my first child. So I was determined to have an epidural this time round. I discussed it with my consultant, and made sure it was put in my notes that this was what I wanted. Then, to be on the safe side, when I arrived in hospital for the induction I told the midwife I didn't want the syn-

tocinon drip to start until the epidural was also at the ready.

But the combination of syntocinon and epidural had one big drawback: I couldn't move off the bed because I was being continuously monitored, and this made the pushing stage extremely hard going. Eventually, after half an hour of pushing, and when I was feeling thoroughly exhausted, the subject of ventouse extraction was raised. My midwife was keen for me to carry on pushing, but I'd run out of energy. Once I'd agreed to the ventouse Sam was out within a couple of minutes, and he appeared to suffer no distress from the procedure.

When forceps are used, you'll be given a local anaesthetic before the curved blunt blades are cradled one at a time around the baby's temples so he or she can be gently delivered.

Ventouse or vacuum extraction is a popular alternative to forceps and involves suctioning the baby out of the birth canal with a cap which is applied to the head. It has the advantage that it can be used before the cervix is fully dilated, whereas forceps require full dilatation of the cervix.

If you have concerns about the possible use of forceps or ventouse, discuss them with your midwife before you go into labour.

CAESAREAN SECTION

A caesarean may be recommended early in your pregnancy because of some foreseen complication, in which case you will be given a date and will know exactly when you are having your baby. An emergency caesarean is carried out when a problem is identified during labour.

The operation can be performed under general anaesthetic or epidural. The epidural has the advantage that you can see your baby as soon as he or she has been removed, and this is very important for some women who feel they are missing out on the birth if they are unconscious. Some doctors, recognizing the strong desire in women to push their babies out physically, will ask you to give a push as they lift the baby out.

If you have a caesarean, expect the following:

- ◆ Your pubic hair may be shaved.
- ◆ You'll have a catheter inserted into your bladder to keep it empty.
- ◆ If you're having an epidural for the operation, a screen will be put up at shoulder level so you won't see the incision being made.
- ◆ Sterile drapes will be arranged around your exposed abdomen and the area will be washed down with antiseptic solution.
- ◆ An intravenous drip will be set up so that additional medication can be given if it's needed.
- ◆ In an emergency caesarean, things may move very quickly.
- ◆ Depending on the hospital's policy, your partner may be asked to leave the room (fainting men just get in the way).
- ◆ If you're awake, you may feel the incision as a sensation of being unzipped – but you should feel no pain.
- ◆ The first cut is made in the lower abdomen, then a second incision in the lower segment of your uterus.

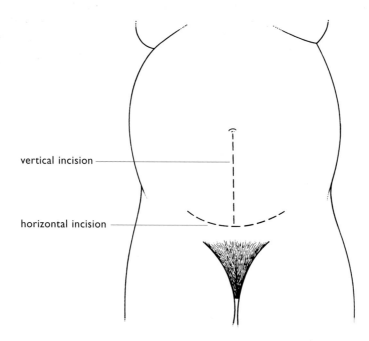

vertical incision

horizontal incision

The horizontal (or low-transverse) incision for a caesarean is made low down near the line of the pubic hair, in the area that would be covered by a bikini.

- The amniotic sac will be opened and any fluid suctioned out.
- The baby is then eased out, manually or with forceps, and you may feel some tugging.
- At this stage, if you want, the screen can be lowered slightly so you can see the baby being delivered, but are spared the gory details.
- The baby's nose and mouth are then suctioned and you'll hear her first cry before the cord is clamped.
- You may be given syntometrine intravenously to help your uterus contract and enable any bleeding to be controlled.
- Don't be too alarmed if your baby is whisked away. Babies born by caesarean often need resuscitation because they haven't had the benefits of a vaginal birth to help stimulate their own respiratory system.

TWINS OR MORE

Many twin pregnancies remain uncomplicated right through childbirth, with a normal vaginal delivery. However, there are still some obstetricians who believe all multiple pregnancies should be delivered by caesarean. And there's definitely more potential for complications during

Delivering twins need not be complicated, although the babies – especially the second – often need more help from the doctor, and will be delivered by senior members of the obstetric staff.

the delivery of twins, so even if a vaginal delivery is scheduled an anaesthetist will be on hand in case a caesarean is needed.

The most likely complication will arise from the babies' positions in the womb during labour. When both babies are head first, a vaginal delivery may be attempted. But one baby may be delivered vaginally and then the other will move and become unturnable, requiring a caesarean. So, as ever, be prepared for the unexpected!

See also the following entries in A–Z of Problems and Solutions: eclampsia, multiple pregnancy, placental problems, polyhydramnios, postpartum haemorrhage.

YOUR QUESTIONS ANSWERED

Q: *Will forceps or ventouse leave marks on my baby's head?*

A: Your baby's head may look swollen and bruised after a vacuum or forceps extraction. But this quickly subsides and rarely causes long-term harm. However, there is a growing awareness that some of the problems thought of as 'normal' in newborns – colic, excessive crying and sticky eyes – are aggravated by compression of the cranial bones during such a birth.

Q: *I've heard that cranial osteopathy can help babies who have been born by forceps or vacuum extraction. Can you explain this?*

A: If your baby seems to have symptoms of cranial irritation (see above), these may be due to a forceps or ventouse birth. However, they may equally be aggravated by the way in which the baby was born (for example she may have had her hand up by her ear during delivery). Cranial osteopathy is a very gentle hands-on therapy which can be used on babies to correct the underlying distortions in the cranial bones caused during a difficult birth. See also p.101.

9 The First Three Months of Motherhood

The early weeks with a baby are a delight – but they can also be a complete shock to the system. No matter how hard you think you've planned and prepared for this new little person in your life, you may be amazed at how demanding your baby seems to be, and how little time – and even less energy – you have for yourself. But, while it's true that your life will never again be as it was, it's reasonable to expect a degree of normality by the time you both attend your six-week check-ups.

THE FIRST FEW DAYS

For the Mother

Afterpains

Strong contractions of the uterus are particularly likely to be experienced when the baby is feeding, but are more common with second, third or fourth babies than with the first one. These pains are a result of the uterus returning to its normal size. If they're so painful that you find yourself dreading the next feed, take a paracetamol tablet about half an hour before you're due to feed. If you're still in hospital, ask your midwife to give you one.

Baby Blues

You may have a couple of days of feeling sad and rather weepy, which usually coincide with your milk coming in. This is not postnatal depression but the 'blues,' caused by the dramatic drop in your hormone levels after giving birth. The blues normally pass fairly quickly and without too much problem, but occasionally they can herald more serious mental illness. See Postnatal Depression (pp.240–43).

BE KIND TO MUMS WITH BABY BLUES

Mothers who have the blues should be allowed the freedom to cry and to express their fluctuating emotions. If they feel miserable they shouldn't be told to pull themselves together, but listened to and reassured that the misery they are feeling will soon pass.

A mother with the blues is very sensitive to anything that medical staff and friends and relatives may say, so tact and empathy are key words for carers at this time.

Bruising

Your vagina has been stretched and the muscles worked hard during labour, and you will naturally feel sore and bruised as a result. An icepack will relieve the pain – and a lot of women find a pack of frozen peas particularly comfortable, as its shape moulds around your body.

Clots of Blood

It's normal to pass clots of blood after the birth. If you do, you should try to retain the clot to show it to your midwife, who will be able to check that it is indeed a clot and not a piece of retained placenta.

Constipation

You lose a lot of fluid in the first few days after giving birth and consequently many women find they get constipated. You'll want to avoid this if you can, as straining on an already delicate and stretched area is extremely uncomfortable. So drink plenty of water and make sure your diet is rich in fibre – bran cereals, fruit and vegetables. Laxatives are not advised, as they can be passed through your breast milk to your baby.

GOING IT ALONE

If you're a single mum with your new baby, remember it's OK not to be Superwoman. You're allowed to feel tired, worn out and longing for your own space. Everyone does – but you may have less opportunity than those women who have the original New Man running around them doing housework, shopping and cooking.

Accept that you can't do all you want to do in a day. Let the house go, and relax. And, if at all possible, make arrangements with friends and relatives who will probably jump at the chances to babysit while you spend some guilt-free time doing something for yourself. Or get them to do your chores while you enjoy your baby!

Bonding is a complex process and despite the popular myth that you will only bond with your baby if you are allowed to hold him straight after delivery, this is not always possible. Women who have had the chance to bond with one baby at birth and not with another, report no difference in their feelings for their children.

Fluid Loss

During pregnancy your body will have stored up excess fluid, which is shed in the first few days after delivery. You'll need to empty your bladder frequently and may sweat heavily too. You're also bleeding from the vagina (see Lochia, below), and beginning to produce milk from your breasts. All in all, you may feel like a leaky sieve! Take showers to help yourself feel more comfortable, and drink plenty of water to help combat constipation. Losing fluid is normal, but do tell a doctor or midwife if it makes you feel unwell.

Lochia

This is the name given to the vaginal bleeding you experience after childbirth. For the first 48 hours it's likely to be quite heavy – much heavier than any period you have ever experienced – and you'll probably need to use large maternity pads. The midwives will let you know if the loss is too heavy or gives cause for concern. After the first two days the flow lessens, but altogether it will continue for anything from two to six weeks after the birth.

Stitches

If you've had stitches, for either a tear or an episiotomy, you'll feel quite uncomfortable for a few days. The scar will feel enormous and swollen, but rest assured that your perineum will probably return to normal in a few weeks. Not so long ago you would have been given a rubber ring to sit on. This is now contra-indicated as the ring can cause congestion and swelling of the damaged and stitched tissues. Soothing remedies such as homeopathic arnica or tincture of Hyper-Cal (which you can put on a pad) help speed up the healing process and reduce soreness.

For the Baby

Blood Tests

A sample of blood will be taken from your baby's heel at around six days old to test for phenylketonuria (a metabolic disorder which can cause mental retardation if not controlled by a special diet), thyroid deficiency and possibly also for hypoglycaemia (low blood sugar level), especially if your baby was small for dates. If the baby has a low blood sugar level you may need extra help and advice about feeding.

The Cord

The stump of the umbilical cord will remain on the baby until it shrivels up naturally and falls off – this usually occurs after about a fortnight. You will be given some powder for the baby to keep the area infection-free during this time.

Jaundice

Any yellow discoloration of the skin should be checked on as it can be a sign of jaundice, which is common in new babies but usually not serious unless left untreated. Frequent feeds will help flush the illness from the baby's system, but if it's already taken a hold the baby may need to be put under phototherapy (see below).

Discovering your newborn baby has jaundice can be upsetting, but it needn't be if you understand the problem.

◆ Nine out of ten babies have jaundice in the first few days of life. Usually it's a minor problem and rarely causes serious concern.

◆ Jaundice normally starts in the second or third day of life, reaching a peak around the fourth day. It gradually disappears, and most babies are better by the age of ten days.

◆ Very occasionally jaundice occurs in the first 24 hours after birth. If this does happen, your baby should be seen by a neonatologist or paediatrician. If you delivered your baby at home, call your midwife or doctor.

◆ Jaundice is caused by a build-up of waste products in the baby's body while he's still unable to remove these properly. It's a waste product called bilirubin which causes the yellow colour.

◆ Bilirubin is produced when old red blood cells are broken down. In an adult red blood cells last for about 120 days, but in a newborn baby they last a shorter time. Babies also have a higher than normal number of red blood cells. As these break down bilirubin is released into the blood, and the newborn baby's liver takes some days to start removing it properly.

◆ Most babies need no treatment for their jaundice, but if there's a lot of bilirubin in their blood they may need phototherapy. This involves the baby being placed naked under a special light which helps break the bilirubin down.

◆ Very high levels of bilirubin can damage the brain, so phototherapy treatment will always be started well before any dangerous level is reached.

◆ Occasionally jaundice lasts beyond the usual ten days – for example if your baby has a condition in which the blood cells break down faster than usual. This is often discovered very soon after the baby is born, or even during pregnancy, but it can be treated.

◆ If the jaundice hasn't disappeared by the time your baby's two weeks old, contact your doctor, midwife or health visitor who will arrange for blood and urine tests to find the cause.

◆ Very rarely, baby jaundice is a sign of a liver problem. If this is suspected, you can get further help and support from the Children's Liver Disease Foundation (see Address Book, p.252).

Meconium

This is the name given to the first stool your baby passes. It is a tarry substance which can be quite difficult to clean up. Once the meconium has passed, though, the baby's stools will change to greenish brown and then yellow, curdy and quite loose if you are breastfeeding, or more solid and smelly if the baby is on a bottle.

Posseting

Most babies posset (vomit) small amounts of their feed, especially when they are being winded. But if your baby appears to be bringing up the whole feed you should check with your doctor – it might just be the result of an infection or a condition known as pyloric stenosis, which causes projectile vomiting.

BONDING

Some authorities say the best way to bond with your baby immediately after birth is to dim the lights and look into his or her eyes, observing the reaction you get. But this is not practical for all women – in an emergency situation for either mother or child, for instance, the baby will be temporarily taken away. In any case, different women have different experiences of bonding. If you are at all worried that your feelings for your baby are not what you expected them to be, just talk to your health visitor. Don't keep things to yourself, and never think you're a failure!

YOUR BODY'S RECOVERY AFTER THE BIRTH

Your profile can still appear distressingly pregnant for the first few weeks after having your baby, but most women are out of their maternity clothes within a couple of months. If you used your pregnancy as an excuse to over-indulge, and have been left with excess weight on your hips, your figure may be slower to return. See pp.212–16 for some effective reshaping exercises, and feel free to walk or swim as much as you like. Some women claim that breastfeeding helps them get back into shape more quickly.

Don't be tempted to crash diet. If you're breastfeeding, you need 500 more calories a day than you did pre-pregnancy – but make sure every calorie counts, packing in fruit, vegetables, pasta, rice and pulses, and leaving out any empty calories like sweets and biscuits.

Even if you're not breastfeeding, you need enough energy to cope with the demands of sleepless nights and frenzied days with your baby. This can be a stressful time, and you must look after yourself.

Slow but steady weight loss, taking exercise when you can and following a sensible diet, is most likely to bring about lasting results. The ideal method is what is known as the Mediterranean diet, which is less about losing weight and more about eating healthily. So you can follow it even if you don't have to lose weight (it will do your partner good, too), so should be seen as a new regime rather than a diet.

Mediterranean Diet

At least 50 per cent of your daily energy should come from complex carbohydrates such as wholegrain rice and pasta and pulses. You should eat 400–800 g (15–30 oz) of fresh fruit and raw or lightly steamed vegetables (not potatoes) every day. And you should also eat more nuts, seeds, pulses and fish, because they are rich in essential fatty acids (not to be confused with fat in general: see below) which help lower harmful blood cholesterol levels.

Less than 30 per cent of your daily energy should come from fat. Use more olive oil (which should be stored in cool dark conditions for it to offer the best benefits to your health) and less butter. Eat fish two or three times a week, try to have one or two vegetarian days every week, and aim to eat red meat no more than once or twice a week. Although you don't have to cut out red meat altogether, research shows that a diet of bread, pasta, olive oil, fish, vegetables, fruit, garlic, fresh herbs and red wine has a significant protective effect against heart disease.

Cooking Methods

If you're aiming for a trim waistline and a healthy body, the best ways to prepare food include:

- Eating fruit and vegetables raw or only lightly steamed.
- Grilling food with only a light brushing of olive or rapeseed oil.
- Baking.
- Steaming.
- Boiling with only minimal water and no added salt.
- Poaching in vegetable stock.

- Stir frying using a light brushing of olive or rapeseed oil.
- Roasting only if the meat is on a rack so the juice and fat run away.
- Making low-fat gravies using granules and vegetable water instead of meat juices.

RECOVERING FROM A CAESAREAN

After a caesarean your body has to recover from two major traumas – childbirth and surgery. Be gentle on yourself. You need plenty of help, especially in the first week, when you shouldn't do any lifting or housework. If you must lift your baby, lift from waist level, using your arms but not your abdomen. If you bend, use your knees and not your waist.

Many women worry that their stitches will burst if they move too much, but there is no danger of this – even though at first you need to support them to avoid pain when you cough, sneeze or laugh. The stitches will come out around the fifth day, but, while they're still in you can wear high-waisted pants and a press-on sanitary towel (for your lochia blood loss: see p.192) to avoid rubbing them.

Your scar will remain sore for a few weeks, but will slowly improve. During this time it's normal to feel brief pains around the scar – these are part of the healing process. Itchiness from the scar is also quite normal. However, persistent pain, redness or discharge are all possible signs of infection, so see your doctor if you experience any of them.

BREASTFEEDING YOUR BABY

Although there will always be mothers who argue vehemently in favour of bottle feeding, today's paediatricians and midwives will encourage you as far as possible to try breastfeeding. And even if you can only stick it for a couple of weeks, your baby will have benefited – although it's a shame to give up now. The most difficult part of breastfeeding is usually the beginning. After that it gets easier and easier.

The advantages of breastfeeding include:

Convenience: breast milk is there whenever you need it. There's no need to fiddle around preparing bottles.

Antibodies: the colostrum which your breasts prepare during pregnancy becomes the baby's first feed, and is full of antibodies which protect your baby from the diseases you've had and have been immunized against as well as safeguarding him from the bacteria which cause gastroenteritis. Bottle-fed babies are more likely to get gastroenteritis, and if you've chosen to bottle feed, or are supplementing breast with bottle, it's vital that the bottle teats are properly sterilized.

It provides everything the baby needs: for the first four months of your baby's life, all the drink and food he needs can be obtained from your breast milk. Your breasts have an amazing ability to manufacture according to the seasons, too, so that in hot weather your milk will quench his extra thirst without compromising on the food aspect of his feed.

It protects your baby from allergies, infections and even obesity.

Your baby's nappies aren't as smelly as those of babies being fed on artificial milk.

It's cheaper than buying formula and bottles.

It is more restful than feeding with a bottle.

It provides closeness which aids the bonding process between you and your baby.

On the downside, you may get leaky breasts (often at the most embarrassing moments). The pads in nursing bras mop up the spills adequately, but they aren't comfortable and you'll probably feel damp and smelly – even though you smell delicious to your baby, and probably your partner.

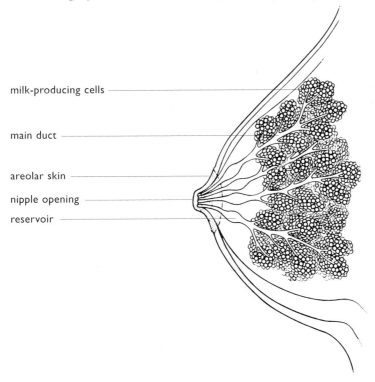

milk-producing cells

main duct

areolar skin

nipple opening

reservoir

The breast is made up of 15 to 20 segments. The cells which make the milk are at the back of the segments and have ducts leading down to the nipple. Just before the ducts open on to the nipple they enlarge slightly to form a reservoir, at the point where the skin darkens into the pigmented ring around the nipple (the areola).

How Breastfeeding Works

Contrary to popular myth, the size of your breasts has little, if anything, to do with the amount of milk you produce. Milk production is controlled by the hormones prolactin (responsible for quantity) and oxytocin (which delivers the milk through the nipples to your baby).

Oxytocin causes the milk-producing cells to contract, squeezing the milk down the ducts and out of the nipple. This is known as the let-down reflex – and is sometimes so efficient that your breasts feel full enough to burst, making the baby's feed time very welcome relief when it comes.

Sometimes the let-down reflex makes milk drip from one breast while you're feeding the baby with the other. If you want, you can catch this milk and freeze it for later use or even enquire about donating it to a Special Care Baby Unit.

Positioning the baby correctly is important. Make sure you're comfortable too – you could be stuck in this position for some time!

Your baby should be facing you sufficiently centrally that he has to tilt his head back to get your nipple in his mouth. When he's correctly positioned you'll see the muscles at his temple moving as he feeds. If his cheeks are going in and out he is not on properly and you'll have to put your little finger into the corner of his mouth, so you can take him off and start again.

Breastfeeding Problems

Afterpains

The oxytocin which triggers your let-down reflex sets up contractions of the uterus (see p.189).

Blocked Ducts

Blocked ducts cause a tender lump and can make you feel feverish. This can follow engorgement (see p.201) or pressure on the ducts – maybe because your bra is too tight, or you are feeding your baby in an awkward position. Even if you're tempted to stop feeding, *don't* – it will make it much worse. Instead, try to massage the lump gently in the direction of the nipple to clear the blockage, apply hot and cold compresses, and offer the breast first at frequent feeds so that the baby's strongest sucking (at the beginning of the feed) will help get the milk moving through the ducts again. If it is difficult for the baby to get a grip, try expressing a little milk first. See also Mastitis (p.201).

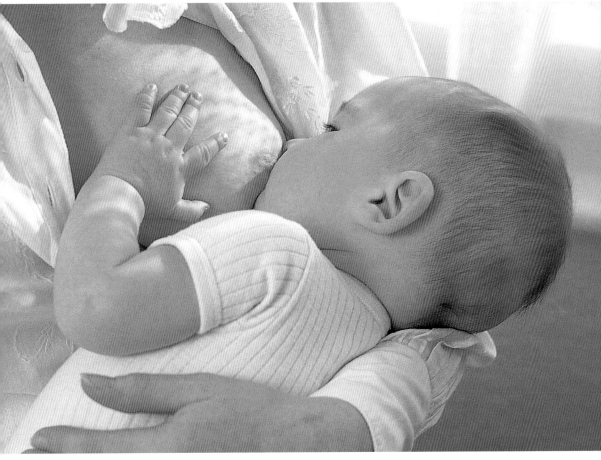

Breastfeeding has many advantages for you and your baby. If you are finding it difficult or painful, trained counsellors (see NCT and La Leche League in the Address Book) can help you overcome your problems. Its worth persevering for at least four months to give your baby the best benefit.

THE DIFFERENT KINDS OF BREASTMILK

The first few feeds of your baby's life are provided by the colostrum your breasts have produced during pregnancy. This is a transitional feed from placental feeding to milk, and is gentle on your baby's new digestive system. After a few days the colostrum is replaced with normal breast milk, which consists of two types – foremilk and hindmilk. The foremilk, which is produced early in the feed, is low in fat and calories and satisfies the baby's thirst. The hindmilk, produced later in the feed, is richer and gives him his meal.

ROSIE'S STORY

As soon as Jamie was born the midwife put him to my breast to take colostrum, and he latched on straightaway. But after that I never seemed to see the same midwife through a feed. One would latch him on and then go off, leaving me wondering whether I was doing the right thing or not. The workshop I attended had told me that breastfeeding would be difficult – but I didn't expect to feel so useless. I couldn't tell whether he was feeding or not, and I didn't understand the signs that seemed so obvious to the midwives.

But the problems really started when my ordinary milk finally came through on the third day after Jamie was born. Michael was driving us home from the hospital and I suddenly felt extremely anxious and tearful. When we got to our flat I wanted to be alone with Jamie, and resented the phone constantly ringing with calls from well-wishers.

Then my breasts, which have always been on the small side, suddenly ballooned into these enormous, rock-hard, conical, throbbing organs. They seemed completely alien to me, and every time I tried to latch Jamie on he'd just slip off. The more upset I became the harder it was to breastfeed, and I remember bursting into tears when a visiting midwife said my nipples were too flat and I'd have to give him a bottle. 'If you go on like this he'll starve to death!' she said, obviously not realizing the devastating effect she was having on me. But I was determined to persevere, and the next day the contents of his nappy were proof that he'd definitely fed properly.

I was so proud, and from that moment on I never looked back. I decided to forget all the advice about feeding on demand. For me and Jamie it seemed to work better to feed every three hours even if it meant waking him – and he quickly became such a good baby, waking like clockwork for his feed.

Even so, the first six weeks were very exhausting – it took me ages to do anything. I'd read that it would be like that, but it was difficult to take on board how completely drained I would feel. It seemed I'd only have a half-hour break between feeding and changing him and we'd be starting all over again.

At the end of six weeks Jamie's routine seemed to be clicking into place and breastfeeding actually became a joy. But then one morning I woke up feeling terrible. I thought it was flu, but as the day progressed my left breast became blotchy and tender. I had a temperature, and my breast was so sore that I had to bite on a face flannel to cope with the pain shooting through me when Jamie fed.

A midwife confirmed that I had mastitis, and said I should carry on feeding regularly as this would help. But, in case I was infected, I should see my doctor as soon as possible as I'd need antibiotics. I wished I'd seen him earlier in fact, because by the time I'd started my treatment Jamie had had blood on his mouth after feeding from one of my sore, cracked nipples, and I was in such tremendous pain that I had to have a glass of wine to relax me before I attempted to feed him.

The next time I got mastitis I was able to recognize the symptoms straightaway, and I got treatment before it had a chance to become a problem.

Engorgement

The increased blood flow to your breasts can make them hot, swollen and hard. Cold compresses will help bring the swelling down, and washing your breasts in warm water before a feed will help the milk to flow quicker, which will also help. The medical herbalist, Carol Rogers, recommends adding one drop of essential oil of rose, geranium, lavender or camomile to the water you use, but be careful to wash off all the oil before you feed the baby.

Mastitis

A few women are affected by mastitis, and it is one of the downsides to breastfeeding. Fortunately the condition doesn't usually last too long providing you are quick to recognize the symptoms and to get the treatment you need.

Mastitis can cause similar symptoms to a blocked duct and may be non-infective, caused by milk leaking from the blocked duct and surrounding tissue. Infective mastitis also has the same symptoms – but you may feel iller. The infection may be caused by a germ in your baby's nose which is transmitted to your breast. Follow the same guidelines for treating engorgement and blocked ducts, and see your doctor about antibiotics (but remember to mention that he needs to choose an antibiotic suitable while you are breastfeeding).

If tests show that your milk is infected, you may have to stop feeding temporarily from the affected breast. Your midwife or health visitor will be able to give you advice about the best way to go about this.

If you are interested in homeopathic treatment for your problem, discuss the following remedies with a practitioner: Belladonna (deadly nightshade) – for inflamed and tender breasts and over-production of breast milk; Bryonia (wild hops) – for breast pain that worsens with the slightest movement but is eased with rest; Hepar sulphuris (Hahnemann's calcium sulphide) – for a single area of mastitis; or Phytolacca (poke root) – for a hard and lumpy breast, and tender glands in the armpit.

Sore nipples

This problem is most common in the first week or so, as you adjust to breastfeeding. You can help prevent it by expressing a few drops of hindmilk at the end of each feed and smoothing it over the nipple and areola.

If it's too late for prevention and you're already suffering, rub in some calendula cream (as recommended by midwives). The aromatherapy alternative is to rub in a little jojoba oil.

CHOOSING TO BOTTLE FEED

The advantages of bottle feeding include:

◆ Someone else can help with feeds.
◆ You will be free to return to work/lead outside activities while your baby is being looked after by a relative, nanny or partner.
◆ No leaky breasts.
◆ You may want to get your baby into an easy routine, and a bottle allows you to do this as the baby is being fed roughly the same amount at regular intervals throughout the day.

SUSIE'S STORY

Laura had nothing but breast milk for the first four months of her life, then I started to introduce pureed vegetables and fruit. I was due to go back to work when she was seven and a half months old, and I was determined to cut the breastfeeding down by this time.

I'd had enough, by then, of wearing a bra in bed, and waking up every morning with big soggy pads. I didn't feel at all sexy, and my breasts were completely out of bounds to my partner. I'd given Laura a healthy start in life and now I wanted my body back, so I cut down the feeds to one at night and one in the morning – and stopped feeding altogether when Laura was nine months old.

Changing from Breast to Bottle

For various reasons many women don't want to breastfeed at all, or wish to switch to bottle feeding after a few weeks. If you're going to bottle feed you'll need about six bottles and teats, and the equipment with which to sterilize these. This equipment doesn't have to be expensive or complicated. You can adequately sterilize bottles by submerging them in a saucepan of boiling water for ten minutes and leaving them there until they're needed. Make sure that bottles are thoroughly washed before you sterilize them, and carry on sterilizing your baby's bottles, cups and dummies until he's a year old.

When you've found a formula milk which your baby is happy with, stick with it rather than swapping brands frequently.

Bottle feeding is something your partner can share with you. Especially if he is working long hours, he may welcome the chance to spend some time with the baby in the evening, while you catch up on your rest.

A typical routine for a newborn baby is to give six 100 ml (3½ oz) bottles per day (though individual babies may need more or less). Providing you have a fridge to store them in, you can make these up in one batch and store the day's supply. If you don't have a fridge you will have to make up the feeds as you need them, because harmful bacteria are quick to grow. And, as a general rule, you should use a feed within an hour of taking it from the fridge (or sooner if you are in very hot conditions).

Making Up Feeds

Sterlize the bottles, and use sterile plastic tongs to handle the teats so as to avoid bacterial infection.

Boil fresh water for the feeds – don't reboil water left in the kettle. Leave it to cool for at least ten minutes, then pour into the bottles, or a measuring jug with a lid. Mix up your feed by adding the powdered milk to the water, not the other way round, and using a ratio of one level scoop (a measuring scoop is provided with the formula) to each fluid ounce of boiled water (round up to 4 oz for a 3½ oz feed).

Allow the feeds to cool completely, and store in the fridge for up to 24 hours.

When you feed your baby, warm the milk by standing the bottle in a bowl of freshly boiled water for a few minutes. Test the temperature on the inside of your wrist before offering it to your baby.

If your baby starts a bottle but doesn't finish it, the same feed can be offered within half an hour of first starting it. After this time, throw away the feed and offer a fresh one.

Always wash your hands before making up feeds and before feeding.

MONITORING YOUR BABY'S HEALTH

Most parents quickly notice changes in their baby's behaviour and condition which may indicate illness. If you're worried, always call your doctor for advice as very young babies can deteriorate rapidly.

Typical Symptoms

- ◆ **The baby's 'not himself'** – for example he's not responding normally, or he's sleeping more than usual.
- ◆ **He has a fever** – see pp.206–207 for ways of reducing his temperature. If the baby cools down and seems otherwise well (i.e. he's feeding and isn't distressed) keep a watch in case his condition changes. If he stays feverish, his arms and legs feel cold, or he has other symptoms, call a doctor immediately.

- **He's not feeding** – call your doctor if your baby takes less than usual for several feeds, or doesn't wake up for feeds at usual times.
- **Vomiting** – especially if it shoots out (projectile vomiting), is green or contains blood, is a sign that you should contact your doctor. See below.
- **Diarrhoea** can occasionally be caused by something you've eaten if you're breastfeeding, but if it continues for several nappy changes, or there are other symptoms, contact your doctor.
- **Dry nappies** may indicate dehydration if a baby hasn't passed urine – especially if he's been sick or had diarrhoea.
- **Difficulty in breathing or feeding** – call your doctor.
- **Persistent coughing** – in spasms, with or without vomiting.
- **Blue lips or tongue** after a bout of coughing or breathing difficulties – seek urgent medical attention.
- **Fits (convulsions)** – all babies jerk their limbs once or twice if they're startled, and this is quite normal. But jerking for a longer period may be a sign of a fit or convulsion, needing urgent medical attention.
- **Screaming** – if the baby is inconsolable and your attempts to feed him, change his nappy and make his clothing more comfortable have no effect, ask your doctor for help.
- **A head injury** followed by vomiting, floppiness or sleepiness should be checked by your doctor.
- **A rash** – most rashes are caused by mild infections, but if your baby seems unresponsive or very irritable, see your doctor.
- If your baby is clearly ill but your doctor cannot come at once, take the child to your nearest **hospital accident and emergency department.**

Why Are Babies Sick?

Posseting is completely harmless, and happens when your baby brings back the last bit of his feed – especially if he's been jiggled around when his stomach's full.

Oesophageal reflux (or hiatus hernia), where the valve inlet to the stomach from the oesophagus isn't working properly, causes the stomach's contents to travel back up towards the mouth. It can be a problem if your baby can't keep anything down, but it helps if you feed him while he's tilted upright in his baby chair, and give him an hour to digest his meal before laying him down. Your doctor can prescribe a medicine if the problem continues.

Projectile vomiting can be a sign of pyloric stenosis, which means that an overgrown muscle at the lower end of the stomach is constricting the opening between the stomach and intestine. The milk has difficulty leaving the stomach to go into the intestine, and is vomited instead. Your baby may need an operation, but it's straightforward, with such a rapid recovery that most babies start feeding normally within hours of surgery.

Gastroenteritis or another infection will cause vomiting combined with other signs of illness: diarrhoea, floppiness, and your baby not being himself. Sometimes he'll have a temperature too, but don't wait for your baby to become hot before seeking help. Vomiting and diarrhoea cause very rapid dehydration, and babies can become dangerously ill within just a few hours.

Allergy to cow's milk or intolerance of gluten (coeliac disease) when the baby is starting on solids can also cause vomiting, but there will usually be other symptoms, such as slow weight gain and smelly nappies. Your health visitor can suggest alternatives to cow's milk and give advice on a special coeliac diet.

WHEN TO TAKE ACTION

- If your baby has a temperature.
- If vomiting is forceful or frequent.
- If your baby has diarrhoea.
- If he doesn't want to feed.
- If he's listless, pale or blue, call an emergency doctor.

Babies' Colds

To stop a baby's cold developing into something more serious such as bronchitis:

- Avoid fluctuating temperatures – don't take him out in the cold unless you have to.
- Use a sling or carry the baby so his face is close to you and not taking in a lot of cold air.
- Raise the head end of the cot mattress slightly to help him breathe more easily.
- Make sure he has plenty to drink so he doesn't become dehydrated.
- Use infant paracetamol to ease symptoms. If taking baby Calpol by spoon makes your baby sick, try droplets (e.g. Infa-drops).
- Call your doctor for advice if you're worried, or the symptoms appear to be getting worse.

Cooling a Baby's Fever

- Keep the air in the room comfortably warm – not too hot, not too cold.
- Lay your baby on your knee and gently remove his clothes, talking calmly and reassuringly.

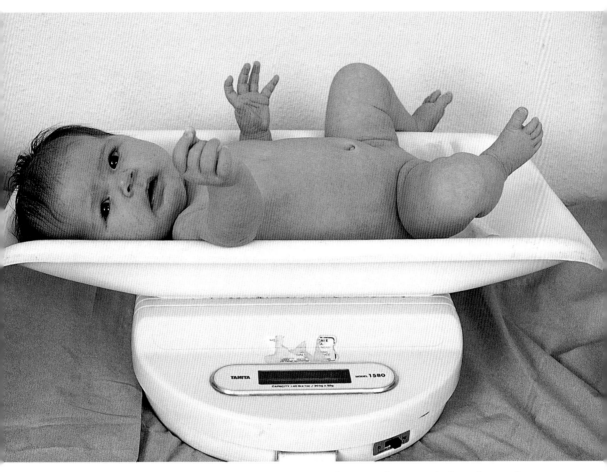

In the first few months your baby's weight gain is likely to fluctuate. Some weeks he will gain about 225 g (8 oz), others he will gain little or no weight at all. This is particularly true of breastfed babies, who control their own intake of milk in various subtle ways.

- ◆ Sponge his body, limbs and face with tepid water – as it evaporates from the skin it will absorb heat from the blood and cool the system.
- ◆ Don't use cold water – it will make the blood vessels constrict and cause less heat to escape, so the baby's temperature will stay high.
- ◆ As the baby cools down, pat him dry with a towel and keep him in a nappy and a cotton sheet.
- ◆ Check him constantly to make sure he's not getting too cold and shivery. If he appears to be getting cold, put some more light clothes on him.
- ◆ If his temperature begins to climb again, repeat the sponging with tepid water.

Meningitis and Septicaemia

Both these conditions are caused by the same bacteria. Meningitis is a dangerous and currently high-profile disease that all mums are naturally concerned about, so it's best to know what to look out for. The classic symptoms of meningitis are:

◆ a rash (although this isn't always present).
◆ drowsiness.
◆ fever and vomiting.
◆ severe headache.
◆ stiff neck.
◆ dislike of bright lights.

But not everyone develops these symptoms, so if in doubt call your doctor or local hospital. Meningitis progresses rapidly and needs urgent medical attention.

In septicaemia, a type of blood poisoning, toxins are released into the blood. These break down the walls of the blood vessels, allowing blood to leak out under the skin. This leaking causes the characteristic rash of purple bruises, blood blisters or blood spots, and reduces the amount of blood reaching vital organs such as the liver and kidneys.

TUMBLER TEST FOR SEPTICAEMIA

Press a glass tumbler firmly against the rash. If it doesn't fade and remains visible through the glass, seek medical advice immediately.

Cot Death

If a baby dies suddenly and unexpectedly, and there is no obvious reason such as being born prematurely, it is called cot death. In the UK two to three of these tragic deaths occur per thousand babies, usually to those between the ages of one month and one year, with most of them taking place between three and six months. To help your baby avoid this possibility:

◆ current medical advice is to put your baby to sleep on his or her back, which has substantially reduced cot death numbers in the UK.
◆ if your baby sleeps a lot, wake him or her regularly for a drink.
◆ don't smoke anywhere near your baby.
◆ don't let your baby get overheated (no electric blankets, for instance). The ideal temperature for a baby's room is 18 degrees C (65 degrees F).

SEX TALK

Your libido may not be what it was during your recovery from giving birth – and that's entirely to be expected. For at least the first six weeks your body's getting over the trauma of childbirth, and your hormones are adjusting too. Your energy is also in short supply and your nerves are likely to be frayed if you're constantly on red alert for a baby who wakes at the slightest noise.

Breastfeeding can further delay your interest in sex or enhance it. Leaky breasts during lovemaking are a turn-off to some couples and there's also the possibility that breastfeeding is unconsciously satisfying your sexual needs.

There's no right time to begin having sex with your partner again – except that it should be when you feel like it. But surveys have found that most women have started having sex again by twelve weeks after giving birth, and about a third have done so by six weeks.

Generally most couples find that they have sex less than they did before the baby was born. Quite apart from the disruption caused by having to get up so often at night to see to your baby, problems you experience may include:

A more relaxed vagina – you may not grip your partner's penis as tightly as before, but, with time, pelvic floor exercises (see pp.42–43) will help you regain your vaginal tone.

Pain – intercourse after childbirth can really hurt. Especially if you've had an episiotomy or tear, the discomfort may continue even after the stitches have healed. Until the pain eases, try some of the following:

◆ a lubricating cream like K-Y jelly to make your vagina more comfortable.
◆ drinking a little alcohol to help you relax – but not too much, or it will tamper with your sex drive!
◆ different positions, such as side to side or woman on top, to give you more control. Or you could try lying with your legs over the side of a low bed and your feet on the floor, so that he can penetrate you very gently.

Some women find intercourse very painful after childbirth. This is called 'dispareunia' and can be caused by stitches which have been inserted so tightly so that the surrounding tissue has become puffy and swollen. Ask your doctor or midwife to look at the sore area as soon as possible. If the pain is higher, near your cervix, the transverse cervical ligaments may be torn – and it takes time for them to repair themselves. Again, it's important to talk to your doctor about the pain and to let him know exactly where it is occuring.

SIX WEEKS ON

Six-week Check-up for the Mother

What the doctor may be looking for:

- Is your weight returning to normal?
- Are your kidneys working properly? A sample of your urine may be tested.
- Is your blood pressure healthy?
- Have your stitches healed? If you still have any discomfort, tell your doctor now.
- Is your womb back to its normal size?
- Are you still bleeding, or do you have any vaginal discharge?
- How are you feeling emotionally? If you're very tired, low or depressed, discuss this with your doctor.

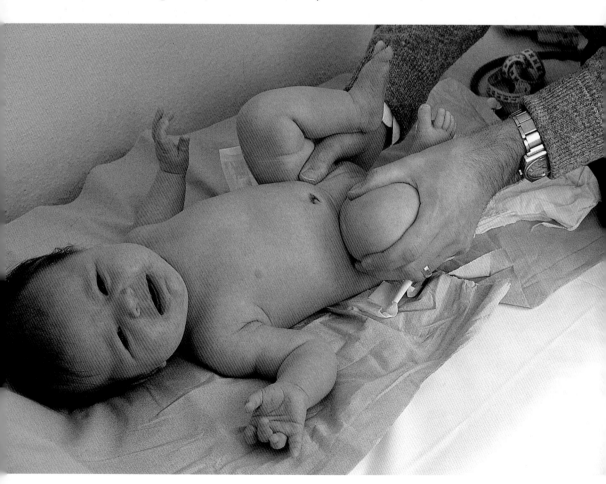

LOUISE'S STORY

The one thing no amount of research can fully prepare you for is the change that the baby brings to his parents' relationship. Bill and I were over the moon during the first month when we were getting used to having little Charlie around. But after that it took a long time to get the dynamic right between the three of us. Books warn that this is difficult – but reading about the problems you have to expect doesn't always help you solve them!

I longed for Bill to come home from work so I could talk to him. But when he got here he was more interested in playing with Charlie, and I sometimes resented that!

Also he wanted to carry on doing the usual weekend things like playing sports – he seemed slower than me to adjust to the difference the baby was making to our lives. And our first big row took place after Bill had taken the day off to accompany me to Charlie's six-week check-up. I thought we'd be spending the whole day as a family – but then I discovered Bill had booked a game of golf with a friend for the afternoon. He didn't get home until really late that evening, and I was absolutely furious!

His argument was that he needed a break too. He was working hard during the week and needed some time for himself. When we talked about it, we could both see each other's point of view – and learned that now we had a baby we had to think much more about each other before making any plans. I suppose that's the biggest step in becoming a family.

Six-week Check-up for the Baby

What the doctor may be looking for:

- Is your baby feeding well?
- Does he have a sleep routine?
- Is he beginning to support his head?
- Does his heart sound healthy? The doctor will listen to it at this check-up.
- Can the baby follow an object with his eyes?
- Does he react to noises? You'll be asked about this now, but tests will be done around eight months to check his hearing.
- Does his hip joint fit properly into the socket? Congenital dislocation of the hips, if detected now, can be treated simply and successfully.

One to two babies per thousand born each year have congenital dislocation of the hips. The exact cause is unknown, although it could be related to hormone changes before birth, or the position of the baby in the uterus.

GETTING BACK INTO SHAPE: EXERCISES YOU CAN DO

The following Pilates (see p.251) exercises are non-jarring, stretching and strengthening techniques (see also p.214). They will help improve your posture and relieve the strain on your shoulders of constantly lifting and carrying your new baby. Set aside twenty minutes three times a week, and you'll really notice the difference.

Warm-up: the Relaxation Position

- Lie on your back, with your legs extended on the floor, arms by your side, and your head resting on a small, flat pillow.
- Bring your knees up to a bent position, one at a time. Your feet should be flat on the floor, hip-width apart.
- Bring your hands to rest on your abdomen, with your elbows open and wide.
- Allow your feet to lengthen and widen so your toes feel long.
- Relax your calf muscles and open your hip joints.
- Soften the front of your pelvis to release your lower back into the floor.
- Try to release your upper back into the floor by softening your breastbone and the front of your shoulders.
- Allow your back to widen out with each breath, so your shoulders melt into the floor.
- Keep your neck long, making sure your jaw isn't clenched.
- Close your eyes, relax your forehead, and observe your breathing without interrupting it.

Navel to Spine – Part One

This exercise will help tone your abdominals.

- Lie on your back with your knees bent, feet hip-width apart and parallel, arms resting on your lower abdomen.
- Have your head on a small, flat pillow, but don't let your pelvis tilt in any direction.
- Breathe in, and, as you breathe out, soften the front of your pelvis, allowing the navel and lower abdominals to hollow out towards your spine.
- Imagine you're lying in a hammock. Hold your abdominals in this hollowed position and feel how your spine lengthens.
- Breathe in and relax.
- Repeat five times.

Navel to Spine – Part Two

This will help tone your abdominals and stretch out your spine.

- Start in the same position as Part One.
- Breathe in, and, as you breathe out, hollow your lower abdominals, drawing your navel back to the spine and lengthening your tailbone away, but keeping it on the floor.
- Still breathing out, slide your right leg away on the floor and take your right arm above your head to touch the floor behind.
- Stretch from your fingertips to your toes, without allowing your back to arch.
- Breathe in as you return your arm and leg to the starting position.
- Repeat on the other side.
- Do five times on each side.

Shoulder Drops

These are good for upper body tension.

- Lie on your back with your knees bent and feet hip-width apart on the floor and flat.
- Keep your neck long, using a small, flat pillow if it helps.
- Raise both arms up to the ceiling, directly above your shoulders.
- Breathe in as you reach one arm up to the ceiling, allowing your shoulder blade to come off the floor.
- Reach through to your fingertips.
- Breathe out as you allow your whole shoulder to release down to the floor.
- Repeat with the other arm, then repeat ten times with each arm alternately.

Leg Lifts

These are good for toning your bottom and thighs and controlling cellulite.

- Lie on your right side in a straight line with your right arm stretched out and your head resting on it.
- Bend your right leg in front of you at the knee – viewed from overhead you'd look like a letter 'h' on its side.
- Use your left arm to support you, and keep lifting your waist off the floor while maintaining the length in your trunk.
- Raise your left leg so that it's in line with your hip, about 15 cm (5 in) off the floor. Don't take the leg behind you.

- Rotate your leg slightly in from the hip and flex your foot towards your face. Breathe out as you slowly lift the leg about 18 cm (7 in), then breathe in and lower it.
- Raise and lower the leg ten times without returning it to the floor. Breathe out as you raise and lower.
- Bend the leg to rest on the bent leg, positioned underneath.
- Turn over and repeat on the other side.

Curl-ups

This exercise will strengthen your tummy muscles, but avoid it if you have neck problems.

- Lie on your back with your knees bent and feet together, flat on the floor, and your knees pressing together.
- Place a tennis ball between your knees and a pillow under your head.
- Squeeze your buttocks.
- Place one hand on the side of your head and the other hand on your abdominal muscles.
- Keep squeezing your inner thighs together throughout the exercise.
- Breathe in, and, as you breathe out, hollow out your lower abdominals, dropping them back to your spine and lengthening the base of the spine. Your tailbone should stay down and lengthen away from you.
- Maintaining the length in the front of your body, slowly lift your head to look at your stomach, gently curling the neck and shoulders, if possible, off the floor.
- Keep the back of your neck long, but don't tuck the chin in. Only go as far as you can keep your stomach hollowed out, then curl back down.
- Don't pull on the neck.
- Breathe in as you slowly curl back down.
- Open your elbow right back to the floor each time you go down.
- Repeat five times, then change hands and do five more.

Pronounced 'pi-lar-tees', the **Pilates method** has been a favourite with ballet dancers for about 70 years, though it's only recently become very trendy, boasting scores of celebrity devotees including Courtney Cox, Madonna and Kate Moss. The exercises are very gentle and can be performed on a mat on the floor. The basic idea is to use the abdomen as a strong anchor from which the rest of the body can be safely stretched and strengthened.

Pilates can help a range of problems, and will also improve your

Use your exercise routine to entertain your baby.

posture (some people claim it adds inches to their height!) and give you narrower hips, trimmer thighs and stronger abdominal and back muscles.

Other stretching methods include:

Method Putkisto – a method of stretching (developed with the help of a chiropractor and a sports doctor), particularly popular with postnatal mothers, which will get you into positions you thought only Olympic gymnasts could manage. After working on one side of the body you will notice the difference in the mirror – your stretched side will be higher than the other. Method Putkisto lengthens the muscles which inevitably become shortened through bad posture, forcing your inner organs into restricted positions. Diaphragm control, at the centre of the technique, improves your breathing, circulation and metabolism so that you feel less tired, gain less fat, and have more energy.

Yoga – now becoming popular with sportsmen, yoga combines stretching exercises with relaxation techniques. It assists organ efficiency and aids digestion, giving you what practitioners call 'an internal work-out', and also strengthens the body against sports injuries. Doing yoga's gentle stretch movements encourages blood circulation and sends more oxygen to your muscles so they can stretch and rotate more easily without the risk of injury. The inner organs – e.g. the kidneys, spleen, ovaries and diaphragm – will be gently massaged to work more fully, giving you a general feeling of wellbeing.

YOUR QUESTIONS ANSWERED

Q: *How do I know my baby's getting enough breast milk?*

A: If the baby's weight gain is steady, his motions are soft and yellow, and he is producing six wet nappies a day without extra fluids, you can be sure he is feeding properly.

Q: *How do I make sure I'm producing enough milk?*

A: Feeding on demand will mean that you tune into your baby's needs and produce the right amount of milk for him. But you can still be quite flexible – wake the baby for part of his feed if you're going out and need to feed him before he's ready. You should also drink to satisfy your thirst (but extra will not help you produce more milk) and make sure you are eating well and regularly.

Q: *Is there anything I shouldn't eat while breastfeeding?*

A: You will be told all sorts of old wives' tales about what you can and can't eat and which foods will make your baby fret. For example, some people say you shouldn't eat tomatoes or spicy foods such as onion and garlic. In fact, this is nonsense. According to the La Leche League which promotes breastfeeding, you can eat as you normally would, but avoid alcohol, and don't take medicine without checking with your doctor that it will not harm your baby.

Q: *How do I go about expressing my milk so the baby can be fed while I'm out?*

A: Expressing milk does take practice, so it's worth starting before you actually need to produce a feed for your baby in your absence. Wash your hands and make sure the pump and any utensils you use are fully sterilized – and, of course, the baby's bottle should also be sterile. The best time to express is first thing in the morning, when your supply is likely to be at its greatest after building up overnight. At the same time feed your baby on one breast, which will stimulate the let-down reflex and make it easier to express from the other breast.

Breast milk can be stored in the fridge for 24 hours, or frozen (in a proper freezer as opposed to the freezer compartment of the fridge) for up to three months. If you do freeze the milk allow it to thaw at room temperature, and never heat or thaw milk in a microwave.

Q: *What's the best way to move my baby on from breast to bottle?*

A: Try to make the change-over slowly. Start by offering your baby a bottle at a lunchtime feed. If he won't take it, try again next day at the same feed. Moistening the teat with a few drops of breast milk may encourage him to take the bottle. Once he's had three lunchtime bottles in a row, replace a second feed with a bottle, and wait another three days before tackling a third feed. Leave the bedtime feed until last. If your baby is over four months old, try a cup.

Q: *I've heard that breastfeeding works as a natural contraceptive. Is this true?*

A: If you are fully breastfeeding and haven't had a period, you're unlikely to conceive in the first ten months. But it can happen – so, unless you're planning to have a second child soon after the first, use contraception from the first time you have intercourse postnatally.

Q: *How soon will my periods start again after I've had my baby?*

A: This depends on whether you're breastfeeding, which suppresses the menstrual cycle (although it's still possible to conceive before your periods have resumed). The exact timing of the first period after giving birth varies among women. Some women who do not breastfeed have a period 28 days after delivery. Others experience a three- or four-month delay. If you're breastfeeding, your periods may resume when you're weaning and giving less breast milk. Or, if you're fully breastfeeding, you may not have a period until you stop even if it is a year or eighteen months after your baby was born.

Q: *Will I be able to use a tampon straightaway?*

A: It's certainly not advisable to use tampons for your postnatal blood loss (because of the risk of infection), and most doctors also recommend that women wait until after the first normal period before using this type of protection. If you find it difficult to hold the tampon in place, it's worth talking to your doctor about specific exercises and instruments to tighten your pelvic floor (these are also discussed in connection with stress incontinence on pp.247–48).

Part 3

A–Z OF
PROBLEMS AND
SOLUTIONS

Anaemia

About 20 per cent of pregnant women suffer from iron-deficient anaemia. Most cases develop around the 20th week, even though you may have been tested for anaemia much earlier in the pregnancy. You are at greater risk if:

◆ you've had excessive morning sickness which has interfered with your nutrition.
◆ you have a multiple pregnancy.
◆ you've had several babies close together.
◆ you haven't been eating properly.

With mild iron deficiency there may be no symptoms, but as the condition deteriorates you may become extremely tired, pale, weak, breathless and faint.

The baby is unlikely to be iron-deficient, even if you are, as his or her nutritional needs are met before yours. But there's a slightly increased possibility that the baby will be small or slightly premature if you don't take iron supplements to make up for your deficiency.

Asthma

Studies have shown that asthmatic women who are under close expert supervision throughout pregnancy have as good a chance of having normal pregnancies and healthy babies as non-asthmatics. However, your pregnancy may change the nature of your asthma. About a third of pregnant asthmatics find their asthma improves, a third notice no change, and the final third (usually those with the most severe cases) find their asthma worsens – usually after the fourth month.

If you have an asthma attack while you are pregnant, treat it with your prescribed drugs to avoid depriving your baby of oxygen. If your medication doesn't work, make sure you get help from your doctor or hospital immediately.

Your asthma will stand a better chance of improving in pregnancy if you have minimal contact with cigarette smoke and take sensible steps to avoid the house dust mite trigger – ideally your house should have bare floorboards and blinds, rather than carpets and curtains, and it should be well ventilated. If you can't avoid the soft furnishings, be sure to clean regularly with one of the dust-sensitive vacuum machines available on the market.

As asthma and other allergies run in families, it's a good idea to breastfeed your baby as this will offer him or her good protection from the disease.

Blighted Ovum

Nobody knows exactly why some women experience a blighted ovum, which means that a pregnancy has started without the formation of its leading player, the fetus. It's thought to be caused by fertilization of a normal ovum by an abnormal sperm, because, in the majority of cases of blighted ovum, the father's sperm count is low and contains more abnormal sperm than usual.

The first signs to you may be that around week 8 of pregnancy you no longer feel pregnant (as hormone levels gradually reduce). Alternatively you may begin to bleed.

It has been estimated that blighted ova constitute as many as 1 in 10 of all human pregnancies. If you've had a previous blighted ovum your doctor may suggest an early scan, at six or seven weeks into your pregnancy, to reveal whether or not a fetus is present. Sadly, a blighted ovum can never develop into a baby, and the only treatment is a D and C (see p.131).

Choriocarcinoma

In about 1 in 20,000 pregnancies, and usually as a result of a hydatiform mole (a benign tumour; see p.230), a malignant tumour develops from the placenta in the uterus. Very rarely it develops after a normal pregnancy, or following an abortion. Occasionally the tumour may not develop until months or even years after the pregnancy.

The first sign may be persistent bleeding. However, some women have no early symptoms and are only diagnosed after the cancer has spread to other parts of the body. If the cancer is suspected, it can be confirmed with ultrasound scanning and measurement of HCG (human chorionic gonadotrophin) levels in your blood and urine.

Untreated, the cancer invades and destroys the walls of the uterus and may spread to the vagina and vulva. Treatment is with anticancer drugs, and nowadays nearly all patients are cured.

CMV

Cytomegalovirus, or CMV, is a common virus which can infect anyone. By the age of forty, 60–70 per cent of the UK population will have had it. But the vast majority won't have had any symptoms, so they won't know they've had CMV. The remainder may experience flu-like symptoms or an illness resembling glandular fever or hepatitis with jaundice. In babies the infection can cause one or more of the following:

◆ hearing loss.
◆ sight problems.
◆ epilepsy.
◆ liver and/or spleen enlargement.

- heart defects.
- cerebral palsy.
- mental retardation.
- brain calcification.

However, of 700,000 births every year in the UK fewer than 2500 babies will be born with CMV, and only a handful of these will be affected. But since there aren't as yet any drugs which deal with this infection it's sensible to take good precautions during pregnancy. CMV is spread through infected saliva and other bodily secretions, so personal hygiene is important for both partners. Also:

- Try to avoid crowds in the coughs-and-colds season.
- Always wash your hands after changing nappies.
- Wear a condom for sex if you're particularly anxious.

Corpus Luteum Cyst

The corpus luteum forms just after ovulation every month, in the space in the follicle left by the recently departed ovum. It produces the hormones progesterone and oestrogen and is programmed by nature to disintegrate in about 14 days, triggering the onset of your period.

In pregnancy the corpus luteum continues to grow and produce the hormones needed to nourish the pregnancy until the placenta takes over. Then, around six or seven weeks after your last period, it begins to shrink and ceases to function around week 10.

But in about 1 in 10 pregnancies the corpus luteum doesn't shrink as expected; instead it develops into a corpus luteum cyst on your ovary. Usually this isn't a problem, but its size will be monitored by ultrasound as a precaution. If it does become unusually large, or threatens to twist or rupture, it may have to be removed. This only happens in about 1 per cent of all corpus luteum cysts, however, and after the 12th week the operation to remove it rarely threatens the pregnancy.

Cytomegalovirus see CMV above.

Deep Vein Thrombosis see Venous Thrombosis on p.250.

Diabetes

Lack of the hormone insulin, which maintains normal amounts of sugar in your blood, can cause these levels to rise. The possible result, diabetes, can create problems for you, and especially your baby.

The hormonal changes in pregnancy increase your blood sugar levels, and most pregnant women produce extra insulin to cope with them.

However, in some women, particularly those who are overweight, this is not effective and the blood sugars start to rise as pregnancy advances.

In some hospitals routine blood tests, including one for blood sugar, may be taken at 28 and 36 weeks. Elsewhere, between the 24th and 28th week a blood test will be taken one hour after you have had a sweet drink.

Those at risk can be identified from their medical history – women who have a family member with diabetes, who have had a previous large baby or have excessive sugar in the urine come into this category. This method is a guide to the advisability of further testing

If either blood tests or medical history suggest high risk, a sugar (glucose) tolerance test will be carried out. If the result is high, diabetes is diagnosed. Getting a diagnosis is important, as raised blood sugar levels in pregnancy are associated with an increased risk of complications, especially to your baby, but treatment reduces these risks. The complications include:

◆ A greater risk of having a large baby, which may cause problems with labour and delivery and increase the chances of having a caesarean or forceps delivery. Large amounts of fluid can also build up around the baby and cause premature labour.
◆ After the birth, the baby is at risk of having too low a blood sugar level. But this is easily recognized, and early feeding prevents any long-term problems. It may mean, however, that the baby will need to be transferred to the special care baby unit for a short time.

Maintaining normal blood sugar levels in pregnancy will reduce the risk of these complications. And most diabetic pregnant women can do so by improving their eating habits. If this doesn't do the trick, you will need a course of insulin injections for the rest of the pregnancy.

If you turn out to be diabetic, a specialist diabetes nurse will show you how to check your own blood sugar levels. You will also be taught how to check your urine at home for the presence of protein and ketones, which are also important factors. You will be expected to improve your diet, with the general aim of keeping the level of sugar in your blood normal and avoiding excessive weight gain.

An acceptable weight gain in pregnancy is 10–12 kg (22–26 lb). If you're overweight the insulin you produce naturally, or inject, is less effective and it will be more difficult for you to maintain a normal blood sugar level. However, you shouldn't attempt actually to lose weight while you're pregnant.

Controlling your blood sugar level is all about the type and amount of food you eat, and the times you eat it.

◆ Avoid sugar and sweet foods.
◆ Go for high-fibre carbohydrates such as pasta, rice and pulses.
◆ Limit the amount of fat you eat.
◆ Eat at regular times.

The labour of a diabetic mother carries no extra risk unless the baby is very large. Providing all is well, and your blood sugars are maintained at normal levels, you'll be allowed to deliver at term. It is unlikely, however, that you'll be allowed to go overdue, and induction at term will probably be recommended. If the baby is a little larger than would normally be expected, or you've needed insulin to regulate your blood sugar levels, you may be induced a week or two early. The potential need for a caesarean is, as already mentioned, slightly greater due to the increased likelihood of a larger baby.

During labour it's important that your blood sugar levels remain normal, so your blood will be checked at two-hourly intervals if you're using diet alone to regulate your condition. If you're insulin-dependent, an intravenous drip will be administered as soon as labour begins, and your blood sugar levels will be checked hourly.

Most women who develop diabetes in pregnancy have perfectly normal blood sugar levels within 12–24 hours after delivery, and insulin treatment can usually be stopped. But some clinics like their patients to take a follow-up glucose tolerance test six weeks after the birth.

Diabetes is very likely to return in any subsequent pregnancies, so try to lose any excess weight before you want another child and tell your doctor or midwife about your past history as soon as you become pregnant.

Eclampsia

This is a more severe version of pre-eclampsia (see pp.243–44). Any woman suffering from pre-eclampsia runs the risk of developing eclampsia, and the fits or convulsions which characterize it.

Fortunately, however, careful monitoring throughout pregnancy now enables pre-eclampsia to be recognized and treated so early that eclampsia itself has virtually disappeared from Britain.

Eclampsia occurs in late pregnancy mostly, but can occur from the 26th week, or may begin in labour or even after delivery. Usually all the signs of pre-eclampsia are also present. These are, notably:

◆ High blood pressure.
◆ Swelling or oedema.
◆ Protein in the urine.
◆ Abnormally high weight gain.

You may also suffer one or more of the following symptoms:

◆ Severe headache, usually in the front of the head, and unresponsive to painkillers.
◆ Visual disturbances such as blurred vision, flashing lights, or even temporary blindness.
◆ Irritability – you're unable to tolerate any disturbance.

◆ Abdominal pain, which feels like severe indigestion in the upper abdomen.

Preventing eclampsia is preferable to treating it, as it remains one of the most dangerous and life-threatening conditions of pregnancy. Even today 1 in 20 women who develop eclampsia don't survive, and 1 in 5 babies die as a result of the mother's condition.

If a woman does suffer eclamptic fits, she will be heavily sedated to prevent further convulsions. It's essential to be in hospital, so any fits experienced at home must be reported to the hospital immediately so you can be sedated and taken to hospital as a matter of urgency. Sometimes the baby of an eclamptic mother will have to be delivered by caesarean or induction. But the labour may start spontaneously and continue easily and rapidly while the mother's convulsions are controlled by sedatives.

Ectopic Pregnancy

A very tiny 1 in 150 pregnancies is ectopic, which means that the embryo develops in the fallopian tube instead of the uterus. The problem occurs when the newly fertilized ovum has not reached the cavity of the uterus by the seventh day after conception and, instead of embedding itself where it should, in the womb lining (endometrium), it settles in the fallopian tube. The embryo can develop for up to eight weeks, but beyond this the fallopian tube is likely to rupture.

The first indication may be pain low down on one side of your abdomen, caused by the fallopian tube contracting in response to the stretching caused by the growing pregnancy. But between weeks 6 and 12 of the pregnancy there's likely to be some bleeding as a result of the fallopian tube rupturing. This is accompanied or preceded by severe lower abdominal pain – you will have to go to hospital immediately so the affected tube can be removed, or the pregnancy removed and the tube repaired. Surgery nowadays is often carried out laparoscopically, which involves a tiny incision and makes for a speedier recovery than the major abdominal surgery which used to be routine.

After one ectopic pregnancy, women naturally worry about having another, especially if the affected fallopian tube has been removed. A second ectopic pregnancy happens to about 10 per cent of women who've previously had one. So, as soon as you know you're pregnant again, you will be checked on ultrasound to make sure the embryo is developing in the uterus, where it should be.

There's a slightly increased risk of ectopic pregnancy if you use a coil for contraception, in which case you may not even suspect that you're pregnant at first. The pain of an ectopic pregnancy can also be confused with that of appendicitis, urinary infection or an ovarian cyst, and the diagnosis may not be made until the pain is extreme.

Faecal Incontinence

Loss of bowel control is an embarrassing and devastating problem, very often caused by accidental damage to the anal muscles and surrounding tissue during childbirth. Sufferers can't control the passage of their bowel contents (stool) and may experience leakages that they're unaware of, or need to go to the loo with extreme urgency and have accidents if they don't get there in time. Another symptom is the inability to stop themselves passing wind.

Damage to the anal sphincter (circular) muscles, which hold back the stools until you get to the loo, is the most common cause of bowel control difficulties that start after childbirth. It happens because the anus is very close to the vagina and, as the baby pushes its way out, it's possible to tear the muscle. Often a tear of this kind can be repaired straightaway. But even after it's been repaired, incontinence can occur. In other cases the damage cannot be seen and may not even become obvious for many years.

Muscle damage is most common after a forceps delivery and episiotomy and if you've had problems after one baby you should get things checked out before planning another pregnancy. Two tests to find out exactly what's happened to the muscle can be done on an outpatient basis at a specialist centre, and take about 30 minutes each. The first checks the nerves and muscles around the anus, and the second looks at the two sphincter muscles (anus and vagina) to see if there's any damage.

Depending on the test results, your doctor may recommend one or more of the following:

◆ Drugs to make the stool firmer and easier to control.
◆ Surgery to repair the sphincter.
◆ Exercises to strengthen weak muscles.
◆ A change of diet to improve your bowel movements.

Fetal Death

It's quite normal to believe at some stage in your pregnancy that your baby has died – usually this is just your anxiety about the baby's safety manifesting itself. And the next movement your baby makes will confirm that everything is OK. You should expect to feel your baby move at least ten times a day.

Occasionally, however, the fetus does die. Usually this is the result of placental insufficiency – because the placenta has either grown inadequately or is diseased, it is no longer able to provide the baby with adequate oxygen and food. Other causes are premature separation of the placenta (placenta abruptio, see p.238), congenital abnormalities of the baby, rhesus disease (see pp.245–46), diabetes (see pp.223–25) and accidents to the umbilical cord.

See also Stillbirth and Neonatal Death on pp.246–47.

Fibroids

These are benign growths which develop, normally in groups, on the wall of the uterus. They are not usually life-threatening, but can grow big (up to about 2 kg/4 lb in weight). Large fibroids may produce some unpleasant symptoms such as backache, pain during intercourse and very heavy periods, at which point treatment becomes necessary and desirable.

Nobody really knows why fibroids occur, but about a quarter of all women develop them, usually before they reach the menopause. Fibroids are more likely in childless women and those who've had children late in life, and they're also more common in younger black women than younger white women – though the reasons for these strange facts are not known.

It's possible to have fibroids and yet go through an uneventful pregnancy and delivery. But some fibroids do cause complications by distorting the uterus and other pelvic organs. Large fibroids may be responsible for premature labour – but they would have to be at least 10 cm (4 in) in diameter to have this effect. They may also lead to excessive bleeding after delivery, so if you're aware of the fibroids' presence steps will be taken to prevent a haemorrhage at this stage (see below).

A very large fibroid can force the baby into an awkward position in the womb. Usually this is resolved naturally before the onset of labour, but if the baby's presentation doesn't correct itself a caesarean may be called for. The fibroid will be removed surgically later – removing it during the caesarean would increase the risk of a haemorrhage.

Fifth Disease

This is one of a group of diseases (including chicken pox) that cause a rash and fever in children. It isn't well known, because its symptoms are mild and often go unnoticed. But caring for a child with fifth disease puts you in the path of infection, and recently this has been linked to a slightly increased risk of miscarriage.

However, most women of childbearing age are already immune because they were infected as children. It's very unusual to contract the infection in pregnancy.

Very rarely, fifth disease may lead to an unusual form of anaemia, similar to that in rhesus disease (see pp.245–46). So, if you do contract the infection in pregnancy, you will be closely monitored by ultrasound for any signs of swelling in the fetus, a classic symptom. If found, treatment will probably be necessary.

Haemorrhage – Antepartum

Any bright red vaginal bleeding after the 24th week of pregnancy may be classified as an antepartum haemorrhage and should be reported to your hospital or midwife. The main causes are placenta praevia (see p.239), placenta abruptio (see p.238), an injury or infection from the genital tract (but not from the site of the placenta), or the onset of labour.

Bleeding may also come from erosion of the cervix. This is very common, affecting 75 per cent of all pregnant women.

Until placenta praevia is ruled out you should be in hospital. Usually an ultrasound scan is performed to determine the site of the placenta, and, if it's found to be a safe distance from the mouth of the uterus, an internal examination may be carried out to check for any erosion – a growth of glandular cells in the cervix caused by the increased hormone levels of pregnancy. Sexual intercourse is also ruled out until investigations are complete and the cause of the bleeding found. If it's just a small amount of cervical erosion, you will probably be able to resume all normal activity.

Haemorrhage – Postpartum

Excessive bleeding after delivery of the baby can threaten the mother's life if not stemmed quickly. Thankfully, due to drugs which help the uterus contract and thus stop bleeding, it is rarely fatal these days.

Causes of postpartum haemorrhage include a uterus which, even after a normal delivery, does not contract satisfactorily, allowing bleeding to continue. An injection of ergometrine or syntometrine (syntocinon with ergometrine), often combined with gentle massage, will help the relaxed uterus contract into a tight ball, at which point bleeding should stop.

If the uterus fails to contract and retract, it's most likely to be because it's exhausted after a prolonged labour or because of overdistension by a multiple birth (see pp.236–37) or polyhydramnios (see p.240). A retained placenta (see p.239) may be another cause of postpartum haemorrhage.

Occasionally a very large fibroid (see above) may hinder uterine contractions, which makes haemorrhage more likely. Repeated injections of ergometrine or syntocinon should quell bleeding.

A large tear in the cervix, maybe because of a rapid or forceful labour, or a very large baby, can cause quite severe bleeding. But the cervix can be stitched and this will stop the bleeding.

Infection can cause a haemorrhage right after delivery, or weeks later. Placenta praevia or abruptio placenta before delivery makes postpartum haemorrhage more likely. Very rarely, the cause is a previously undiagnosed bleeding disorder which interferes with the blood's ability to clot.

The symptom of postpartum haemorrhage is any abnormal bleeding after delivery. This means any bleeding that saturates more than one pad an hour for a few hours or is bright red any time from the fourth day after giving birth – especially if it doesn't slow down when you rest. Foul-smelling lochia (see p.192), large blood clots, pain and swelling in the days after delivery also need to be reported to your midwife. In the worst case, a blood transfusion will be needed to replace lost blood.

Hydatiform Mole

Very rarely, a defective egg cell with no nucleus becomes fertilized and begins to develop as if it were a normal pregnancy. This is called a hydatiform mole. There is no embryo, but the placenta develops as if there was – producing pregnancy hormones and making you feel pregnant – until around 8 to 16 weeks, when the body realizes there is something wrong and the mole is miscarried.

In the UK, mole pregnancies occur at the rate of 1 in 1000 registered births. The pregnancy is known to go wrong at the time of fertilization of the egg by the sperm, but we don't yet know why this happens. What results is that the trophoblast – the layer of cells that line the gestational sac – convert into a mass of clear, frogspawn-like vesicles instead of a healthy placenta. Without its placental support system, the fertilized ovum deteriorates.

There are two types of mole. In the 'complete mole' there is no baby at any time; instead the placenta grows as a series of cysts which look rather like grapes (hydatid means 'watery cyst'). The 'partial mole' pregnancy contains a fetus, but the baby cannot survive.

The first sign of a molar pregnancy is usually an intermittent, though sometimes continuous, brownish discharge. Frequently the normal morning sickness of pregnancy becomes abnormally severe.

By the beginning of the second trimester the uterus may be larger than expected and feels doughy rather than firm. No fetal heartbeat can be detected. An ultrasound scan will confirm the absence of a fetus and may also show enlarged ovaries due to high levels of HCG (human chorionic gonadotrophin, one of the hormones which maintain pregnancy), which characterize the condition.

Treatment requires a D and C (see p.131) to remove the contents of the uterus. Because of the risk of mole tissue persisting, growing and spreading, special tests are done after such pregnancies to show whether or not the mole is dying out. In 90 per cent of women affected, HCG levels return to normal and there are no further problems.

It's generally recommended that attempts to conceive again be postponed for a year or two. A subsequent pregnancy will need to be carefully monitored because of the risk of another mole developing.

Hyperemesis Gravidarum

Severe vomiting in pregnancy is called hyperemesis gravidarum. It affects 5–10 in 1000 women and can interfere with your nutrition, fluid and essential mineral balance. Symptoms include:

- ◆ Weight loss.
- ◆ Vomiting several times a day.
- ◆ Being sick for a number of days.
- ◆ Feeling weak, tired and unable to work.

- ◆ Looking grey and emaciated.
- ◆ Having headaches caused by dehydration.

Hyperemesis was once fatal, but the advent of the intravenous drip changed all that. If you can't keep anything down, even sips of water, you may have to go into hospital to be rehydrated on a saline drip containing glucose, drugs to stop you vomiting, and possibly vitamins to correct any deficiencies resulting from your condition. Usually symptoms improve within 24 hours. As your attacks of vomiting decrease you'll be given a liquid diet; when you can tolerate this you'll be moved on to semi-liquids, and eventually food. Once you're eating and keeping your food down, you'll be able to go back home.

It's important to be sure that vomiting is due to pregnancy alone. You may be offered an ultrasound to check you haven't got a molar pregnancy (see Hydatiform Mole, above) or multiple pregnancy (see pp.236–37).

Hypertension

Blood pressure is the force of blood pumping around your body. It is measured in your upper arm with an inflatable cuff and recorded as two numbers. The first and higher of them shows the pressure when your heart beats; the second, lower figure shows the pressure between beats.

There are variations in blood pressure from one person to another and also changes throughout the day, depending on what you are doing. An average pressure of 110/70 or 120/80 is common, but yours may be slightly higher or lower and still be completely normal for you.

Your midwife will discover your usual blood pressure at your first antenatal check, and it will be checked at every subsequent appointment. This is because raised blood pressure can be an early sign of a pregnancy illness called pre-eclampsia (see pp.243–44). She will also check it between appointments if you feel unwell.

It's common for blood pressure to fall around the middle of pregnancy, then return to normal in the last few weeks. If it keeps on rising beyond your normal level, you may be getting pre-eclampsia and will need extra checks. There is no cut-off point between normal and high blood pressure, but a reading of 140/90 or more would usually give cause for concern.

Incompetent Cervix

Having an 'incompetent cervix' means that the cervix, which should remain closed until labour starts, has become weakened. As a result the weight of the fetus may cause it to begin to open around the 12th week of pregnancy, when it should be staying closed until you go into labour. Cervical incompetence is normally suspected if a woman has had two or more miscarriages after the 14th week of pregnancy, and about one in five women who have recurrent miscarriages have cervical incompetence.

Ultrasound scanning or an internal examination may show the consultant that the cervix is incompetent. If so, during the fourth month of pregnancy you can have the cervix stitched closed. Under either epidural or general anaesthetic a stitch is tied around the cervix like a purse string. It is left in place until the end of the pregnancy and then cut so that you can deliver the baby normally.

Incontinence see Faecal Incontinence on p.227, and Stress Incontinence on pp.247–48.

Infertility

The various causes of infertility are discussed in Chapter 1. The treatments available depend on your own particular reason for not being able to conceive.

A Problem with your Partner?

There may be various problems and shortcomings with your partner's sperm. Each condition has its own treatment.

Donor insemination: if your partner is not producing enough good-quality sperm, you can be treated with a sample of sperm from a donor.

Success rate: 5 per cent per treatment cycle.

Intra-cytoplasmic sperm injection (ICSI): if your partner produces quality sperm but the quantity is low, single sperm can be isolated and injected into individual eggs, then inserted straight into your womb.

Success rate: 30 per cent per treatment.

Intra-uterine insemination (IUI): the most active sperm is collected and injected into the womb on the day of ovulation.

Success rate: 30 per cent over six to eight months of treatment.

Struggling Sperm

Your doctor may offer to collect a sample of your mucus, a few hours after intercourse on the day of ovulation. This will be checked to see whether the sperm are able to move normally through your mucus.

Gamete intra-fallopian tube transfer (GIFT): the egg and sperm are placed in the fallopian tube using laparoscopy, bypassing the cervix.

Success rate: 25 per cent per cycle.

Intra-uterine insemination may be offered, as above.

Are You Producing Eggs?

Blood tests can check whether or not you're ovulating. An ultrasound scan or biopsy of the womb lining may be necessary to pinpoint the cause.

Fertility drugs: clomiphene (Clomid) tablets can restore ovulation but can only be used for six cycles of treatment. If you still don't ovulate you may be offered more powerful injectible fertility drugs.

Success rate: About a third of women get pregnant with clomiphene.

Keyhole surgery to the ovaries avoids the need for drugs.

Success rate: restores regular ovulation in 65 per cent of cases.

Are Your Fallopian Tubes Blocked?

Damage to the fallopian tubes can prevent conception taking place. Tests will tell your doctor whether there's a total or partial blockage.

Keyhole surgery can treat mild disease of your tubes, but if the damage is severe you'll need IVF.

In-vitro fertilization (IVF) was developed as a treatment for blocked tubes but is now used for most forms of infertility. Under general anaesthetic you'll have your eggs collected with a laparoscope – a long fibre optic tube inserted through a small incision made near the navel. The eggs are then fertilized in the laboratory, after which a maximum of three embryos are placed in the cavity of the womb.

Success rate: 20 per cent chance of the embryos surviving.

If No Problem Can Be Found

About 28 per cent of couples are told they're infertile with no obvious cause because they haven't conceived after two years of trying. But 80 per cent of couples who've been trying for three years are likely to conceive in the following eighteen months, and even if you've been trying for five years without success there's still a 30 per cent chance you'll conceive without treatment.

ALTERNATIVE TREATMENTS FOR INFERTILITY

Aromatherapy has been used successfully in the treatment of both male and female infertility.

For female infertility, rose oil is recommended for regulating the reproductive system; geranium regulates the menstrual cycle; while bergamot balances hormones. For male infertility thyme, cumin, sage, clary sage and basil are all recommended.

Cranial osteopathy (see p.101) can be particularly effective for women with fertility problems as it can help the hormone-producing pituitary gland to function properly.

Herbal medicine: Teas and tinctures can restore the regularity of the menstrual cycle and improve the tone and strength of the reproductive system. They may improve the male reproductive system too, and will certainly benefit both partners' general health and wellbeing.

Homeopathic treatments are tailored to meet the needs of the practitioner's 'picture' of a patient's health problem, but there are remedies to treat both male and female infertility. For example, sepia or pulsatilla may be prescribed to strengthen a woman's reproductive system; and either sex may be treated with tin, iron or calcium for a chemical imbalance.

Hypnotherapy has proved successful in treating unexplained infertility, and can also treat spasmodically blocked fallopian tubes by removing the woman's anxieties and enhancing her self-esteem.

Reflexology has a particularly good record in treating infertility, especially in women, although it can be useful for both partners when stress is a factor.

IUGR

Intra-uterine growth retardation is diagnosed when the fetus is not growing as rapidly as it should. Suspicions may be raised at an antenatal visit when the 'height of fundus' is checked and found to be inconsistent with the age of the pregnancy – for example, if you are 28 weeks pregnant, but your height of fundus is that of 26 weeks.

IUGR is more common in first pregnancies and fifth and subsequent ones, and also among women who are under 17 or over 34. The cause is that the uterus is not adequately nurturing the growing baby. This may be because of illness in the mother, poor nutritional status or placental insufficiency (see pp.239–40).

If the condition remains undiagnosed the baby will be born 'small for dates', but once identified medical care may reverse the problem. Your baby's growth and health will be closely monitored via ultrasound and fetal heart monitoring, and you will be advised about lifestyle and dietary changes including giving up smoking and drinking. Occasionally, if you have an IUGR baby who is failing to thrive, your delivery may be brought forward if doctors think he stands a better chance of survival outside the womb.

Even when prevention of IUGR and treatment of the condition are unsuccessful and a baby is born smaller than normal, his or her chances of survival and even excellent health are nowadays increasingly good. And low birth weight babies often catch up with their peers.

Listeriosis

The bacteria *Listeria monocytogenes*, found in some unpasteurized cheeses and cook-chill foods, may give rise to a mild, flu-like illness, which, although not serious in itself, can lead to miscarriage or stillbirth. But the condition is extremely rare, occurring in only 1 in 20,000 live and stillbirths, and can be avoided (see p.37).

Miscarriage

The spontaneous loss of a baby at any time up to the 24th week of pregnancy is known as a miscarriage (after 24 weeks it becomes a stillbirth). This experience, which leaves women feeling lonely and bereft, is particularly upsetting when doctors are unable to explain exactly why the miscarriage occurred.

Causes

It is often difficult to pinpoint the exact cause, but the possibilities include, in the first 8 weeks, ectopic pregnancy (see p.226); and, in the first 12 weeks, blighted ovum (see p.222). More than 20 per cent of pregnancies end in miscarriage in the first 12 weeks.

In the first 16 weeks, the following may be responsible:

Hormonal problems: high levels of luteinizing hormone (LH), particularly likely if you have polycystic ovaries (a hormone imbalance), can increase the likelihood of miscarriage. Daily urine tests will detect a high level of LH, and treatment can be prescribed to prevent too much being secreted.

Low levels of either progesterone or HCG (human chorionic gonadotrophin), the hormones which help maintain a pregnancy, may be the cause.

Incompetent cervix (see pp.231–32).

Hydatiform mole (see p.230).

After 16 weeks, the causes are likely to be:

Fibroids: (see p.228).

An irregular-shaped uterus can mean that there isn't enough room for the baby to grow. This can result in miscarriage as the baby gets bigger, often between 14 and 28 weeks. It may be possible for a surgeon to improve the shape of your uterus for a future pregnancy. However, many doctors will instead encourage you to hang on to the next pregnancy by taking plenty of bed rest and possibly medication to help relax the muscles of your uterus as the baby grows.

Is It a Miscarriage?

Spotting or bleeding – anything from a brownish discharge to a period-like loss – are early signs of miscarriage, but neither symptom means that a miscarriage is inevitable. You may also experience a period-like cramp or backache, and loss of the morning sickness or breast tenderness which first told you you were pregnant. But only 1 in 10 women will go on to lose their baby. In some cases even heavy bleeding may settle down and stop, and a scan may show that the pregnancy is still developing normally.

After a Miscarriage

Following a miscarriage you may have a D and C to clear out the womb thoroughly. Your likelihood of going through a successful pregnancy next time round is slightly lower if you've had one miscarriage, but most women do go on to have a healthy pregnancy without any treatment.

Coping with the Loss of Your Baby

Every couple copes differently with miscarriage. For some, the only way of coming to terms with what has happened is to see the baby (if the miscarriage took place late enough in the pregnancy for this to be possible), to hold the child and to keep a photograph. Naming the baby and holding a memorial service gives him or her a place in the family. This is vital for many parents and, with an increasingly sympathetic hospital service, usually possible nowadays.

Others have no desire to see the baby they've lost, but will find some other way of putting their miscarriage into perspective. Even so, most women and many partners need time to grieve. This process will involve feelings of sadness, anger, depression, jealousy of other women with babies, loneliness, tiredness, feelings of guilt and failure, and a loss of interest in everyday life and can be particularly strong around the time the baby would have been born.

Expressing your feelings is important. Bottling up your emotions can make things worse – and sometimes feelings return long after you thought you'd dealt with them. The Miscarriage Association (see p.252) will give the kind of support you need for as long as you need it, and all volunteer contacts have had experience of miscarriage.

Multiple Pregnancy

Approximately 1 in every 73 pregnant women deliver twins annually in the UK – that's around 10,000 sets of twins, and the number has increased substantially since about 1980. Infertility treatment is partly responsible, making multiple pregnancies more likely. The rate of triplet births has also gone up – 317 sets were born in the UK in 1995.

If you're told you're expecting twins it's a good idea to meet, as soon as possible, other couples who've had twins. They will be able to give you some advice on what to expect in the next year.

In a twin pregnancy your hormone levels are much higher and you carry more fluid than in a single pregnancy. Your body changes are more noticeable and you're more likely to have greater discomfort due to sheer size. With one baby your womb reaches your ribcage by the 36th week. With twins this happens earlier – often by the 32nd week. This can mean that you slow down, and feel much more tired than many of your friends who are expecting single babies. Pay good attention to the advice in Chapters 2, 3 and 4 on coping with heartburn and on looking after your diet and posture, which will help relieve pain as far as possible.

The average length of a twin pregnancy is 37 weeks, compared to 40 weeks for a single pregnancy. Most twins are born within a week or two either side of this date, which means some are premature and need special care in hospital until they reach a good weight. Premature labour can be a problem with multiple pregnancies.

Try to get as much rest as possible from 25 weeks, and especially between 30 and 34 weeks. Some consultants routinely admit mothers from 30 weeks to try to reduce the risk of prematurity though research has shown this does not affect outcome.

See the advice on forceps/ventouse deliveries (p.184) and caesareans (pp.185–87), as these eventualities are more likely with a twin birth. Twins are usually delivered by the most senior and experienced staff, and there are likely to be several experts present in the delivery room with you. Most are there to help, but some are there to learn. If you don't like the idea of extra people watching, let the staff know in advance.

The best position for twins to arrive is for both to be head (vertex) first. But often one twin will be head first and the other breech (buttocks first), in which case a caesarean may be advised. If you don't want a caesarean, discuss this with a good midwife or obstetrician.

Obstetric Cholestasis

Although quite rare, obstetric cholestasis could account for a significant proportion of unexplained stillbirths. An abnormality of liver function, probably due to the high steroid load of pregnancy, it results in a build-up of bile acids and this is what causes the condition's characteristic skin itch. Some itching is normal in pregnancy, centring on the breasts and abdomen. But with obstetric cholestasis, the itching starts on the arms and legs before moving in more centrally. Sufferers tend to be more disturbed by it at night, and will use anything – hairbrushes are common – to scratch themselves to bits. You might also notice that you pass dark urine and even have some jaundice, but itching is by far the major symptom.

Except in very extreme cases, there is not much risk to the mother. But the baby can be stillborn – especially, although it is not known why, if the birth takes place after 38 weeks of pregnancy.

If you suspect you have the symptoms, make sure your doctor or midwife runs a liver function blood test for bile salts. If your suspicions are confirmed, treatment with ursodeoxycholic acid will turn the condition round and stop the itching within a couple of days. This drug is not licensed for use by pregnant women in the UK because it has never been officially tested on them, but no problems have been recorded and it can be given with the patient's consent.

Ovarian Cysts

These abnormal, fluid-filled swellings in the ovaries are very common, but nearly always benign (non-cancerous). Many disappear without treatment, but some have been known to grow up to an extraordinary 50 cm (20 in) in diameter. The larger they become, the more pain and swelling they cause as they press on other organs. Usually it is possible to have the cyst removed without damage to the ovary.

If a large ovarian cyst (more than 6 cm/2 in) is found in early pregnancy it will be removed at the earliest opportunity, to avoid the risk of twisting which, in later pregnancy, could cause your health to deteriorate rapidly. The operation can cause a miscarriage, but this is rare, and the risk is much less than that to the mother and her baby of a twisted cyst later on.

Ovarian Hyperstimulation Syndrome

Very rarely, as a result of fertility drugs, a potentially life-threatening condition known as ovarian hyperstimulation syndrome (OHSS) develops. It's caused by the ovary producing large numbers of follicles – sometimes as many as eighty as opposed to the normal one or two – in response to the drugs given. The side-effects can be alarming. Symptoms range from abdominal pain and marked ovarian enlargement in the less severe cases (3–5 per cent of women undergoing fertility treatment) to the severe form, which affects up to 23.3 per cent of such women.

Severe OHSS results in fluid from the follicles collecting in the abdomen – as much as 65 litres (14 gallons) has been recorded. This leads to weight gain, difficulty in breathing, a fall in blood pressure, fluid in the lungs and an abdomen severely swollen by all the fluid it contains. The woman also becomes dehydrated and may have problems with her essential mineral balance. Her blood will be more concentrated and therefore liable to clot too readily. There's a risk of thromboembolism – a blockage in a blood vessel caused by a broken-off piece of blood clot – and heart failure.

With her ovaries having grown to as much as 8–10 cm (3–5 in) when their normal size is 3 cm (1 in) there's a real risk of rupture. Any examination will therefore have to be carried out by very gentle ultrasound alone. Very occasionally the ovaries have to be removed to control a haemorrhage as a result of a rupture.

Ovum, Blighted see Blighted Ovum on p.222.

Placental Problems

Placenta Abruptio

This is an extremely rare condition in which the placenta becomes prematurely separated from the uterus. Responsible for about 1 in 4 cases of bleeding in late pregnancy, it's more common in older mothers who've had babies before, and in those who smoke, have hypertension, have been taking aspirin late in pregnancy, or have had a previous problem with abruptio placenta. Occasionally, though, a short umbilical cord or an accident may cause the separation.

If the separation is small the amount of blood loss may be similar to a period – but there may be no bleeding at all. Bed rest for a few days should be enough to stop the bleeding, and, with luck and within reason, you'll be able to resume many of your normal activities. A moderate separation causes heavier bleeding with severe abdominal pain from strong uterine contractions, and both mother and baby may show signs of blood loss.

When more than half the placenta separates from the wall of the uterus the symptoms are similar to those of a moderate separation, but more severe. This is an emergency situation for both mother and baby. But with prompt medical attention, including transfusions and immediate delivery, virtually all mothers and over 90 per cent of their babies survive the trauma.

Placenta Accreta

In this condition the placenta grows into the deeper layers of the uterus wall, becoming so firmly attached that it will not separate during the third stage of labour. This is most likely if your uterus wall is already scarred from previous deliveries or caesareans.

In most cases the placenta must be removed surgically to stop the bleeding. Very occasionally, a hysterectomy will become necessary.

Placenta Praevia

The placenta should normally be situated in the upper part of the uterus, usually on the posterior wall. Occasionally, however, and often due to scarring of the uterus wall, the fertilized ovum can't implant where it is expected to, and does so in the lower part of the placenta.

A scan at 18 weeks may reveal that the placenta is low-lying, but this doesn't mean you have placenta praevia. Many placentas lie low early on, but by the end of the pregnancy, when the wall of the uterus has stretched and enlarged, they are usually in the right place in the upper part of the uterus.

Only 6 per cent of low-lying placentas turn out to be lying over the cervix, meaning vaginal delivery will be impossible.

Given a diagnosis of placenta praevia you may have to remain in hospital, or take supervised bed rest, until delivery. This is chiefly because of the risk of heavy bleeding before and during labour, which will need prompt treatment.

Placenta – Retention

Usually the placenta separates and is delivered spontaneously a few minutes after the baby is born. But in about 1 per cent of deliveries the placenta doesn't separate and is called a retained placenta. Its presence prevents the uterus from contracting after the birth, which increases the risk of a haemorrhage – so removing it becomes a matter of urgency. This can be done manually, or by a D and C (see p.131). But very occasionally, if the placenta has grown into the wall of the uterus (see Placenta Accreta above), a hysterectomy may be the only option.

Placental Insufficiency

A healthy placenta is vital for a healthy baby, as this is essentially his or her lifeline in the uterus. The placenta reaches full maturity around 32–34 weeks of pregnancy, and afterwards starts to becomes more inefficient. The process is very gradual, however, so that even at 40–42 weeks it can still provide the baby with all his or her needs.

Two types of placental insufficiency may arise during the pregnancy. The first happens early, when the placenta may not produce enough hormones to keep the pregnancy going. This results in miscarriage (see pp.234–36). The second happens later in pregnancy when the placenta fails to provide for the baby's needs, resulting in IUGR (see p.234) and putting the baby's life at risk.

Polyhydramnios

Most pregnant women carry about 1 litre (1¾ pints) of amniotic fluid at term. But more than 2 litres (3½ pints) is a sign of polyhydramnios, a potentially dangerous condition but one which only occurs in about 3 per cent of pregnancies.

Acute polyhydramnios – rapid enlargement of the uterus, so that you suddenly look three months more pregnant than you did a week earlier – is rare and invariably starts around the 24th week of pregnancy and must be reported to your midwife or hospital urgently. Treatment is not always successful and premature delivery may be unavoidable.

Chronic polyhydramnios is usually discovered around the 30th week of pregnancy when the uterus is much larger than expected for dates. It's caused by the vast increase of fluid in the uterus, but there's usually no pain until the uterus is so large that its size causes discomfort.

Causes include:

◆ twin pregnancy.
◆ diabetes.
◆ pre-eclampsia.
◆ congenital abnormality of the fetus.

However, no cause can be found for more than 50 per cent of women with the condition.

The large quantity of fluid in the uterus predisposes you to an early labour – best avoided by taking plenty of bed rest. During labour you'll need extra-careful monitoring as your uterus is distended, rendering contractions inefficient and increasing the likelihood of a prolonged labour and even a forceps delivery. Continuing weak contractions during the third stage may predispose you to bleeding after delivery, so it's important to accept the syntocinon injection after delivery as it will prevent a post-partum haemorrhage (see p.229).

Having had polyhydramnios doesn't harm your baby, and there's no evidence to suggest it will recur in a later pregnancy.

Postnatal Depression

Surprisingly little information about postnatal depression (PND) is given to expectant mothers. Yet 10 per cent of recently delivered mums go on to develop this unfortunate illness. But remember: all cases of PND do eventually pass and, although some women need psychiatric help and drug therapy, you needn't be separated from your baby during your illness and recovery.

But the taboo which still surrounds PND puts many women off speaking up about their fears that they may be postnatally depressed. And this can make matters worse – they are not getting the support they need, and in effect have to suffer in silence. So how can you recognize the symptoms and deal with them?

After giving birth, many mums experience what are known as the baby blues (see p.189). These feelings of emotional turmoil and unexplained tearfulness are largely due to the sudden hormone changes that occur at this time. If these feelings seem to be getting worse, and the symptoms are becoming more distressing, depression could be developing – although for some women the baby blues pass and then, several weeks after the birth, depression starts to set in. But in fact it isn't always easy to recognize that you're depressed because, since the baby's arrival, everything has changed – and it is easy to blame your symptoms on the new demands on your time and energy. However, it's possible you're suffering from some degree of depression if:

- You feel permanently tired and lethargic.
- Simple household chores seem too much effort.
- You can't be bothered to bath, dress properly or take care with your appearance.
- You suffer from head, neck or back pain.
- You feel generally unwell.
- You're anxious – worrying unjustifiably about the baby and other members of the family.
- You can't cope with meeting friends or even answering the door.
- You experience confusion or panic in everyday situations.
- You can't relax, no matter how much you know you should.
- You develop obsessional thoughts.
- You can't concentrate on books, television programmes or even conversation.
- You sleep badly.
- You lose all interest in sex.

Sometimes the care of a small baby is too much to cope with, and you shouldn't be afraid to ask for help from a relative, friend or neighbour while you recover. Ideally you'll want someone to come and help with the domestic chores, giving you time to rest. Being separated from your baby is likely to exacerbate your depression – and it's unlikely anyone will suggest this when an alternative can easily be found.

Medical Help

If you think you may be suffering from postnatal depression you should see your doctor or Health Visitor. Request a home visit if you can't bear to visit the surgery.

Your doctor may prescribe tranquillizers or antidepressants – antidepressants are preferable as they aren't addictive. They may make you feel drowsy, but this usually wears off as you continue to take the drug. If the drugs make you feel worse in any way, consult your doctor to see if you need a stronger or milder dose, or a different form of treatment.

Although using antidepressants can seem quite frightening, these drugs have an important role to play in buying time for your recovery. They make the unpleasant symptoms fade until they go completely.

Severe cases of postnatal depression may require a stay in hospital while you recover. There are now special mother and baby units where depressed mothers can receive treatment while keeping their babies with them. Your doctor will be able to tell you where these are and to help you get a place in one if it's appropriate for you.

Self-help

During your recovery you can help yourself a lot by believing in your ability to get better. But you need patience, and you have to understand that recovery will take time.

Take as much rest as you can. This is important, because tiredness seems to make depression worse. If you can, try to rest on your bed (sleeping if possible) every day. Avoid late nights and try to get someone else to feed the baby if you can. Some doctors believe that peace and quiet after the birth can help to prevent postnatal depression – so rest must play an important part in your convalescence.

Try not to go without food for long periods, as hypoglycaemia – low blood sugar – can make things worse for a depressed mother. If you're trying to diet to help get back into shape, cut down on sweet, starchy foods and eat plenty of fruit or raw vegetables when you're hungry.

Finding small chores you can easily complete will help occupy you as soon as you are ready, and will take away those feelings of uselessness which come with having nothing to do when you are depressed. This is sometimes known as 'polish your shoes' advice – but, done slowly and steadily, simple tasks can help restore order to your life as well as being therapeutic.

Talk to Someone

Many women with postnatal depression find it helpful talking about their problems with someone who's been through the same thing and who really understands how they feel. Support groups exist specially for mothers who have been postnatally depressed (see Association for Post

Natal Illness and Meet a Mum Association in the Address Book). The women you'll meet there will have had a range of experiences, some of which may make you feel you aren't doing so badly after all. Others will jolt you into understanding that, yes, you do have a problem which deserves all the time and care you can lavish on yourself.

See also Puerperal Psychosis on p.245.

Pre-eclampsia

This condition, sometimes called toxaemia, is the most dangerous of the common complications of pregnancy.

Basically a placental disorder, it's caused by partial failure of the blood supply to the placenta, which has knock-on effects on the mother and baby. The mother's problems are signalled by general circulatory disorder, usually manifested as hypertension (high blood pressure) and/or protein-uria (protein in the urine), with or without oedema (swelling). This leads to complications such as eclampsia (see pp.225–26), kidney failure, brain haemorrhage and a condition of the blood and liver known as HELLP syndrome.

Pre-eclampsia affects 1 in 10 pregnancies overall, and as many as 1 in 5 first pregnancies. Most cases are mild, but one first pregnancy in 100 is so severely affected that there's a serious risk to the life of both baby and mother.

The condition causes the deaths of around a thousand babies in the UK every year – many die as a consequence of extreme prematurity. It also kills between seven and ten mothers a year. But as many as nine out of ten of these maternal deaths are associated with substandard care. It's there-fore essential to understand pre-eclampsia, and to be sure that your pro-fessional carers are also fully aware of the symptoms and treatment.

How You Can Help Yourself

Diagnosing pre-eclampsia early makes it easier to keep you and your baby safe. Treatment can be given to help lower your blood pressure, and your baby may be delivered early. Pre-eclampsia won't get better until after your baby is born, when you should get better quickly.

◆ Keep all your antenatal appointments.
◆ Report bad headaches, flashing lights or spots in front of your eyes to your doctor immediately.
◆ Report pain below your ribs, especially on your right side, to your doctor.
◆ Watch out for any swelling of your hands, face or feet.

Your blood pressure and urine should be checked at every antenatal appointment, and any abnormal findings followed up with more frequent and detailed monitoring. First-time mothers are most at risk, and their risk is increased by:

◆ hypertension, diabetes, kidney disease and (to a lesser extent) migraine.
◆ age – particularly if you're over 35.
◆ short stature.
◆ twin or multiple pregnancy.

Pre-eclampsia can occur for the first time in a second or later pregnancy – particularly after a change of partner. The risk of recurrence after a first attack is 1 in 20, with early onset (before 30 weeks) posing the highest risk. But recurrent pre-eclampsia is often milder than the first attack.

The condition can develop at any time after the 20th week, but is most common in the third trimester. The following symptoms may alert your doctor or midwife to the problem:

Raised blood pressure – usually the level of blood pressure mirrors the severity of the disease, but not always. Moderate or mild hypertension, and very rarely normal blood pressure, have been found in women with severe pre-eclampsia.

Oedema (swelling) – ankle oedema occurs in a high proportion of normal pregnancies, but the oedema of pre-eclampsia tends to be linked with rapid weight gain and swelling of the face and hands.

Proteinuria – this usually appears after hypertension, but it can precede it too. It must therefore never be ignored, and you should question any antenatal check-up at which your urine is not tested.

IUGR – sometimes pre-eclampsia affects the unborn baby before the mother, and growth retardation may be the first sign (see p.234).

Most cases of pre-eclampsia are detected at antenatal check-ups before the symptoms start to show. But you should call your doctor immediately if you experience any of the symptoms listed on p.243.

Because pre-eclampsia is caused by the placenta it doesn't get any better until after the birth, when the placenta comes away. That's why most women with pre-eclampsia have their babies delivered early. However, while you remain pregnant drugs which control high blood pressure can help to prevent complications.

If you have pre-eclampsia in your first pregnancy, you may get it in subsequent pregnancies and should be offered frequent check-ups next time. But you're most likely to have a normal pregnancy.

Premature Babies

In the UK about 7 per cent of pregnancies end in a premature birth (before 37 weeks). The survival rate of premature babies has improved tremendously in recent years, but there are still many babies who die because they are born before their systems can cope with life outside the womb.

Sometimes these babies also have congenital malformations which make it impossible for them to survive.

The more premature a baby is at delivery, the less chance he or she has of surviving and growing into a healthy child. Prematurity is the most common cause of babies dying in their first week of life, and premature babies are at particular risk of complications such as:

- respiratory distress syndrome, due to immature lungs.
- bleeding of the fragile blood vessels in the brain (intraventricular haemorrhage).
- infections – their immune systems are immature and they may be overwhelmed by an infection very quickly.

Being small for dates increases the risk to a premature baby.

Nobody knows why some premature babies survive and others do not. Some babies seem well at birth, but then become very ill. Because their systems are so small and fragile premature babies can go through rapid ups and downs, recovering and becoming ill again very fast.

Improved technology has meant that some severely handicapped babies can be kept alive, although their quality of life is likely always to be poor. And in some ways the technological innovations in neonatal care have made parents' and doctors' decisions about tiny babies more difficult. Do you decide to give your baby a chance even though, after intensive treatment, you may still lose him? Or do you decide that because your baby is severely handicapped, and will have poor quality of life, you should not fight to keep him alive? These can be extremely distressing decisions to have to make – they need very careful thought, counselling and discussion with your doctor and with each other.

Puerperal Psychosis

This is the name given to a mental illness such as manic depression which manifests itself for the first time just after you have had a baby. It isn't caused by childbirth, but happens because you are already predisposed (as are 1 in 4 of the population) to mental illness; the pregnancy, birth or postnatal period put you under the strain that triggers an attack. In most cases any other emotional disturbance of similar severity would act as an equal trigger.

Rhesus Factor

If your blood group is rhesus negative and your baby's father's is rhesus positive, there's a good chance your baby will be rhesus positive too. This usually causes no problem during a first pregnancy, but there may be some exchange between your blood and your baby's during delivery, causing your blood to respond by producing antibodies to rhesus positive blood. When this happens, subsequent pregnancies will pose problems if the babies have rhesus positive blood. Your antibodies will regard the baby's blood as a foreign body and try to break it down, causing the baby's haemoglobin levels to drop – often so low that he or she will require a blood transfusion at birth. However, treatment with an 'Anti D' injection following a first delivery (or miscarriage) can pre-empt these problems.

In a first pregnancy Anti D should be given if there is any bleeding during the pregnancy or any procedure known to carry a risk of feto-maternal transfusion, i.e. your baby's cells getting into your blood. Many centres are now advising one injection of Anti D to all Rhesus negative first-baby mums at 28 weeks as well as after the birth.

Stillbirth and Neonatal Death

In the UK around nine thousand babies a year die after the 20th week of pregnancy, at or shortly after birth. A stillbirth refers to a baby born dead after 24 or more weeks. Babies born dead after 20–23 weeks are referred to as 'late fetal losses'. Neonatal deaths are babies born alive but who die before they are 28 days old. They are divided into 'early neonatal deaths' (under seven days) and 'late neonatal deaths'.

Causes include:

♦ Placental problems (see pp.238–40) such as placental insuffiency or failure, placenta abruptio, placenta praevia, antepartum haemorrhage (see pp.228–29), or hydatiform mole (see p.230).
♦ Uterus problems such as an incompetent cervix (see pp.231–32), fibroids (see p.228) or an abnormally shaped womb.
♦ Problems in the mother caused by pregnancy, e.g. eclampsia (see p.225).
♦ Infections in the mother such as toxoplasmosis (see p.249) or listeriosis (see p.234).
♦ Problems to do with the mother's health, such as diabetes or epilepsy.
♦ Problems to do with the baby's development, e.g. chromosomal abnormalities, rhesus disease, congenital heart problems or neural tube defects.
♦ Problems during labour, such as prolapsed cord or fetal distress.

But many stillbirths are unexplained, and this can make the loss worse.

In the early days after losing a baby, you may experience the physical feelings of grief: tiredness, heaviness or pain in the chest, and a need to take deep, sighing breaths. Some people have palpitations, 'butterflies' or aching arms. Others have difficulty eating and sleeping. Drugs may be offered to help you sleep, but cannot deal with your sadness and may only postpone and prolong your pain.

Sadly, your body won't recognize that your baby's died and your breasts will continue to produce milk. Try to resist the temptation to express this milk, which will only make your breasts produce more. Instead, use ice packs to relieve the pain. Within a few days your breasts will be more comfortable, and your body will soon reabsorb the milk.

Your emotional recovery will be much slower than your physical recovery. But the Stillbirth and Neonatal Death Society (see Address Book) offers support, through a network of local groups and a range of publications, to parents who have experienced a late miscarriage, a stillbirth or a neonatal bereavement.

Immediately following a stillbirth you should see and cuddle your baby – many hospitals have a special parents' room where you can all spend time alone. You may also want to take your baby home to familiar surroundings, and this can be arranged too. However, don't worry that you'll be pressured into doing anything you don't want to.

Ask the hospital for mementoes to remember your baby by. Photographs, your baby's identification band, locks of hair, foot or hand prints and any cards and letters you've been sent will be of comfort when you look at them in the months and years to come. If you don't have a camera, many hospitals will take pictures for you.

Hold a funeral for your baby – it may help to dress your baby in his or her own clothes and to put mementoes like a family photo, letter or poem in the coffin. If you don't want to hold a funeral, a memorial ceremony may help you come to terms with your loss – many parents have found this comforting in the years afterwards.

Stress Incontinence

After childbirth, when the pelvic floor muscles are weakened, 'leaking' urine may become a problem – especially when you laugh, cough or sneeze. It's embarrassing to live with and difficult to discuss. But doctors are very used to treating incontinence, so don't be put off making an appointment to talk through the problem. In most cases treatment will be very straightforward.

Before going to the doctor, ask yourself the following questions and keep a note of your answers.

- Do you 'leak' when you laugh, cough or sneeze, or when you move suddenly or bend to lift something?
- Do you frequently suffer with dribbles?
- Do you often not reach the loo in time?
- How often do you go to the loo?
- Once you have the urge to go, how long can you hold on?
- Does your bladder empty without warning?
- Do you wet yourself at night?
- If so, does it wake you, or are you unaware of it until morning?
- Has your flow of urine changed – is it not as good as it once was?
- Do you often feel thirsty?
- Are you taking any drugs? If so, which ones?

Your doctor will need the answers to these questions (and he may have others too) for clues about what's causing your incontinence. He may also ask you to keep a chart showing how much you've eaten and drunk in a day, and how often you've passed urine. He may order tests to establish further or rule out the cause of your incontinence. The tests will tell him whether you have diabetes or an infection, or if your incontinence is a response to medicine you are taking.

You may be referred to an incontinence adviser and a gynaecologist and physiotherapist. Drug therapy can also be prescribed to help recapture and maintain continence.

What a Continence Adviser Can Do

Your continence adviser, if you're referred to one, will help you make the best of the health care available – getting the right appliances, garments, bedding and care that you need.

What a Physiotherapist Can Do

A physiotherapist will give you exercises to do which will strengthen your muscles. You may also be offered electrical stimulation, for instance interferential therapy, which makes muscles relax and contract. This treatment is given in an outpatient department, but there is an alternative, functional electrical stimulation, which you can be trained to use at home.

What You Can Do for Yourself

- Make sure you do the exercises you're given, and work at any bladder retraining you're told to do.
- Use vaginal weights, available from your continence adviser, to increase vaginal tone.
- Keep charts to monitor your progress.
- Use your district nurse and continence adviser – they're there to help you, so don't be afraid to ask them for help.
- Try to get your bladder completely empty every time you go to the loo – pressing a tissue firmly against yourself and waiting a few seconds will encourage those last drops to come.
- Wear clothes which are simple to remove, and nothing that's too tight around the stomach or bladder where it can increase the pressure to go to the loo.
- At night go to the loo just before getting ready for bed, and then again just before going off to sleep, so that your bladder is quite empty.
- If late-night drinks make a difference, take your last one earlier in the evening – and keep a drink by your bedside in case you're thirsty in the night. If you do have a drink in the night, go to the loo before going back off to sleep.

Toxaemia see Pre-eclampsia on pp.243–44.

Toxoplasmosis

A positive test for toxoplasmosis during pregnancy can lead to a great deal of anxiety. There are measures you can take to protect yourself against the disease (see Chapter 2), but infection can go unnoticed.

Having a positive test result doesn't mean that your baby is definitely at risk, but the degree of risk depends on when in the pregnancy you caught toxoplasmosis. French research suggests that an infection caught shortly before conception carries a 1 per cent or below risk of transmission to the fetus, but a high risk of miscarriage if it does transmit. If the baby were infected, the degree of damage would be severe.

Infection during the first trimester (up to 13 weeks) results in a 10–25 per cent chance of fetal infection, with a high risk that, if severely affected, the baby would be miscarried, stillborn, or born with some or all of the severest symptoms of congenital toxoplasmosis – brain damage and blindness.

Infection during the second trimester (weeks 13–26) could result in severe damage. The chance of the infection transmitting is 25–40 per cent, although it's unlikely to cause miscarriage.

The rate of infection during the third trimester (26 weeks and on) may be as high as 70 per cent, but the damage is less severe. It is usually eye damage, which is not apparent at birth but may develop later in life.

A specific antibiotic, spiramycin, is used to treat toxoplasmosis in pregnancy. While being relatively ineffective against the parasite, it has a 60–70 per cent chance of preventing the infection from transmitting to the baby. Spiramycin is not licensed in the UK, but if your consultant recommends it he can obtain it for you.

If the baby is found to be infected, you can take stronger antibiotics to help limit the damage to him or her, although they cannot undo any damage already done. These drugs are a combination of pyremethamine and sulphadiazine, taken with folinic acid to reduce the worst side-effects.

Amniocentesis, cordocentesis (a test on blood taken from the umbilical cord) and ultrasound scan tests can find out whether the baby is damaged, but they will not show how severe the damage is. The option of terminating a pregnancy may be offered to you if fetal damage has been identified.

If you go ahead with the pregnancy your baby will have a thorough examination after birth, and follow-up blood tests during the first year of life.

Uterine Inversion

Rarely, when the placenta doesn't detach completely after delivery of a baby, it pulls the top of the uterus with it, like pulling a sock inside out. This is a potentially dangerous situation known as uterine inversion and causes excessive bleeding and shock.

You are at slightly increased risk if:

◆ You've had many babies.
◆ You've had a prolonged labour (more than 24 hours).
◆ The placenta is implanted across the top of the uterus.
◆ You were given magnesium sulphate in labour (sometimes used in the treatment of pre-eclampsia).
◆ The uterus is over-relaxed or the fundus isn't firmly held in place while the placenta is coaxed out in the third stage of labour.

Usually the uterus can be replaced by hand – though occasionally surgery is necessary. If you've lost a lot of blood, you may need transfusions.

Venous Thrombosis

Sometimes, in the pregnant mother's body's efforts to prevent a bleed, the opposite happens and the blood over-clots. You're more susceptible to thrombosis, when a clot develops in a vein, in pregnancy – particularly just after giving birth, because the body's natural clotting ability increases in order to prevent heavy bleeding at this time. You're slightly more at risk of developing a clot if:

◆ You're over 30.
◆ You've had three or more previous deliveries.
◆ You've been confined to bed for long periods.
◆ You're overweight, anaemic or have varicose veins.
◆ You've had a forceps or caesarean delivery.

Superficial clots are called thrombophlebitis and occur in 1–2 per cent of pregnancies. The main symptom is tenderness (usually redness too) near the surface of the thigh or calf. Treatment usually consists of rest and ointments.

Deep vein thrombosis is more serious. Untreated, it can lead to the clot moving to the lungs and becoming life-threatening. It is much less common than thrombophlebitis, and the symptoms are more severe – a heavy, painful feeling in the leg, tenderness in the calf, and often swelling. Ultrasound can diagnose the blood clot and you will be treated intravenously with an anticoagulant drug (usually heparin), for up to ten days, until labour begins. At this point treatment is stopped, to be resumed several hours after delivery.

Because of the serious nature of deep vein thrombosis, get urgent medical attention if you have symptoms such as chest pain, blueness of the lips and fingertips, or you are coughing up blood-stained sputum, which could be signs that the clot has moved to the lungs.

Further Reading

AYNSLEY-GREEN, Professor A., *The Great Ormond Street New Baby and Child Care Book* (Vermilion 1997)

BOURNE, Gordon, *Pregnancy* (Cassell 1995)

CLIFFORD, Frances R., *Aromatherapy During Pregnancy* (C.W. Daniel Company Ltd 1997)

CURTIS, Glade B., *Your Pregnancy Questions and Answers* (Element 1997)

EISENBERG, Arlene, Heidi E. Murkoff and Sandee E. Hathaway, *What to Expect When You're Expecting* (Simon and Schuster 1991)

ENKIN, Murray, Marc J.N.C. Keirse, Mary Renfrew and James Neilson, *A Guide to Effective Care in Pregnancy and Childbirth* (Oxford 1995)

GRIFFEY, Harriet, *The Really Useful A–Z of Pregnancy and Birth* (Thorsons 1996)

JAMIL, Tanvir, *Complementary Medicine – A Practical Guide* (Butterworth-Heinemann 1997)

KITZINGER, Sheila, *The New Pregnancy and Childbirth* (Penguin 1997)

PUTKISTO, Marja, *Method Putkisto* (Headline 1997)

ROGERS, Carol, *Women's Guide to Herbal Medicine* (Hamish Hamilton 1997)

WEBB, Dr Peter, *The Family Encyclopedia of Homeopathic Remedies* (Robinson 1997)

WESSON, Nicky, *Alternative Infertility Treatments* (Vermilion 1997)

WESSON, Nicky, *Morning Sickness* (Vermilion 1997)

Other books of interest published by Ward Lock

BARBIRA FREEDMAN, Françoise and Doriel Hall, *Yoga for Pregnancy*

FEINMANN, Jane, *Surviving the Baby Blues*

HOLLYER, Beatrice and Lucy Smith, *Feeding: The Simple Solution*

HOLLYER, Beatrice and Lucy Smith, *Sleep: The Secret of Problem-free Nights*

NATANSON, Jan, *Learning Through Play*

PILIA, Irene, *The Working Parent's Survival Guide*

SCATTERGOOD, Emma, *The First-time Parents' Survival Guide*

SCATTERGOOD, Emma, *Your Pregnancy Workout*

Address Book

UK

Action on Pre-Eclampsia
31–33 College Road, Harrow, HA1 1EJ

The Active Birth Centre
25 Bickerton Road, London N19 5JT

Alcohol Concern
275 Gray's Inn Road, London WC1X 8QF

Association of Pilates
17 Queensberry Mews West,
London SW7 2DY

Association for Post Natal Illness
25 Jerdan Place, London SW6 1BE

British Acupuncture Association and Register
34 Alderney Street, London SW1V 4EU

The British Diabetic Association
10 Queen Anne Street, London W1M OBD

The British Homeopathic Association (BHA)
27a Devonshire Street, London W1N 1RJ

The British Liver Trust
Central House, Central Avenue, Ransomes
Europark, Ipswich, IP13 6EL

CHILD
Charter House, 43 St Leonards Road, Bexhill-
on-Sea, East Sussex, TN40 1JA

The Children's Liver Disease Foundation
138 Digbeth, Birmingham B5 6DR

Congenital CMV Association
69 The Leasowes, Ford, Shrewsbury, SY5 9LU

Foundation for Study of Infant Deaths (Cot Death)
14 Halkin Street, London SW1X 7DP

International Confederation of Midwives
The Barley Mow Centre, 10 Barley Mow
Passage, Chiswick, London W4 4PH

ISSUE – The National Fertility Association
509 Aldridge Road, Great Barr,
Birmingham, B44 8NA

La Leche League of Great Britain
Box BM 3424, London WC1N 3XX

Marie Stopes International
108 Whitfield Street, London W1P 6BE

Meet a Mum Association (MAMA)
c/o 58 Malden Avenue, London SE25 4HS

MIND (National Society for Mental Health)
22 Harley Street, London W1N 2ED

The Miscarriage Association
c/o Clayton Hospital, Northgate,
Wakefield, WF1 3JS

The National Childbirth Trust
Alexandra House, Oldham Terrace,
London W3 6NH

Natural Medicines Society (NMS)
Edith Lewis House, Back Lane, Ilkeston,
Derbyshire, DE7 8EJ

Neal's Yard Remedies
15 Neal's Yard, London WC2 9DP

Osteopathic Centre for Children
19A Cavendish Square,
London W1M 9AD

QUIT (National Society of Non-Smokers)
102 Gloucester Place, London W1H 3DA

Right Baby Ltd (Patrick Schoun)
PO Box 101, Chipping Norton,
Oxon, OX7 4PT

Royal College of Midwives
15 Mansfield Street, London W1M OBE

SATFA (Support around Termination for Abnormality)
73–75 Charlotte Street, London W1P 1LB

Stillbirth and Neonatal Death Society (SANDS)
28 Portland Place, London W1N 4DE

The Toxoplasmosis Trust
61 Collier Street, London N1 9BE

Twins and Multiple Birth Association
PO Box 30, Little Sutton,
South Wirral, L66 1TH

The United Kingdom Central Council for Nursing, Midwifery & Health Visiting (UKCC)
23 Portland Place, London W1N 4JT

AUSTRALIA

Australian College of Midwives
1st Floor, 3 Bowen Crescent, Melbourne,
Victoria 3000

CANADA

The Alberta Association of Midwives
1616-20 A St N.W., Calgary, AlbertaT2N 2LS

Association of Ontario Midwives
562 Eglinton Avenue East – Suite 102,
Toronto, Ontario M4P 1B9

Midwives' Association of British Columbia
219-1675 West 8th Avenue, Vancouver, British
Columbia V6J 1V2

NEW ZEALAND

New Zealand College of Midwives
P O Box 21106, Christchurch

SOUTH AFRICA

Society for Midwives in Southern Africa
P O Box 91981, Auckland Park 2006,
Johannesburg

USA

Midwives' Alliance of North America
78 Chester, Fairfax, CA 94930

American College of Nurse Midwives
818 Connecticut Avenue NW – Suite 900,
Washington DC 20006

Index

Page numbers in *italic* refer to the illustrations

abdomen: itchy 77
  pain 72, 93
  ultrasound scans 114, 129
abnormalities, 58, 113–22
abortion 130–3
abortion pill 130–1
acne 48
Active Birth Centre 141–2, 173
acupuncture 100, 154
aerobics 41
afterpains 189, 198
age: and fertility 27–8
  at first pregnancy 58–9
air travel 88
alcohol 17, 30, 209, 217
allergies 206, 221
alpha-fetoprotein (AFP) 114–16, 122
Alzheimer's disease 124
amniocentesis 116–17
amniotic fluid 165, 240
anaemia 34, 72–3, 95, 221
anaesthesia: caudal 157
  epidural 156, 157, 185–6
  pudendal block 157
  spinal 156
anencephaly 113, 122, 126
ankles, swollen 77, 95, 244
antenatal clinics 32–4
antenatal screening 113–29, 115
antepartum haemorrhage 228–9
anterior presentation 97, 99
'Anti D' injections 246
antibiotics 201, 249
antibodies: breastfeeding 196
  rhesus factor 245–6
antidepressants 242
anus: faecal incontinence 227
  fissures 78
anxiety 57
Apgar score 172, 177
areola 46
aromatherapy *51*, 110, 154, 233
Artificial Rupture of Membranes (ARM) 166
aspirin 87
asthma 221

baby: bonding with *191*, 194
  death 208, 246–7
  monitoring health 204–8
  newborn babies 172, 176–7, 192–4
  premature babies 112, 121, 244–5
  six-week check-up 211
  tests 172, 177, 192
  see also fetus
baby blues 189–90, 241
Bach flower remedies 154
back, strengthening exercises 82
'back labour' 101, 167

backache 73–4
badminton 41
Bart's test 117
baths, temperature 61
bearing down 166, 168
bed: getting out of 73
  labour in 176
bicycling 41
bilirubin 193
biochemical screening 120
biophysical profile 117–18
birth *see* labour
birth defects 58, 113–22
birth partners 140
birth plans 161
birthing pools 153, 173–4, *174*
birthing stools 176
bladder: catheters 173
  stress incontinence 104, 247–8
  ultrasound scans 134
blankets, electric 89
blastocyst 25
bleeding: cervix 80
  during pregnancy 59, 86, 102, 228–9
  incomplete abortion 131
  lochia 192
  miscarriage 235
  placenta abruptio 238–9
  postpartum haemorrhage 229
  rectal 78–9
blighted ovum 222
blocked ducts, breastfeeding 198
blood: fetal cells in maternal blood 120
  gender tests 120
  hospital phobia 140–1
  rhesus factor 245–6
blood clots 77, 190, 250
blood poisoning 208
blood pressure 34, *35*, 74–6, 231, 244
blood sugar levels 49, 56, 192, 223–5
blood tests 34, 117, 192
'blues' 189–90, 241
body odour 71
bonding *191*, 194
bones, ultrasound scans 129
bottle feeding 172, 202–4, 203, 217
bowels: constipation 48, 94, 190
  faecal incontinence 227
Bradley approach 144
brain, ultrasound scans 126
bras 87, 197
Braxton Hicks contractions 46, 93, 106, 109
bread 38
breastfeeding 196–201, *197*, *199*, 216–18
  after birth 172
  diet and 194–5
  problems 198–201
  and sex 209

switching to bottle feeding 202, 217
breastmilk 196, 198, 199
breasts: after stillbirth 246–7
  bras 87, 197
  during pregnancy 46–8, 59
  engorgement 201
  'leaking' 76, 197
  soreness 48, 80
breathing: Bradley approach 144
  exercises 141
  in labour 142, 165
  pain relief 153
breathlessness 76
breech delivery 181–2, *181*
breech presentation 97, 99–100
brow presentation 100–1
bruising 190

caesarean section 185–7, *186*
  breech presentation 99, 181, 182
  fibroids and 60
  recovery after 196
  vaginal birth after 59, 148–51
caffeine 14, 17, 54
calcium 16, 53, 77
camomile oil 110
cancer, choriocarcinoma 222
car seat belts 88
carbohydrates 195
cardiotocogram 118
carpal tunnel syndrome 78
catheters 173
caudal anaesthesia 157
cephalic presentation 96–8, 97
cereals 38
cervix: bleeding 80
  dilatation 164–5
  erosion 229
  incompetence 31, 231–2
  mucous plug 106, 164–5
  mucus at ovulation 20
  prolonged labour 180
  smear tests 34
  tears 229
cheese 38
chicken pox 64
childbirth *see* labour
childbirth classes 141–4, *143*
childbirth education philosophies 144–5
chlamydia 37, 62
chlamydiosis 37
chloasma 70
cholestasis, obstetric 237
choriocarcinoma 222
chorionic villus sampling (CVS) 118–19, 132
choroid plexus cysts 126–7
chromosomes: chorionic villus sampling (CVS) 118–19
  conception 25
  cordocentesis 120
  Turner's syndrome 128
classes, childbirth 141–4, *143*
cleft lip/palate 114, 127

clinics, antenatal 32–4
clomiphene 232
clothes: baby's 144
  during pregnancy 87
clots, blood 77, 190, 250
club foot 114, 129
clumsiness 69
coeliac disease 206
coils *see* IUDs
cold compresses, pain relief 153
colds, baby's 206
colostrum 76, 196, 199
complementary therapies, pain relief 154–5
compresses, pain relief 153
conception 21–5, *24*
  difficulties 26–8
  planning 13–23
condoms 29
constipation 48, 94, 190
contraception 29, 217
contraceptive pill 29, 59
contractions: afterpains 189, 198
  Braxton Hicks 46, 93, 106, 109
  contraction stress test 120
  first stage 165
  hypertonic action 178–9
  insufficient contractions 178
  pain 152
  second stage 168–9
convulsions 205, 226
cooking methods 195–6
cord *see* umbilical cord
cordocentesis 120
corpus luteum cysts 223
cot death 208
coughing, baby 205
counselling: genetic 114
  hospital phobia 141
  termination of pregnancy 132
cramps 60, 77
cranial osteopathy 101, 188, 233
cravings 48–9
curl-ups 214
cycling 41
cystic fibrosis 113, 118
cystic swellings, ultrasound scans 127
cysts: choroid plexus 126–7
  corpus luteum 223
  ovarian 237
cytomegalovirus (CMV) 64, 222–3

D and C 131, 235
D and E 130, 132
dairy products 38
death: cot death 208
  fetal death 227
  miscarriage 234–6
  pre-eclampsia 243
  premature babies 245
  stillbirth and neonatal death 246–7

deep vein thrombosis 250
dehydration 205, 206
delivery 169–70
  fetal distress 180
  see also labour
dental problems 76
depression, postnatal 240–3
desks, sitting posture 73, *75*
diabetes 223–5
diaphragmatic hernia 129
diarrhoea 48, 205, 206
Dick-Read, Grantly 145
diet: after pregnancy 194–5
  before conception 13, 14–17
  during pregnancy 37–40, 46
  food hygiene 36–7, 40
dieting, during pregnancy 57,
    62
dilatation and curettage (D
    and C) 131, 235
dilatation and evacuation (D
    and E) 130, 132
discharge from hospital 177
discharges, vaginal 79
distraction, pain relief 153
dizziness 49
DNA 25
Domino scheme 177
donor insemination 232
Down's syndrome 58, 113,
    118, 119, 121, 122–4,
    132–3
drawbridge exercise 42–3
dromedary droop exercise 84
drugs: fertility drugs 232
  pain relief 157–8
  pre-conception 30
Duchenne muscular dystrophy
    113
ducts, blocked 198
dwarfism 114, 129

eclampsia 225–6
ectopic pregnancy 25, 226
eggs: ectopic pregnancy 226
  fertilization 21–5, *24*
  hydatiform mole 60, 230
  implantation 25, 43
  infertility 27, 232–3
electric blankets 89
electrolysis 89
electronic fetal heart monitor-
    ing 118, *119*, 162–3, *163*
embryo, implantation 43
emergency delivery 169–70
emotions: baby blues 189–90,
    241
  miscarriage 235–6
  in pregnancy 57, 87
  stillbirth and neonatal death
    246–7
endometrium 25
endorphins 153, 154
enemas 173
energy, during pregnancy 70,
    105
engagement, head 90, 105,
    106, 112
engorged breasts 201
Entonox 155–6
epidural anaesthesia 156, 157,
    185–6

episiotomy 161–2, 169, 192,
    209
ergometrine 174, 229
estimated date of delivery
    (EDD) 32–3, *33*
exercise: after childbirth
    212–16
  antenal classes *143*
  before conception 17–19
  first trimester 40–3
  second trimester 70, 82–5,
    83
exomphalos 129
expressing milk 217
external cephalic version,
    breech presentation 100

face (baby's), ultrasound scans
    127
face (mother's), puffiness 95
face presentation *100*, 101
facial clefts 127
facial massage 52
faecal incontinence 227
faintness 49, 140
fallopian tubes 24, 25, 226,
    233
falls 86
false labour 106
fathers, help in labour 160
fatigue, during pregnancy 49,
    94–5
fear of labour 138–41
feet: club foot 114, 129
  reflexology 137–8
  swollen 77, 95, 244
  ultrasound scans 129
fertile times 19–21, *19*
fertility 26–8
fertility drugs 232
fertility treatment 232–3
fertilization 21–5, *24*
fetal death 227
fetal distress 180
fetal heart monitoring 118,
    119, 162–3, *163*
fetal tissue sampling 121
fetoscopy 121
fetus: first trimester 43–4, *45*
  movements 66, 69, 93–4
  presentation 96–102, *97*,
    181–3
  second trimester 65–9, *68*
  third trimester 90, *92*
fevers: baby 204–5, 206–7
  mother 64
fibroids 60, 182, 228
fifth disease 64, 228
first trimester 32–64
fish 38, 195
fissures, anal 78
fits *205*, 226
flatulence 50
fluid loss 192
fluid retention 77, 95
flying 88
folic acid 14–15, 30
food *see* diet
food aversions 50
food cravings 48–9
food poisoning 36–7
footling breech 181

forceps delivery 161–2,
    184–5, *184*, *188*
foremilk 199
forgetfulness 70
frank breech 181
fruit 38, 195
funerals, stillbirth and neo-
    natal death 247

gamete intra-fallopian tube
    transfer (GIFT) 232
gas and oxygen 155–6
gastroenteritis 196, 206
genetic counselling 114
genital herpes 34
genital warts 62
genitals: engorgement 80
  itchy 77
  see also vagina
German measles *see* rubella
gluten intolerance 206
golf 41
gonorrhoea 62
grief: miscarriage 235–6
  stillbirth and neonatal death
    246–7
  termination of pregnancy
    133

haemophilia 113
haemorrhage: antepartum
    228–9
  postpartum 229
  see also bleeding
haemorrhoids (piles) 48, 78–9
hair: colouring or perming 88
  electrolysis 89
  lanugo 66, *171*
hands: carpal tunnel syndrome
    78
  swollen 95
  ultrasound scans 129
HCG (human chorionic gona-
    dotrophin) 26, 61, 122, 235
HCG test 121
head: engagement 90, 105,
    106, 112
  ultrasound scans 126
head injuries 205
headaches 50–2, *55*
heart: abnormalities 114
  cardiotocogram 118
  Down's syndrome 123–4
  fetal distress 180
  ultrasound scans 129
heartburn 52
heat rash 71
height, and pelvis size 34
hepatitis 34, 64
herbal medicine 30, 233
hernia, diaphragmatic 129
herpes, genital 34
hiatus hernia 205
high blood pressure 74–6,
    231, 244
hindmilk 199
hips, congenital dislocation
    210
HIV 34, 62–3
home birth 137, 147–8
homeopathy: breech presenta-
    tion 100

for infertility 233
  mastitis 201
  pain relief 154
  preparation for childbirth
    152
hormones: baby blues 189,
    241
  implantation of fertilized
    egg 25
  miscarriage 235
  Turner's syndrome 128
hospital birth 145–7, 177
hospital phobia 140–1
hot compresses, pain relief 153
human gonadotrophin 117
hydatiform mole 60, 222, 230
hydrocephaly 114, 126
hygiene 36–7, 40, 76
hyperactive children 101
hyperemesis gravidarum 53,
    230–1
hyperpigmentation 71
hypertension 74–6, 231, 244
hypertonic action 178–9
hyperventilation 153
hypnotherapy 154–5, 233
hypoglycaemia 192
hypotension 74
hypotonic inertia 178

identical twins 25
immune system 13
implantation, fertilized egg 25,
    43
incompetent cervix 31, 231–2
incomplete abortion 131
incontinence: faecal 227
  urinary 104, 247–8
incubators *183*
indigestion 52–3
induction of labour 166, 173
infections 63–4
infertility 26–8, 232–3
inhibin A 122
insemination, artificial 232
insomnia 110
insulin 223–5
intercourse *see* sex
internal examinations 34
intra-cytoplasmic sperm injec-
    tion (ICSI) 232
intra-uterine insemination
    (IUI) 232
iron 16
  deficiency 49, 54, 221
  supplements 34, 72–3
itching 77, 237
IUDs (intra-uterine devices)
    29, 61, 226
IUGR (intra-uterine growth
    retardation) 234, 244
IVF (in-vitro fertilization) 233

jacuzzis 61
jaundice 193–4
jogging 42

kicking, baby 66, 69, 93–4
kidney abnormalities 114, 129
Kitzinger, Sheila 173

L/S ratio 121

labour: 'back labour' 101, 167
  birth plans 161
  breech delivery 181–2, *181*
  caesarean section 185–7, *186*
  delivery 169–70
  emergency delivery 169–70
  false labour 106
  father's help 160
  fear of 138–41
  first stage 164–5
  forceps delivery 184–5, *184*, 188
  home birth 147–8
  hospital birth 145–7
  induction 166, 173
  length of 168
  natural preparation 151–2
  pain relief 152–8
  positions *142*, 165, 168, 176
  prelabour symptoms 105–6
  premature labour 107–9
  preparing for 137–63
  prolonged labour 178–80
  second stage 168
  signs of 164
  termination of pregnancy 132
  third stage 169
  transition stage 166
  triggers 104–5
  twins 188
  vaginal birth after caesarean 148–51
  ventouse delivery 184–5, *184*, 188
  water birth *139*, 173–4, *174*
  what to take with you 158–60, *159*
lactic acid 152
Lamaze approach 145
lanugo 66, *171*
'late' babies 109, 152, 173
laxatives 190
lazy dog exercise 82
lecithin 121
legs: cramps 77
  leg lifts 84, 213–14
  oedema 95
  sciatic nerve pain 87
  varicose veins 31, 56
  venous thrombosis 250
let-down reflex 198, 217
libido 53, 81, 209
lifting children 62
ligaments, abdominal pain 93
limbs, ultrasound scans 129
linea nigra 70
listeriosis 37, 234
liver, obstetric cholestasis 237
lochia 192
lovemaking *see* sex
low birth-weight babies 13, *183*, 234
low blood pressure 74
low-lying placenta 78
lungs, ultrasound scans 129
luteinizing hormone (LH) 21, 61, 235
Lyme disease 64

mandarin oil 110
'mask of pregnancy' 70, 88
massage *107*
  aromatherapy 154
  facial 52
  pain relief 153
  perineum 151
  reflexology 137–8, 233
mastitis 200, 201
maternity belts 93
meat 38, 195
meconium 180, 194
Mediterranean diet 195
memory problems 70
meningitis 208
menopause 27
menstrual cycle 19–21, *19*, 33
mental illness 245
Meptid 157
Method Putkisto 216
microwave ovens 88
midwives 32, 147–8, 161, 177
milk: allergies 206
  bottle feeding 202–4
  breastfeeding 196, 198, 199, 216
  expressing 198, 217
  milk intolerance 53
miscarriage 234–6
  causes 61, 89
  IUDs and 61
  risk of 64
  signs of 59, 235
  subsequent pregnancies 29
Miscarriage Association 236
mittelschmerz 21
mole, hydatiform 60, 222, 230
monitoring, fetal heart 118, *119*, 162–3, *163*
mood swings 57, 87
morning sickness 53–4, 63
morula 25
mosaicism 119
movements, baby's 66, 69, 93–4
MRI (magnetic resonance imaging) 120
mucous plug, cervix 106, 164–5
mucus, cervical 20
multiple pregnancy 25, 188, 236–7
multivitamins 30
muscles: leg cramps 77
  pelvic floor 42–3, 218, 247–8
muscular dystrophy 113

National Childbirth Trust 141, 142
natural pain relief 153
natural preparation for childbirth 151–2
nausea 53–4, 63
neck, ultrasound scans 127
neck relaxer exercise 84
neonatal death 246–7
neroli oil 110
nerves: carpal tunnel syndrome 78
  sciatic nerve pain 87

neural tube defects 15, 122
newborn baby 172, 192–4
nipples: breastfeeding 198
  soreness 201
  starting labour 152
  stimulating to deliver placenta 172
nitrous oxide, pain relief 155–6
nonspecific vaginitis 62
nose problems 64
nuchal fold screening 121
nuchal translucency scan 121
nursing bras 197
nutrition *see* diet

obesity 62
oblique lie 182
obstetric cholestasis 237
obstetricians 63
occipito-anterior presentation 97, 101
oedema 95, 244
oesophageal reflux 52, 205
oestriol 117, 122
oestrogen 52, 223
oils, aromatherapy 110
oral contraceptives 29, 59
oral hygiene 76
oral sex 80
orange blossom oil 110
orgasm 21, 60, 81, 112
osteogenesis imperfecta 129
osteopathy, cranial 101, 188, 233
ovarian hyperstimulation syndrome (OHSS) 238
ovaries: cysts 223, 237
  infertility treatment 232
  polycystic 61, 235
overdue babies 109, 152, 173
overheating 96
ovulation 20–1, *20*, 28, 223, 232
ovulation kits 21
ovum, blighted 222
oxygen, fetal distress 180
oxytocin 105, 120, 168, 174, 198

pain: abdominal 72, 93
  afterpains 189, 198
  'back labour' 167
  Braxton Hicks contractions 109
  bruising 190
  ectopic pregnancy 226
  fear of labour 138–9
  painful intercourse 209
  pubic pain 110
  sciatic nerve pain 87
pain relief 137, 140, 152–8
  complementary therapies 154–5
  during pregnancy 87
  natural pain relief 153
  orthodox methods 155–8
paracetamol 87
parentcraft classes 144
pelvic floor muscles 42–3, 218, 247–8
pelvic lift 82
pelvis: in labour 168

prolonged labour 180
pubic pain 110
  size of 34
perinatologists 63
perineum: bruising 190
  delivery 169
  episiotomy 161–2, 169, 192, 209
  massage 151
  perineal pressure 78
periods 26, 46, 217–18
perspiration 71
Pethidine 157–8
phenylketonuria 192
phobia, hospital 140–1
phosphorus 77
phototherapy 193
physiotherapy, stress incontinence 248
pica 48–9
pick-me-up, ten-minute 85
picking up children 62
pigmentation changes 70–1
Pilates exercises 212–16
piles (haemorrhoids) 48, 78–9
the pill 29, 59
placenta: bleeding 102
  delivery 169, 170, 174–6
  hydatiform mole 60, 230
  low-lying 78
  overdue babies 109
  placenta abruptio 238–9
  placenta accreta 239
  placenta praevia 78, 228–9, 239
  placental insufficiency 227, 239–40
  pre-eclampsia 243, 244
  retention of 239
PMS (premenstrual syndrome) 57
polycystic ovaries 61, 235
polyhydramnios 240
positions during labour 165, 168, 176
posseting 194, 205
post-mature babies 109
posterior presentation 97, 101, 179
postnatal depression (PND) 240–3
postpartum haemorrhage 229
postural hypotension 74
postural tilting, breech presentation 100
posture 73, *75*
potatoes 38
pre-eclampsia 74, 95, 243–4
pregnancy tests 26
prelabour symptoms 105–6
premature babies 112, 121, 181, *183*, 244–5
premature labour 107–9
presentation, baby 96–102, 97, 181–3
progesterone 25, 42, 52, 223, 235
projectile vomiting 194, 205–6
prolactin 152, 198
prolapse, umbilical cord, 102, 183

prostaglandins: induction of labour 166
termination of pregnancy 132
triggering labour 104–5, 152
protein 38
proteinuria 244
psychophysical approach 145
psychoprophylactic approach 145
psychosis, puerpural 245
ptyalism 54
pubic hair, shaving 173
pubic pain 110
pudendal block 157
puerpural psychosis 245
PUPPP (pruritic urticarial papules and plaques of pregnancy) 96
pushing, delivery 166, 168
pyloric stenosis 194, 205–6

rashes 205
raspberry leaf tea 151
rectal bleeding 78–9
red blood cells 13, 193
reflexology 137–8, 233
relaxation: head-to-toe 86
neck relaxer exercise 84
pain relief 153
Pilates exercises 212
posture 74
rest 49, 94–5
rhesus factor 245–6
rose oil 110
rubella (German measles) 17, 29, 34, 64

saliva, excessive 54
salmonella 37
sandalwood oil 110
saunas 62
scars: caesarean section 186, 196
episiotomy 192
sciatic nerve pain 87
screaming baby 205
screening, antenatal 113–29, 115
seat belts 88
second trimester 65–89
semen 21, 152
septicaemia 208
serotonin 56
serum testing 122
sex: after childbirth 209
bleeding after 102
conception 21–3, 26, 28
during pregnancy 53
maternal blood test for gender 120
in second trimester 80–1
starting labour with 152
in third trimester 104, 112
sex of baby 23, 134
shaving, pubic hair 173
shopping list, baby basics 144
shoulder drop exercise 213
'show' 106, 164–5
sickness: babies 205–6
morning sickness 53–4, 63
posseting 194, 205

single mothers 190
sitting posture 73, 75
six-week check-up 210–11
skin: baby's *171*
during pregnancy 48, 70–1, 96
rashes 205
stretch marks 96
skin tags 71
skull, cranial osteopathy 101, 188, 233
sleep problems 49, 54–6, 110
'small for dates' babies 234, 245
smoking 14, 17
sore nipples 201
soreness, vulva 110
sperm 21, 23–5, *24*, 28, 222, 232
spermicides 62
sphingomyelin 121
spider naevi 56
spina bifida 15, 114, 122, 126
spinal anaesthesia 156
spine, ultrasound scans 126
spiramycin 249
spotting, in third trimester 102
squatting 84, *142*, 168
standing posture 73, 74
STDs (sexually transmitted diseases) 17, 62–3
steptrococcus, Group B 64
stillbirth 13, 234, 246–7
Stillbirth and Neonatal Death Society 247
stitches: caesarean section 196
episiotomy 162, 192
incompetent cervix 232
painful intercourse 209
stomach, heartburn 52
stress incontinence 104, 247–8
stretch marks 96
stretching exercises 212–16
sun tans 88
sunbeds 88
support tights 95
sweating 71
swelling, oedema 95
swimming 42, 70, *71*, 85
swollen feet 77, 95, 244
syntocinon 166, 174, 178, 229
syntometrine 172, 174–6, 229
syphilis 34, 62, 64

tampons 218
tanning 88
Tay-Sachs disease 118
tears: cervix 229
perineum 161–2, 192
temperature: at ovulation 20–1
confirming pregnancy 26
fevers 64, 204–5, 206–7
hot baths 61
overheating 96
saunas 62
ten-minute pick-me-up 85
tennis 42
TENS (transcutaneous electrical nerve stimulation) 138

terminating pregnancy 130–3
tests: antenatal 34, 113–29, 115
newborn baby 172, 177, 192
pre-conception 29
pregnancy 26
third trimester 90–112
thrombophlebitis 250
thrombosis 250
thyroid problems 123, 192
tights, support 95
tiredness, during pregnancy 49, 94–5
tooth problems 76
toxaemia *see* pre-eclampsia
toxoplasmosis 17, 36, 64, 249
tranquillizers 242
transition stage, labour 166
transverse lie 102, *181*, 182
travel, flying 88
'trial labour' 181
triple test 117
triplets 236
Trisomy 18, 126–7
tryptophan 56
tumours, choriocarcinoma 222
Turner's syndrome 113, 127, 128
twins 25, *187*, 187–8, 236–7

ultrasound scans 125–9, *127*, 134
umbilical cord: after birth 192–3
cordocentesis 120
cutting 169, 170, 172
prolapse 102, 183
round baby's neck 169
unstable lie 102, 182
urination, during pregnancy 50
urine: pregnancy tests 26
protein in 244
stress incontinence 104, 247–8
tests 34
uterus: afterpains 189, 198
Braxton Hicks contractions 46, 93, 106, 109
contractions 165
delivery of placenta 169, 174–6
fibroids 60, 182, 228
implantation of fertilized egg 25, 43
insufficient contractions 178
and miscarriage 235
orgasm 81
placenta abruptio 238–9
placenta accreta 239
placenta praevia 239
polyhydramnios 240
postpartum haemorrhage 229
uterine inversion 249–50
vaginal birth after caesarean 151

vacuum aspiration, termination of pregnancy 130

vacuum (ventouse) extraction 184–5, *184*
vagina: after childbirth 209
antepartum haemorrhage 228–9
bruising 190
discharges 79
internal examinations 34
lochia 192
lovemaking 80
painful intercourse 209
ultrasound scans through 134
vaginal delivery: after caesarean 148–51
breech presentation 181
see also labour
vaginitis 62
varicose veins 31, 56
vegetables 38, 195
veins, changes during pregnancy 31, 56
venous thrombosis 250
ventouse delivery 184–5, *184*, 188
vernix 69, *171*
vitamin A 17, 30
vitamin B6 17
vitamin B12 15, 17
vitamin C 16, 73
vitamin D 16
vitamin K 172, 176
vitamin supplements 30
vomiting: baby 205–6
hyperemesis gravidarum 53, 230–1
morning sickness 53–4, 63
posseting 194, 205
projectile 194, 205–6
vulva, soreness 110

waistline expansion 57
walking 42, 74
warm-up exercise 212
warning signs, during pregnancy 79–80
warts, genital 62
water: drinking 95
pain relief 153
water birth *139*, 173–4, *174*
waters, breaking 164, 165
weight: after pregnancy 194–5
baby's weight gain 207, 216
birth weight 13, 17
gain during pregnancy 33–4, 57, 72
IUGR (intra-uterine growth retardation) 234
low birth weight 13, *183*, 234
obesity 62
wind 50, 227
womb *see* uterus
work, during pregnancy 30-1, 105
wrists, carpal tunnel syndrome 78

X-rays 63, 180

yoga 31, *83*, *142*, 216

zinc deficiency 50